Blood Politics

Blood Politics

Race, Culture, and Identity in the Cherokee Nation of Oklahoma

Circe Sturm

UNIVERSITY OF CALIFORNIA PRESS
Berkeley · Los Angeles · London

University of California Press
Berkeley and Los Angeles, California

University of California Press, Ltd.
London, England

© 2002 by the Regents of the University of
California

Library of Congress Cataloging-in-Publication Data

Sturm, Circe, 1967–
  Blood politics : race, culture, and identity in the
Cherokee Nation of Oklahoma / Circe Sturm.
    p.   cm.
Includes bibliographical references and index.
  ISBN 0-520-23096-5 (Cloth : alk. paper)—
ISBN 0-520-23097-3 (Paper : alk. paper)
  1. Cherokee Indians—Ethnic identity.   2.
Cherokee Indians—Mixed descent.   3. Cherokee
Indians—Social conditions.   4. Ethnohistory—
Oklahoma.   I. Title.
E99.C5 S88   2002
305.897'55—dc21   2001005772

Manufactured in the United States of America
11 10 09 08 07 06 05 04 03 02
10 9 8 7 6 5 4 3 2 1

The paper used in this publication is both acid-free
and totally chlorine-free (TCF). It meets the
minimum requirements of ANSI/NISO Z39.48–
1992 (R 1997) (*Permanence of Paper*). ∞

To my beloved, Randolph Lewis

We are all of the household of the Cherokee family and of one blood . . . embracing each other as Countrymen, friends and relatives.

Chief John Ross

I have Indian blood in me, and I have just enough White blood for you to question my honesty!

Will Rogers, aka "The Cherokee Kid"

Contents

Illustrations

Acknowledgments

Writing a book is a lengthy process, and I have incurred many debts of gratitude over the years. First and foremost, I want to extend my heartfelt appreciation to the hundreds of Cherokee people who put up with my presence in their lives and who patiently answered my seemingly endless questions. They have proven to be the most excellent of teachers, and I greatly admire their willingness to address the issues presented here with such honesty and insight. I wish that I could thank each of them individually, in print, for their own unique contributions to this project. Although I cannot do so out of a need to protect their anonymity and to distance them from what are my own interpretations, I am comforted by the fact that when they see their words reflected in these pages they will know who they are, if they do not already.

I am also grateful to the Cherokee Nation proper, whose officers gave me permission to conduct research on such a sensitive topic. Beginning with the Mankiller administration up through the present, many people at the tribal complex have helped me along the way. I want to especially thank Richard Allen, in the Cherokee Nation's Office of Research, who kept me laughing and thinking and whose intellectual guidance proved to be invaluable.

To the many archivists and librarians who directed my research efforts with such expertise, a very special thanks. In particular, I want to acknowledge Delores Sumner and Vickie Sheffler at Northeastern State University's Special Collections, Margaret McCoy and Tom Mooney at the Cherokee National Historical Society, and John Lovett and Don Dewitt at the University of Oklahoma's Western History Collections. I also greatly appreciate the kindness of attorney Jim Goodwin, in Tulsa, who generously agreed to give me access to his personal papers on the Cherokee freedmen legal cases. These papers were the primary source of data for chapter 7, an earlier version of which appears as "Blood Politics, Racial Classification and Cherokee National Identity: The Trials and Tribulations of the Cherokee Freedmen" in a special issue of *American Indian Quarterly,* 22 (1–2): 230–258. This material is copyrighted by the University of Nebraska Press, 1999, and is used by permission.

The seeds of this book began to take root while I was a graduate student in the departments of anthropology and Native American Studies at the University of California, Davis. I owe a great deal to those professors who encouraged my intellectual endeavors during that time. Carol Smith supported this project when it was little more than an idea. She guided my intellectual and personal growth during graduate school and continues to be a mentor in the truest sense of the word. I want to especially thank her and the other members of my doctoral committee, including Aram Yengoyan, Inés Hernandez-Avila, and James Brooks. I am grateful for their careful readings, critical comments, and general support.

I also owe an immeasurable debt to my friends and colleagues at UC Davis, the University of Oklahoma, and elsewhere but especially to those who served as proofreaders, whose suggestions saved me enormous amounts of time and effort. In particular, I want to thank Deb Cahalen, Norman Stolzoff, Patricia Erikson, Margaret Bender, Morris Foster, Ari Kelman, Julia Ehrhardt, Francesca Sawaya, and Josh Piker for their generosity. I am also grateful for the thoughtful and incisive readings that both Karen Blu and Pauline Turner Strong gave to an earlier version of this manuscript while it was being considered for publication. Even my acquisitions editor, Monica McCormick, made time to read chapters of this manuscript and managed to guide me through what is often a harrowing process with kindness and enthusiasm. Other people should be so lucky to have such wonderful colleagues, supporters, and friends, and although this manuscript has improved greatly from the collective insights of all these people, I alone am responsible for its contents.

For financial support, I extend my deep appreciation to the National Science Foundation for a Dissertation Improvement Grant, to the University of California at Davis for a Graduate Humanities Research

Award, and the University of Oklahoma for a Junior Faculty Summer Research Fellowship. All three awards helped cover the expense of various stages of fieldwork in the United States between 1995 and 1998. In addition, short-term fellowships from UC Davis's College of Graduate Studies and a research fellowship from the College of Arts and Sciences at the University of Oklahoma allowed me to finish writing in a timely fashion.

Finally, I want to thank my family for their love, patience, and unfailing confidence in my abilities. To my mother, who kept me grounded, and to my father, who kept me dreaming, you are both simply wonderful. But I owe the deepest gratitude to my husband, Randy, who has always nurtured my endeavors with a gentle, loving spirit. Not only does he happen to be the world's greatest editor, but his love, wisdom, support, and seemingly unending patience are what have sustained me for the duration.

Note to the Reader

In the ethnographic sections, I have tried to incorporate what I would call a southern storytelling aesthetic. This is familiar to me because of my own experiences listening to my father in the evenings. Although I grew up in an age of television, I always preferred these regular, almost nightly storytelling sessions, where I could hear an old favorite or listen to my father's latest yarn with rapt attention. I chose this stylistic tool because it comes easily for me and allows me to present an angle on events, experiences, and even myself that I otherwise could not.

I also have chosen to use this voice because I think it makes several interesting theoretical points about ethnography, which is itself a form of storytelling that, although not fictionalized, is still highly subjective. In these passages, I parallel historians and anthropologists who view their written work as narratives or "stories." These unassuming substitutes for history and anthropology do not seek to represent a single truth (White 1978, Ankersmit 1989). Within anthropology this tradition is well entrenched in the works of Marcus and Fischer 1986, Clifford and Marcus 1986, Abu-Lughod 1986, 1990, and Ruth Behar 1993 to name but a handful.

Michel de Certeau has described the practice of ethnography as a "heterology," or science of the "other," a journey into difference that results in a narrative that is as much about oneself as it is about the meaningful interaction between self and "other" (1986: 68–70). I hope that the narrative southern voice will keep the reader aware of the crafted, filtered, and subjective nature of these descriptions and of the whole ethnographic project. I am always in these descriptions, although never in the first person. These are my experiences, but they have been filtered through my own subjectivity, the ethnographic gaze, anthropological theory, and time. Even though experience has always been a great source of legitimization for anthropologists, I find it is more honest to acknowledge these filters up front. Nevertheless, I believe that I have new and different insights as a result of these filters and that I can communicate in ethnographic writing things that otherwise would be unavailable, such as a sense of place, the texture of a conversation, or the details of a cultural moment.

I have frequently chosen to protect the anonymity of my consultants. Many offered to waive that right, preferring to have their name included, but in some cases the material is particularly sensitive and reveals confidential information about other individuals. I have exercised my own discretion in these instances. All quotes are taken from either taped or hand-recorded interviews during the course of my fieldwork conducted in the Cherokee Nation, northeastern Oklahoma, between the fall of 1995 and the summer of 1998.

CHAPTER ONE

Opening

In a back room outside a bar stand two men estranged by chance
from one another, a grandfather and his grandson, tentatively speaking
their first words. Otis Payne, the elder of the two, is an imposing
African-American man with intense eyes, a wide girth, and a round,
soft face. His grandson barely resembles him and is bookish, shy, and
uncomfortable. Otis literally owns the space, a bar he has lovingly
tended for twenty-five years. But he also owns the space with his
presence, which floods the room like warm summer light. He is standing
with his grandson in a shabby, makeshift museum, a memorial to the
Black Seminoles, a tribe of Native and African Americans who after
intermarrying and exchanging their cultures and identities became
a single people. Old lithographs, newspaper clippings, and photos cover
the wall, each placed on the dingy whitewash with careful precision.
The grandson wants to know how his grandfather got interested "in all
this." Otis explains that these are their people, that Paynes are looking
back at them from all corners of the room.

"Does that mean we're Indian?" the grandson wants to know.

"By blood," Otis says, "but blood is what you make of it."

Blood has so many layers of meaning and is such a familiar metaphor
that this exchange between Otis Payne and his grandson causes me to
smile with recognition whenever I think about it. The scene is taken
from John Sayles's 1996 film, *Lone Star*, about race relations in a Texas

border town. For me, the vignette between Otis and his grandson em-
bodies an archetypal American relationship, showing how dominant
ideas about race and culture shape the identities of multiracial individuals in different ways.[1] I have heard conversations like this one many
times before, not only in southeast Texas, where I lived for the first
twenty-five years of my life, but also in rural northeastern Oklahoma,
the site of my anthropological fieldwork during 1995 and 1996 and in
the summer of 1998. These conversations raised many questions in my
mind about the roles of race and racism in ethnic identity formation,
culminating in this book on Cherokee identity politics.

In this book, I examine how Cherokee identity is socially and politically constructed and how that process is embedded in ideas of blood,
color, and race that permeate discourses of social belonging in the
United States. Of particular interest to me is the relationship between
racial ideologies and identity among individuals of multiracial heritage.[2]
I want to explain how racial ideologies are constructed and then filter
from the national level to the local level, where they are simultaneously
internalized, reproduced, manipulated, and resisted in different ways in
various Cherokee communities. At the heart of these processes are the
sociohistorical categories of blood, color, and race, which are conflated
with each other and with culture at national and local levels in a variety
of sociopolitical discourses and legislation so that "race-thinking"
touches all Americans in one way or another.

Racial ideologies are particularly problematic for Native-American
communities, of which the Cherokees are one prominent example. For
instance, the federal government through the Bureau of Indian Affairs
(BIA) continues to use blood quantum as both a metaphor and measure
of "Indian" identity to manage tribal enrollments and determine eligibility for social services. Native Americans who wish to receive benefits
such as health care, housing, and food commodities must meet a biological standard, usually set at one-quarter or more Indian blood, and
must also present a certificate degree of Indian blood (CDIB) authenti-
cated by their tribe and the BIA.[3]

In spite of these racial restrictions, the Cherokee Nation has a large
and diverse multiracial population. Of its more than 175,000 enrolled
members, as many as 87,223 have less than 1/16 degree of Cherokee
blood (Cherokee Nation Registration Department, 1996). According to
tribal law, Cherokee citizens must be lineal descendants of an enrolled
tribal member, but no minimum blood quantum is required. Not quite
a century ago, blood degree varied among tribal members from "full-

blood" to 1/256. Today, the range is far greater—from full-blood to 1/2,048. This development raises questions about the symbolic significance of blood and the degree to which blood connections can be stretched and still carry any sense of legitimacy.

Along with blood, color is another arena for the contestation of Native-American identity. When phenotypically "black" or "white" individuals of multiracial heritage claim to be Cherokee, even if they have the necessary documentation of blood descent to enroll officially in the tribe, they are often rejected by some tribally enrolled Cherokees and other federally recognized Native Americans. This complex and emotional situation raises some thorny questions. To what degree can multiracial individuals claim Native-American identity and still be considered socially "authentic"? In other words, what markers of Native-American identity outweigh the dominant tendency to classify according to phenotype? These issues need to be addressed since the legitimacy of racially hybrid Native Americans is questioned more than that of other ethnic groups.

A case in point is that in many universities, applicants for affirmative action programs who identify themselves as Native American are required to provide documents proving their tribal affiliation. This is not the case for other underrepresented groups. This special treatment acknowledges the federal government's unique relationship with Native-American nations as semisovereign entities. However, it is also a reaction to the diverse and increasingly multiracial Native-American population that falls outside of society's and social science's enduring cultural and racial boundaries. According to Russell Thornton, a Cherokee sociologist and demographer, Native Americans are marrying outside their ethnic group at rates higher than any other Americans (Thornton in Bordewich 1996: 46). More than 50 percent are already married to non-Indians, and Congress has estimated that by the year 2080 less than 8 percent of Native Americans will have one-half or more Indian blood (Bordewich 1996: 46).[4] This fact also raises several questions, such as how much "racial blending" can occur before Native Americans cease to be identified as a distinct people, and what danger is posed to Native-American sovereignty and even continuity if the federal government continues to identify Native Americans on a racial instead of a cultural or more explicitly political basis.

To answer these questions, we need to examine the impact of racial ideologies on Native-American identity politics, including how race serves as a basis for the exclusion or inclusion of mixed bloods within tribal communities. More importantly, competing definitions of ethnic identity and social belonging often result in personal, political, and social conflict as Native Americans wrestle with the perplexing questions— who is really Indian, how do we know, and who gets to decide?[5] These are important concerns for both tribal communities and U.S. society as a whole, where questions of identity are one of the great issues of contestation in an increasingly multicultural and multiracial society.

ORIGINS

In early spring 1994, a group of Native-American women gathered in the living room of a friend's apartment for their weekly meeting. The women were trying to organize a local powwow, and afterward held a "talking circle," where they could discuss personal issues and share advice with one another. That evening a newcomer named Viola had joined the group. She had dark hair that flowed down her back, with thick bangs shadowing her black, almond-shaped eyes. She was from Oklahoma, and unlike the others in the room, she talked in an incessant stream of joking commentary.

"Hey, Sammie, you from a northeastern tribe, or what?" Viola blurted out.

"What do you mean, 'cause I look sorta' white?" Sammie giggled softly, shifting awkwardly in her seat.

"No, no," Viola continued, explaining that it had something to do with Sammie's eyes and her broad nose, and the way Sammie kind of reminded her of someone she knew from that area. With that spur, the conversation took off and suddenly everyone was talking about the little ways they knew to tell whether or not someone with ambiguous ancestry was really "Indian"—straight hair, flat feet, fingerprint whorls, broad noses, Mongolian spots, Asian eyes, earlobes connected at the base, and shovel shaped incisors.[6]

"Which teeth are your incisors, your front teeth or your Dracula teeth?" "Does *shovel-shaped* mean scooped out?" Suddenly, Viola asked if she could feel Sammie's front teeth. Although Viola had been raised within a tribal community and appeared "Indian" to most people, she seemed insecure about her identity and wanted the other women in the room to feel her teeth too, to see if they were the right type, the "Indian" type. As their fingers darted into one another's mouths, the room filled with nervous laughter, sighs of relief, sighs of disappointment.

I was one of those women. I came to this group through my work as a graduate student in the departments of anthropology and Native American studies at the University of California, Davis. I entered graduate school to work with Mayan languages and to pursue a Ph.D. in linguistic anthropology. But at the end of my first year, I began taking classes in Native-American studies to find out more about my own Native-American heritage. Through classes, mentors, and a wide social network, I gradually became better educated and understood for the first time my own racialized history, in all its complexity, in the context of this country. Within a year, I had switched from linguistic to cultural anthropology and also had enrolled in a program in Native-American studies, where I could pursue a topic that was closer to home.

Home meant many things. By doing a project on Native-American identity politics in Oklahoma, I would not work on foreign soil. I would live in an area of the United States where I was raised and would share a regional culture with the people I was "studying." I would also be an object of my own research, because I was of multiracial/Native-American heritage and was subject to the same racial ideologies and discourses of identity. This final point raised many concerns about my ability to examine this topic objectively. I struggled with these concerns for some time but eventually reasoned that, because our sense of self is so complex and multiple in nature, anyone who conducted anthropological research in a sensitive manner would find points of convergence with and divergence from the people with whom they worked.[7] Participant-observation has always mandated a conscientious movement between subjective and objective experience, and it has been the ongoing recognition of these complex differences and similarities that has guided the development of anthropological theory. This is not to deny power differentials or the colonial and Eurocentric baggage of the discipline but to point to the fact that anyone who seeks to represent anyone, including himself or herself, is caught in this tension between self/other, sameness and difference.

Still, as can be expected, to navigate these troubled waters so close to home was disorienting as often as it was rewarding. For example, I had always known that my paternal grandmother was Mississippi Choctaw on her mother's side and very distantly Cherokee on her father's side. I was only vaguely aware of this heritage as I grew up, having no exposure to a tribal community and little knowledge of Choctaw culture. Although I thought of my father as German with a Choctaw twist, I mostly identified myself as a Sicilian and Texan because of closer familial and cultural ties with my mother's kin. Over several years, my sense of identity began shifting as a result of my experiences at the university and in the field. My Choctaw identity moved front stage next to the Sicilian and Texan, while the German receded. The process was both personal and social. Other Native Americans on the university campus and in Oklahoma assigned me different degrees of Native-American identity depending on the circumstances and the people involved.

At the extremes were moments when individuals argued either that I was a victim of internal colonialism, denying my Native heritage, or that I "hadn't grown up on a 'rez' and hadn't a clue." The truth, I think, can be found somewhere in between. I believe that most of the time other Native-American students viewed me as a white woman with some Native-American ancestry. In the last few years, I reached out to my extended family and learned far more about my Choctaw relatives and their life experiences. At the same time, I investigated whether or not I was eligible for tribal enrollment through my grandmother. I was surprised to find that the Choctaw Nation in Oklahoma had no minimum blood quantum requirement and only asked for proof that my great-grandmother had moved to Oklahoma and was listed on an earlier tribal roll. However, my grandmother had been born in Mississippi, the original homeland of the Choctaw people, and had never moved west. Moreover, even with proper records, I failed to meet the Mississippi Choctaw Nation's minimum racial standard of one-half Choctaw blood or more. Had my grandmother moved to Oklahoma, I would have been in, but because she stayed in Mississippi where the racial definitions were stricter, I was out.

This frustrating experience is a common one for Native Americans whose identities are administered and verified through what are often rather haphazard paper trails leading to racially quantified ancestors. For instance, some Native Americans who speak indigenous languages and are phenotypically "Indian" are not federally recognized because they lack proper documentation. Usually, their ancestors resisted formal enrollment because they viewed it as a tool of political, cultural, and social assimilation. Many who witness this pervasive focus on documentation and genealogical descent are shocked at the degree to which culture is ignored in the enrollment process.[8] Although culture is not a primary consideration when federal or tribal governments assign Indian identity, for most Native Americans culture is the litmus test of "Indianness." But culture is also subjective and embedded within the race concept—so much so that cultural identifications can be as arbitrary as racial ones. One incident in particular, which happened during my time in Tahlequah, Oklahoma, demonstrates this point.

Sitting across from this Cherokee man in his late fifties, she wondered why he kept switching the topic, kept directing the questions back at her. He was a sly and crafty one—a trickster.

He had the bearing of a prominent man who knew that he was well respected in the community. He was confident that if he broke into a Cherokee song, thousands of Cherokee Baptists would flock to hear him sing like so many times before. Cherokee language flowed in his songs and in his jokes, and even though she couldn't understand him, he loved to tease, loved to watch her squirm, loved to wrestle her own questions away from her. After some time, she realized that the tease was a standard test to see how white she was, how defensive, how much the outsider. If she could laugh it off and throw out a few good ones, she'd pass the test, and if not, well, at least she'd be tolerated. Maybe.

She could tell it bugged him that he couldn't place her, that he didn't quite catch her last name. So, she teased him in return, avoiding questions that were brilliantly indirect, replacing them with her own, and through the mutual teasing, their exchange grew warmer and kinder. Their laughter began to ring, filling his office, flowing through the open door and into the corridors of the Cherokee Nation tribal complex. Finally, he relented, having grown more curious in the course of their cat-and-mouse conversation.

"Are you part Indian?" he asked point blank.

"Funny, how people always ask me that around here. Yeah, I'm part Mississippi Choctaw through my father's mother, but mostly I'm Sicilian and German," she answered. She thought he must have liked her response, because she could see the man change. His body opened a little. He shifted forward in his seat and touched her lightly on the arm.

"Are you enrolled?" he asked in a soft tone.

"Oh, no. I'm not eligible because my grandma stayed in Mississippi and they say I don't have enough blood there."

"You should look into that," he said pulling his head back sharply. "I think the Oklahoma Choctaws in Durant sometimes recognize Mississippi Choctaws and it's important for you to connect up with your people. What did you say your family's name was?"

"Well, our Choctaw name is Wesley, " she replied.

"Oh, I know lots of Wesleys down there. That's a real common Choctaw surname. Well, it's not Tubbee, but I bet you might even have family right here in Oklahoma," he chuckled. "You know, my first wife was Choctaw. That's how I know." He paused a minute and then said, "Now, let's see. You said you were married. Well what about your husband?"

"Uh. Do you mean is he Indian? Well, no. He's an Irish boy from New Jersey," she said.

His brow furrowed and released. He leaned forward, met her gaze directly and said, "Does your husband understand your culture?"

She was dumbfounded. A hundred questions ran through her mind. Was he sincerely worried about her marriage? Did this really matter to him? Or was he just kidding, again?

My questions about racial and cultural belonging originate in life experiences such as this. Through them I have become sensitized to the role that ideologies of race and culture play in ethnic identity formation, particularly among Native Americans of multiracial heritage. These experiences guide my intellectual endeavors and inform the choices I make. But I am no more biased or objective than the next person, and I make no claims to cultural insiderism. Like many Americans, I am reminded daily that racism continues to plague and divide our society at the national and local levels. And although this continuity with a racist past alarms me, it is not the whole story of our country, even if at times it seems to be the most obvious. This research provides a window into one community where, like other communities in this country, complicated systems of racial classification are simultaneously created, internalized, manipulated, and resisted.

CHEROKEE LANDSCAPES

When people who are unfamiliar with the state think of Oklahoma, they conjure up images of "the West," a dusty, dry, and barren landscape filled with cowboys and Indians where the iron-red topsoil steadily erodes under the heavy breath of the all-too-animated wind. True, parts of western Oklahoma fit this profile, but the state's cultural and physical geography is much more diverse. In its northeastern corner, Oklahoma is surprisingly green and lush, with rolling hills and dozens of lakes and streams. Here, the Cherokee Nation lies in the foothills of the Ozark Mountains, a region characterized by dense forest, poor soil, and dra-

matic displays of weather. During the course of my fieldwork, summer-
time highs pushed the thermometer to the century mark, with humidity
forcing people without air conditioning to retreat to their open-air
porches or down to the nearest swimming hole. Fall brought an early
chill, the smell of wood-burning stoves, and leaves in an endless kalei-
doscope of color. Winter lows brought ice storms and thin layers of
snow that kept me and the school-aged children at home when the roads
become nearly impassable because of the inadequacy of local plowing
equipment in a state with long roads and relatively few people. In spring
the rains were unrelenting, and there was always the possibility of a
twister appearing out of the blue on the horizon. I came to appreciate
the common expression in Oklahoma, "Hey, if you don't like the
weather, stick around and it'll change."

The ecology of eastern Oklahoma has also changed in the past century from what the Cherokees once described as "forests with trees so
big and so wide spaced that through them you could see a man on
horseback a quarter mile away" (Wahrhaftig 1975: 30). After Oklahoma statehood in 1907, white settlers increasingly took control of the
land and over several decades logged the forests and leased the land to
hundreds of cattlemen and thousands of tenant farmers. As a result of
this high tenancy on a land unsuitable for agriculture, the already poor
soil was soon exhausted and the game hunted to depletion (Wahrhaftig
1975: 30). Shortly after, in the 1940s and 1950s, the Army Corps of
Engineers, in a flurry of dam building, created what is now known as
Green Country, a so-called paradise for sportsmen of bass-filled lakes
and game-rich woodlands. Green Country has brought an increase in
tourism, but Cherokees are rarely the direct beneficiaries of those dollars. Instead, Cherokees are left with "scrub choked, tick-infested secondary growth woods, fishing lakes with the sites of once-cohesive Indian settlements at the bottom, and a displaced population" (Wahrhaftig
1975: 31).

For many decades, the desperate situation in Ozarkia (a region similar
to Appalachia in its poverty and isolation) forced the rural economy of
eastern Oklahoma to revert to an Appalachian subsistence model. Many
Native-American, black, and white families with limited access to the
tourist industry depended heavily on hunting, fishing, and small garden
plots for food, on the forests for wood to heat their houses, and as the
century progressed, on the state for welfare assistance (Thompson 1993:
17). Fortunately, financial conditions began improving steadily in the
region throughout the 1980s. In 1980, the per capita income of largely

Figure 1.   Cherokee landscape. Outside Welling, Oklahoma, Cherokee
Nation. Photograph by Sammy Still (Cherokee).

Cherokee Adair County was considerably less than half that of the
state.[9] But by 1987, "all the northeastern counties in the Cherokee Nation had seen an increase in per capita income relative to the state as a
whole," (Cherokee Nation, Office of Research and Analysis 1993[4]:
2). Still, in 1989, 53 percent of white households in the fourteen-county
area had earnings in excess of $25,000 compared with only 37 per-
cent of Native-American households. Cherokees, then, are poorer than
their white neighbors, and according to 1989 statistics, 27 percent of
Native Americans in northeastern Oklahoma continue to live below the
poverty line (Cherokee Nation, Office of Research and Analysis
1993[4]: 2).

While Cherokee people have never known much in the way of material wealth, they have had one thing in abundance—each other. The
Cherokee Nation is the largest tribe in the United States, with over
200,000 enrolled citizens, and continues growing in leaps and bounds

with well over a thousand people applying for tribal membership each month. According to the Cherokee Nation's Registration Department, in 1996 roughly 39 percent of Cherokee citizens lived outside Oklahoma, but most resided within the state, with over 87,000 remaining in the historical boundaries of the Cherokee Nation. The core of the Cherokee population resides in seventy or so identifiable Cherokee settlements distributed throughout northeastern Oklahoma (Wahrhaftig 1975: 25). Historically, Cherokees have lived in these small and cohesive communities of relatives, and many continue to do so today.

Cherokee communities are the "wealth" of the Cherokee Nation because they represent historical and cultural continuity in the imaginations of many Cherokees who are the first to claim the importance of social bonds. These communities are old social units that have tended to be semi-autonomous in their decision making and political leadership yet fluidly connected to the tribal body as a whole. In 1838, when the Cherokees were forced to move to Oklahoma (known then as Indian Territory), whole towns moved on the Trail of Tears and resettled together under the direction of their own leaders, with scouts selecting new locations that were similar to the ones they had left behind. Some of the Oklahoma settlements bear the names of these old towns, and several Cherokee dialects continue to exist today (Wahrhaftig 1975: 28). These communities are the sites where Cherokee continues to be spoken as a first language by over 10,000 individuals, where survival is based on mutual support and cooperation. Here, the pace of life seems to slow down, refusing to be rushed by anything but the most dire of circumstances. Here, people stop to notice things, to feel themselves walking firmly on the ground.

SOUTHERN VOICES

One hand fans the program guide back and forth in a desperate attempt to create a little wind, while the other rubs an ice cube from her now empty wax-paper cup across the back of her neck. It's the height of summer, and the infrequent breeze offers little relief. Fidgeting in her chair with impatience, waiting for the second act to begin, she looks around in boredom, noticing the stars peeking through the clouds high above the amphitheater. But her seat is so high and the rows are so steep, that with her head leaning back she begins to feel vertigo, as if at any second she's going to fall over. So, she rights

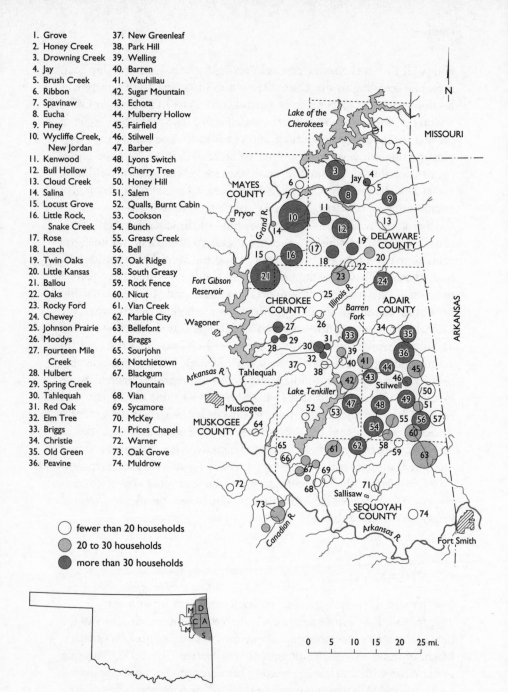

1. Grove
2. Honey Creek
3. Drowning Creek
4. Jay
5. Brush Creek
6. Ribbon
7. Spavinaw
8. Eucha
9. Piney
10. Wycliffe Creek, New Jordan
11. Kenwood
12. Bull Hollow
13. Cloud Creek
14. Salina
15. Locust Grove
16. Little Rock, Snake Creek
17. Rose
18. Leach
19. Twin Oaks
20. Little Kansas
21. Ballou
22. Oaks
23. Rocky Ford
24. Chewey
25. Johnson Prairie
26. Moodys
27. Fourteen Mile Creek
28. Hulbert
29. Spring Creek
30. Tahlequah
31. Red Oak
32. Elm Tree
33. Briggs
34. Christie
35. Old Green
36. Peavine

37. New Greenleaf
38. Park Hill
39. Welling
40. Barren
41. Wauhillau
42. Sugar Mountain
43. Echota
44. Mulberry Hollow
45. Fairfield
46. Stilwell
47. Barber
48. Lyons Switch
49. Cherry Tree
50. Honey Hill
51. Salem
52. Qualls, Burnt Cabin
53. Cookson
54. Bunch
55. Greasy Creek
56. Bell
57. Oak Ridge
58. South Greasy
59. Rock Fence
60. Nicut
61. Vian Creek
62. Marble City
63. Bellefont
64. Braggs
65. Sourjohn
66. Notchietown
67. Blackgum Mountain
68. Vian
69. Sycamore
70. McKey
71. Prices Chapel
72. Warner
73. Oak Grove
74. Muldrow

○ fewer than 20 households

◐ 20 to 30 households

● more than 30 households

Figure 2. Map of Cherokee communities in northeastern Oklahoma, 1963. After Wahrhaftig 1968: 511. Courtesy of Albert L. Wahrhaftig.

herself, fixes her eyes straight ahead on the dense and ratty foliage tumbling from the woods behind the stage, and gulps down an ice cube hoping to quell the nausea in her belly.

After a moment, the lights go up with a single spot brightening around a young female figure primping before a mirror. The anthropologist tries to focus her attention on scene after scene of young people, both white and Indian, both with long black wigs, playing Cherokees. After all, this is the history of the Cherokee Nation—the tourist version—the story of the Trail of Tears told for all the world to see. She keeps trying, but she's bored, hot, and impatient. Her mind wanders and she thinks how lucky she is that her friend in the cast gave her complimentary tickets, how thankful she is that she didn't have to pay nine dollars for admission. She thinks of how much flack this version has gotten in Cherokee communities, how people used to protest it and still it hasn't changed—the same old celebration of Oklahoma statehood, the same old conclusion that the Cherokee Nation had to die for Oklahoma to live.

These thoughts bring on another bout of nausea. And then she realizes scene thirteen is about to begin, the infamous Ceremony of War: the Civil War. This scene stops the fidgeting and draws her attention, as prominent Cherokee Stand Watie swears allegiance to the Confederacy, stating that the Cherokees are southerners at heart, that their interests are the same. Is black slavery the issue here, he demands, because Cherokees are a slaveholding people? It doesn't seem so when Chief John Ross refuses to breach the loyalty he feels toward the United States. The Cherokees on stage divide, a majority on the side of the South, the rest with the North. She gapes as they start to sing "Dixie" and wave the rebel flag—Cherokees! Then, the fighting begins. Brothers kill each other. Children die. She sits so still. This scene always pulls at some deep place within her, as if her own southern roots were ripped out of the ground and exposed.

The Trail of Tears drama at the Cherokee Heritage Center is not the only place where one hears southern voices in the course of this project. I, too, expected northeastern Oklahoma to have a western feel and was surprised not only at the marked differences between the eastern and western regions of the state, but also at the distinctly southern quality of the Cherokee Nation. Most scholars would argue that northeastern Oklahoma is not a part of the South proper, but there are several facts of Cherokee history, geography, culture, and identity that cause me to question this assertion.

First, the Cherokees originally lived in the southeastern woodlands of the United States in an area encompassing parts of what is now Georgia, North Carolina, Tennessee, and Alabama. There, many Cherokees adopted from their white neighbors a mostly Baptist version of Christianity and a system of black slavery that they slightly modified to suit their own economic needs. When the Cherokees were forced to leave their homeland for Indian Territory, those who were Christian slaveholders took their religion and black slaves with them. In Indian Territory, this same group of slaveholding Cherokees fought on the side of the Confederacy, at times against other non-slaveholding Cherokees who had joined forces with the Union. The Cherokee Nation was torn apart by violence during the Civil War and, after its defeat, was left vulnerable to outside manipulations in the period between reconstruction and statehood.

The historical divide between slaveholding and non-slaveholding Cherokees mirrors cultural divisions that continue to this day, most of which will become apparent in the course of this book. Some Cherokees proudly proclaim that they have always been a southern people, while others disdain this "white man's" label. Nonetheless, most Cherokees live in a region bordered on the east by Arkansas and on the south by "Little Dixie," the southeastern portion of Oklahoma that many historians include in their maps of "the South." Most Cherokees consider Oklahoma their home in the fullest sense of the word, but almost all look back to the South, to their original homeland. Like many displaced peoples, Cherokees long to return to their roots. Some make temporary pilgrimages or save money to buy land, while others ask to be buried there. Many never get a chance to go back, but those geographic, historical, and cultural origins continually visit their imaginations and shape their identities in complex ways.

UNDERSTANDING "RACE"

In the stable but diverse Cherokee communities of northeastern Oklahoma, race is also a part of the landscape, and it intersects with Cherokee identity in important ways. Thus, to understand better the relationship between race-thinking and Cherokee identity, we need to examine critically the concept of race and how it has been treated in the scholarly literature. Race is not a natural, biological, or scientific cate-

gory. Instead, it is a social, historical, and political category defined in
biological terms. This biological aspect, which is only one of many other
features, has made race the subject of much scientific inquiry, particularly within the social sciences. Anthropology bears partial responsibility
for the scientific legitimization of race-thinking, though today most anthropologists recognize that race is a politically charged, highly variable
social construct.

Nevertheless, anthropological research historically has tended to
dodge the centrality of the issue of race by subsuming it into other social
paradigms such as class, ethnicity, or nation (Omi and Winant 1994).
The most common of these paradigms conflates race with ethnicity.
When race is employed in the anthropological literature, it serves as a
variant of ethnicity, connoting biological distinctions and social divisions based on skin color, phenotype, and genotype. When ethnicity is
used, it substitutes for race and brings to mind "style-of-life" distinctions
based on cultural differences such as religion, language, food, and clothing (Alonso 1994). Besides confusion, the conflation of race with ethnicity results in the neglect of race as an autonomous field. This move
is "power-evasive" when we consider that within the context of U.S.
history racially defined minorities have almost always been treated in
qualitatively different ways from ethnically defined minorities (Frankenberg 1993). Fortunately, in the past ten years, a new wave of anthropological literature focusing on race as its specific point of departure has
swept the discipline.[10]

However, both race-thinking and the scientific buttressing of race as
a biological category continue to this day with profound effects on social
reality. It is in this context that race is both a falsehood and a fact, being
false in its biological, scientific sense and factual in its very real effects
on lived experience. With this in mind, I have found most useful the
literature that views race as a Western social construct used to explain
difference and to justify political and social inequality, a construct whose
meaning varies over time because it is embedded in shifting relations of
power and struggle (Frankenberg 1993, Gilroy 1987, Goldberg 1990,
and West 1993b). I particularly appreciate those scholars who use this
framework to grapple with the complex notions of race underlying the
identity formation process and who then relate that process to ideological domination and resistance (Hall 1986, 1991, Omi and Winant
1994, San Juan 1992, Gregory and Sanjek 1994, and West 1993a).

Another body of literature critical to this project examines the relationship between racial ideologies and nationalism. Cherokees are bi-

nationals, identifying as citizens of both the United States and the Cherokee Nation. The literature on race and nationalism suggests that virtually all nations, including the United States, have normative racial ideologies that homogenize cultural diversity and shape discourses of social belonging (Alonso 1994, Gilroy 1987, Malkki 1992, and Williams 1989, 1991, 1993). I argue that the same can be said of Native-American nations. Like other Native Americans, Cherokees employ a complicated ideological matrix where two mutually embedded sets of racial ideologies associated with two different national identities articulate with one another. It is in this matrix that Cherokee identities take shape.

Brackette Williams's work on race and nationalism helps us understand this process. In an important essay, "A Class Act: Anthropology and the Race to Nation across the Ethnic Terrain" (1989), she summarizes the dominant ideologies of Western Euroamerican nationalism and argues that nations are constructed around myths of racial and cultural homogeneity. Because discourses of nation-state formation underlie current forms of political and economic power, they constrain contemporary cultural processes including the formation of indigenous identity. Thus, ethnopolitical activism often reproduces dominant ideologies in its own discourses and structural forms. For instance, Cherokee cultural activists might choose to portray their communities as culturally "authentic" or homogeneous, even going so far as to invoke biological difference and "natural" superiority to create the sense of unity deemed necessary for a collective, national front.

According to Williams, ideologies of nationalism conflate race, class, and culture, producing "concepts which locat[e] the source and meaning of cultural differences in the 'bloods' of different human populations" (1993: 162). In other words, people belong to a race and share a common blood, and it is that blood that then becomes the basis of a "primordial" culture passed on genetically from one generation to the next. During the course of my fieldwork, this pattern of thought was apparent when the vast majority of Cherokees I interviewed mentioned "Cherokee blood" as a potent symbolic medium connecting all Cherokees to one another.

This "symbolics of blood," as Carol A. Smith (1997) has termed it, originates in earlier conceptions of race and blood purity from the colonial period in the Americas. At that time, notions of blood purity were associated with honor and legitimacy and used to control women's sexuality in different ways along class lines (Martínez-Alier 1974, Williams

1993). However, in the early national period these meanings shifted, producing an even more virulent form of racism that was used to legitimate class and gender inequalities (Martinez-Alier 1989, Smith 1995, Stolcke 1991). Thus, during colonial and capitalist expansion, Western ideologies of race, class, gender, and culture spread throughout the world, providing ideological justifications for national sovereignty based on "logically integrated notions of territoriality, biological purity, cultural homogeneity, and status stratification" (Smith 1995: 728). These theoretical formulations help explain how some indigenous expressions of nationalism come to reproduce dominant forms. This phenomenon can be observed in the Cherokee Nation's own state structure in Tahlequah, Oklahoma, which mimics the state structure of the federal government.

Because Cherokees throughout their history have made political choices that have had transformative effects on their own society, we need to pay attention to how Native-American agency not only reproduces but also mediates and potentially refigures ideological structures inherent in both U.S. society and tribal nations. Several authors have chronicled how Native-American resistance to U.S. domination has been forged around issues of autonomy, sovereignty, and self-determination expressed in the pan-Indian movement (Clifton 1990, Cornell 1988, Deloria 1969, Dowd 1992, Hertzberg 1971, Jaimes 1992b, Nagel 1996). My research builds on these and other works, paying close attention to the ways in which racial identity becomes a rallying-point of collective resistance as well as a source of political and social factionalism (Clifton 1989 and 1990, Feraca 1990, Green 1988, Hagan 1985, Isaacs 1975, Peterson and Brown 1985, Tanner 1983). In the past, the scholarly literature has largely ignored the effects of racial ideologies on alliance building within heterogeneous Native-American populations. My objective is to extend this literature to investigate whether or not Cherokees have built collective fronts around ideologies that recognize cultural and racial difference.

This type of analysis is rare for multiracial populations in the United States, which are largely ignored because of racial typological boundaries. These boundaries have been criticized as a colonial legacy that obscures the complex relationships within and between communities of study (Anzaldúa 1987, Lowe 1991, Root 1992, Smith 1997, Spickard 1989). This critique is particularly valid concerning Native Americans, who are becoming increasingly multiracial as a result of high rates of exogamy. Some earlier research does treat Native Americans of multiracial heritage, but it focuses on either assimilation or tribal factionalism around economic resources (Brewton 1963, Gulick 1973, Gist and Dworkin 1967, Unrau 1989, Wax 1971). In general, the tendency has been to reduce tribal populations to only two categories—the culturally authentic "full-bloods" or the assimilated "mixed-bloods." Mixed-bloods are often portrayed as "race-traitors," so that lower blood degree becomes directly associated with cultural loss that allegedly results from "white Indian" political domination. In fact, the association of racial mixing with cultural loss has so permeated the literature that some writers have gone so far as to ask whether or not there are "real Indians" in Oklahoma.[11] The mere suggestion that Native Americans are "real" only if they look "Indian" calls into question the cultural and political continuity of the whole southeastern tribal complex.[12] Many of these ideas bias contemporary research on Cherokee identity politics, limiting its scope and depth, with virtually no ethnographic research having been conducted among the Oklahoma Cherokees for the past twenty-five years.[13]

New research on multiracial Native Americans is beginning to acknowledge the complexity of these communities and no longer assumes a priori that blood degree correlates with cultural authenticity or ethnic identity (Calloway 1986, Crowe 1975, Forbes 1988, Hagan 1986, Mulroy 1993, Nagel 1996, Vaughan 1982). The most insightful studies examine tri-racial communities with Native-American, African-American, and Euroamerican heritage (Blu 1980, Campisi 1991, Forbes 1993, Sider 1994). Blu and Sider have written important ethnographies on the tri-racial Lumbee of North Carolina, who recently fought for federal recognition as an indigenous people. Sider specifically deals with the relationship between ethnohistory and cultural identity and the way in which Native-American people actively produce their own histories and cultural boundaries. What these writers share is recognition of the historical constraints of dominant ideologies on Native-American identity formation, balanced with an emphasis on Native-American agency. I follow the lead of these authors by emphasizing both ideological domination and resistance as it relates to the "racial formation" of Cherokee identities (Gilroy 1987, Omi and Winant 1994). For example, in chapter 2, I discuss the rise of Cherokee nationalism in the nineteenth century, particularly the ways in which Cherokees internalized ideas of race and then used them to their own political advantage in the process of nation building. However, this ongoing process of ideological accommodation and resistance is apparent in all the chapters and weaves its way from the Cherokee past through the present.

THEORETICAL DEPARTURES

NEO-GRAMSCIAN PERSPECTIVES ON RACE AND RESISTANCE

As we begin to explore the racial formation of Cherokee identities, it is important to recognize up front that ideological domination and resistance are not distinct categories. They overlap with one another and cannot be divorced from the material and political conditions of lived experience. Traditionally, scholars have viewed power mechanisms within state structures and other economic and material factors as the primary influences on ideology. Today, however, most scholars recognize the need to avoid this type of determinism by reembedding agency within studies of power and domination. Many have tried to resolve the tension between structure and agency by searching for a middle ground, but all too often this results in quixotic conclusions that raise more questions than they answer. Several theorists, however, informed by the writings of Antonio Gramsci, have managed to use this tension productively to make major contributions. The best of these analyses keep structure and agency in dialogue by employing the Gramscian concepts of "hegemony" and "contradictory consciousness," which allow for ideological domination and resistance to co-construct one another.

A case in point is the groundbreaking work of Michael Omi and Howard Winant (1994), two sociologists who analyze racial formation in the United States from a Gramscian perspective. According to Omi and Winant, racial formation occurs through historically situated, racial projects. They define racial projects as hegemonic explanations of racial dynamics linked to efforts to redistribute resources along particular racial lines. In the U.S., we are all subject to these racial projects and learn the rules of racial classification and racial identity without any obvious conscious inculcation. In this manner, we are inserted into a social structure that varies in content over time but nonetheless remains inherently racial. Race then becomes a "common sense" way of explaining the world (1994: 55–61). These racial projects collectively mediate between the "discursive or representational means in which race is identified and signified on the one hand, and the institutional and organizational forms in which it is routinized and standardized on the other" (1994: 60). An example of a racial project would be the way in which federal, state, and tribal bureaucracies have routinely used the idiom of blood in Native-American census records as a quantifiable measure of Indian identity.

In the United States, racial formation has occurred as an uneven historical process that has "moved from dictatorship to democracy, from domination to hegemony. In this transition, hegemonic forms of racial rule—those based on consent—eventually [have come] to supplant those based on coercion" (1994: 67). As a result, today we find ourselves the subjects of an ongoing, "messy," and incomplete racial hegemony that shifts as needed to justify the existing social order. However, Omi and Winant argue that racial projects buttressed by common sense are not inherently racist unless they specifically link essentialist representations of race to structures of social domination (1994: 71–72). Defined in this manner, racism is both ideological and structural, and to oppose it we must remain conscious of race while at the same time challenging the common sense presuppositions of racial rule.

While I agree with these points and use Omi and Winant's insightful concept of racial formation as a theoretical foundation for exploring Cherokee identity politics, I find that they fail to address sufficiently the role of contradictory consciousness and counterhegemonic resistance in this process. So I return to Gramsci's original writings to draw attention to problems in Omi and Winant's adaptation of his theory. Gramsci (1971: 333) suggests that contradictory consciousness has a dual nature whose aspects are always in tension—one aspect being implicit, critical, and as I read it, possibly counterhegemonic "good sense," which arises from lived experiences and material conditions of oppression; the other being explicit, hegemonic "common sense," which is uncritically absorbed and arises from ideological domination by a more powerful class. To clarify this distinction, good sense might be foregrounded when a Cherokee meets a white or black neighbor who also speaks Cherokee. In this instance, the common sense presuppositions that blacks or whites cannot be Cherokee or that racial mixing necessarily means cultural loss might be challenged by the counterhegemonic experience of a common language. While Gramsci suggests that all people share contradictory consciousness, his notion of hegemony as common sense most directly accounts for the presence of dominant ideas in the consciousness of subordinate peoples.

Like Omi and Winant, I believe hegemony is a powerful explanation for race-thinking in contemporary U.S. and Cherokee society, but I find

it perplexing that they do not follow Gramsci's lead by specifically linking hegemony to contradictory consciousness. This is a major drawback,
since it is contradictory consciousness and not hegemony per se that
mediates between the implicit and explicit realms of culture, the material
and ideological realms of lived experience. It is the contradictory nature
of consciousness that makes hegemony partial, messy, and incomplete,
that allows for the possibility of counterhegemonic resistance, and that
accounts for contradictions in contemporary debates around Native-
American identity.

But Gramsci's framing of contradictory consciousness still leaves several questions unanswered, questions that also are not addressed in Omi
and Winant's writings. Gramsci argues that the common-sense aspect of
contradictory consciousness is hegemonic, but he is less explicit when it
comes to good sense. This raises the first of two limitations in Gramsci's
theory: hegemony seems to limit agency at an intellectual level, because
hegemony is "uncritically absorbed" (1971: 333). This has often been
interpreted as consent to rule by a subordinate class. I find Omi and
Winant's focus on consent disturbing at times and would argue that the
difference between "consent to rule" and the uncritical absorption of
dominant ideas is an important distinction (1994: 67). Consent seems
to blame the victim, implies permission, and suggests that subordinate
peoples are complicit in their own oppression because they "self-police."
I would argue, at least among Cherokees, that few have any *consciousness* that they are reproducing dominant ideas in ways that either sub-
jugate themselves or others. Not only would conscious awareness imply
the agency necessary for consent or permission, but it also might be the
critical link that stimulates counterhegemonic practices.

The second and most important limitation of Gramsci's framework
comes from his statement that counterhegemony is always embedded *in*
hegemony (1971: 328). This raises two related concerns for my research:
are Native Americans constrained from formulating ideologies outside
of dominant ideas, and if a critical counterideology emerges, then is it
necessarily hegemonic? In other words, do ideas that unite a diverse
Native-American population in an effective political coalition actually
homogenize that population, or can there be unifying ideas that recognize difference? This latter point is most explicit in Gramsci's discussion
of a collective will forged around a single unifying principle, which Omi
and Winant apply in their analysis of historical transformations in the
U.S. racial order (1994: 88–89, 98–99, 111).

In order to retain the useful parts of Omi and Winant's explanatory framework while avoiding the residual limitations from Gramsci's original writings, I will take a slightly different approach. First, since Omi and Winant's discussion of counterhegemonic resistance is limited, I will focus on the contradictory nature of resistance and how collective resistance might coalesce around *multiple* unifying principles. For instance, Cherokees might simultaneously unite around ideas of national sovereignty and cultural difference rather than a single monolithic principle like class oppression. Second, although I believe that most counterhegemonic resistance reproduces hegemony to some extent (often in the actual terms of the debate), I will allow for the *possibility* of nonhegemonic resistance. By this I mean that Cherokees may engage in resistance that is framed against dominant ideas but not necessarily within them. Here, an example might be Cherokee resistance around cultural or national difference that specifically disarticulates itself from race.

FROM IDEOLOGY TO HEGEMONY AND BACK AGAIN

In addition to Gramsci's ideas about hegemony, I also use the concept of ideology to examine Cherokee identity politics. Ideology has been defined as everything from the social determination of thought to the deployment of false ideas in the interests of a ruling class or from the ways in which signs, meanings, and values reproduce a dominant social power to any conjuncture between discourse and politically charged interests. Ideology always relates to the subject, and each theoretical framing of ideology has a correspondingly different understanding of subjectivity. Thus, to understand the ways in which racial and national ideologies work in Cherokee society, one must also understand the effects these ideologies have on the self-consciousness of Cherokee individuals and how they potentially shape Cherokee collective action.

While ideology would seem to be an important theoretical concept, particularly for this project, in recent years it has been seriously challenged to the point that its use in contemporary studies is considered almost passé. In particular, postmodern theorists have built on Foucault's insights, insisting that all social relations are constituted in discursive practices. Postmodern theory does make important contributions in showing how discourse shapes identity, consciousness, and social relations in complex ways. However, because it questions the existence of truth, while at the same time suggesting that all discourse is equally interested and power laden, it becomes virtually impossible for scholars to pinpoint social ideologies. Then, radical movements are as "interested" as those of archconservatives, and ideology as a concept loses its political punch.

Recently some theorists have begun to return to the concept of ideology, hoping to sharpen its critical edge. I follow in their footsteps because I believe ideology provides an important tool for social and cultural criticism. Ideology does make a series of assumptions about the existence of truth, reason, and responsibility, but these are significant social considerations that have been too readily dismissed in recent theorizing. I do not mean to imply that there are simplistic notions of truth or reason that can be divorced from power relations or history, only that there are some falsehoods worth denouncing (e.g., women are inferior to men, some races are superior to others, or race-mixing equals cultural loss). Even if our justification for doing so is more in the realm of politics than epistemology, it is Gramscian good sense. All individuals make evaluations that are interested and even irrational but still useful in a political, personal, and social sense. In light of power relations and history, these evaluations are necessary for social theorists and activists to assign responsibility for societal ills and to locate avenues of critical investigation that might lead to potential remedies.

With this overall goal in mind, I use the concept of ideology to show how people, as agents, can promote ideas with powerful effects. I see ideology as explicit and conscious, at the level of the "said," and as not necessarily the possession of a particular class, although it does justify relations of dominance in general. Hegemony, on the other hand, is another useful concept that allows for ideological processes that are not always conscious and explicit. Instead, with hegemony, these processes are multiple, complex, and contradictory, occurring at different levels of awareness. Ideology occurs as a more specific and explicit site within hegemony, and these concepts used together allow us to examine complex, messy, and partial forms of domination and resistance.

In a similar vein, Jean and John Comaroff make important distinctions between ideology and hegemony by combining a Bordieuian framework with a Gramscian one (1991: 21–22). The Comaroffs examine how dominant ideologies and state structures are both mediated and reproduced by individuals in the context of missionization in colonial South Africa. They suggest that individuals always act within a particular cultural field—a field including embodied forms of knowledge and thought that are implicit and uncritically absorbed and that have a material aspect, observable in the way people unconsciously sit, walk, talk, and behave. If we extend these insights to the case at hand, when

Cherokees resist dominant ideas in discourse and practice, because they unconsciously resist within a cultural field, culture shapes their choices of behavior. These habitual or hegemonic forms of culture, then, can be a cohesive force between state structures and acting Cherokee agents that insures their reproduction of and engagement with certain types of racial domination.

The Comaroffs argue that we need all three concepts—hegemony, ideology, and culture—because when culture is aligned with power, whether intentional or not, systems of meaning get rooted in habit. Ideology would be an intentional expression of power in culture, whereas hegemony would be an implicit and unintentional form of self-policing, also rooted in cultural practice (Comaroff and Comaroff 1991: 22–25). When there are disruptive changes in power relations, hegemony can erupt into conscious awareness and become part of the explicit political discourse. At that point, however, it immediately shifts from being hegemony and becomes either ideology or counterhegemony (Comaroff and Comaroff 1991: 28).

To ground these theoretical ideas in the case at hand, *Indian* originally was an external label of colonial oppression that incorporated diverse indigenous nations into a system of racial and social classification. "Racing" Native Americans rationalized their oppression. Race, then, was an overt discourse, the ideology of a dominant white, colonial class that helped maintain and obscure power relations. But racial ideologies often double back on themselves, and when they become habit and are no longer in the realm of discursive struggle, they slip to a tacit level and are hegemonic once more. In this instance, people began to take "Indianness" for granted, and over time it became an "unquestionably" racial category.

These historical processes shape and sometimes even constrain ideological formations in the present. However, the intersections of history, ideology, culture, and hegemony are not static. Sometimes, a hegemonic idea, like that which says Native-American cultural authenticity is frozen in the past, might erupt into consciousness when challenged by life experiences. If one experiences Cherokee culture as a fluid and dynamic social medium in the present, then one is likely to develop a critical awareness that this culture is not solely a thing of history. As a result, critical consciousness about Cherokee culture may become complicit in an overt way with dominant ideas (ideology), or it might oppose dominant ideas to gain access to resources or power (counterhegemony). Hegemony and ideology are complex, contradictory, and "best visualized as two ends of a continuum," with a permeable boundary between levels of agency and degrees of consciousness (Comaroff and Comaroff 1991: 28).

Because people are constituted in multiple ways, we also need to recognize the numerous hegemonic struggles taking place simultaneously within each Cherokee individual. By this I mean that ideology and hegemony do not work on a singular subject. Because individuals are always clothed in culture, certain aspects of subjectivity such as race, class, gender, sexuality, regional identity, and national identity get constituted within culture in different ways. So I am suggesting that we need to take the same basic process—the hegemonic complex—and multiply it, so that it occurs around different nodes of consciousness simultaneously. With historical depth, this theoretical formulation would then allow for the heterogeneity of consciousness, its multiple subjectivity, and the constant slippage between ideology, hegemony, and counterhegemony that takes place over time.

At the same time, we need to keep in mind that subject formation, counterhegemonic coalitions, and ideological maneuvers occur almost exclusively within the context of social groups. There are eccentric individuals who create innovative change, but this still happens in relation to other people. Within each individual there are sites where ideas coalesce around a particular subjectivity, such as race or nationality. These sites provide points of divergence and convergence, or difference and sameness, with other people. When these sites overlap, then we have the basis of a coalitional subjectivity—or as Gramsci would put it, an articulatory principle—that can then be used to unite a diverse group of people around a particular political project. Allowing for the ways subjective, ideological processes happen coalitionally provides us with a more accurate and politically grounded theoretical framework. With such a framework, Cherokee society can be visualized as a diverse body of multiply constituted individuals who coalesce in socially significant ways around one or more subjectivities, or different aspects of identity.

Thus far, I have argued that we need to build on Omi and Winant's theory of racial formation, adding to it a more nuanced understanding of Gramsci's hegemony and counterhegemonic resistance. We also need to salvage the concept of ideology from postmodern theory and use it in conjunction with hegemony and culture. Together, these ideas provide an excellent point of departure, but one that still needs to be modified to include hegemonic processes occurring within multiply constituted individuals in relational ways. This is critically important, since it is the very nature of multiple subjectivity that allows for resistance. There is always some aspect of a person's consciousness that runs counter to whatever dominant ideology is foregrounded at a given moment. Furthermore, I would argue that since no one is constituted in a unified way, no one is entirely subject to any prior or existing system of power and knowledge.

With this theoretical framework in mind, this project can begin to examine the full spectrum of Cherokee identity politics. We can pay attention to identity itself and how it is always contingent and relational, a shifting negotiation of multiple subjectivities. We can focus on how identities coalesce and break apart in socially significant ways and what happens to individuals and communities when identities are forcibly policed. These are complicated matters that are hard to imagine without a grounding in specific historical and ethnographic case studies. I hope to provide those case studies in the course of this book, so that we can begin to imagine what it means to be Cherokee, and why the stakes are so high in this political debate. By focusing on racial identity as an important site of contestation and by applying this theory to the largely multiracial Cherokee community, I hope to provide some critical insights into the ideological terrain of race, which continues to homogenize and divide this country, often, paradoxically, at the same time.

CHAPTER TWO

Blood, Culture, and Race

*Cherokee Politics and Identity
in the Eighteenth Century*

It's nearly midnight at the Cherokee ceremonial grounds in the
backwoods of Adair County, not far from the border of Arkansas. She
and her Cherokee friends have been dancing all night around a
sacred fire, and they have every intention of continuing until the early
hours of the morning. But it's late July and the midsummer's night
is hot and still, and they need a moment to rest, catch their breath,
and cool down a little. Standing beside the Bird Clan arbor, the
anthropologist and her two companions, both men in their thirties,
laugh and tell jokes as they watch the next round of dancing begin.
Mostly, however, they make note of all the different Cherokee people
who have come from near and far to celebrate the occasion. On
Red Bird Smith's birthday, some come to honor the Keetoowah
traditions, others to visit with family and friends, and still others
to connect with a sense of themselves as Cherokee people.[1] As people
arrive, the crowd swells to nearly four hundred, rivaling the turn-
out on Labor Day weekend during the Cherokee national holidays.
With her friends, she rests and visits, watching the people around
them.

"Hey, Bobby, you know Luanne over there from Stilwell?" one of
the men asks the other.

"No," says Bobby looking off at the woman in the flickering
shadows, "Who's her mother . . . Where's she from?" The conversation
continues like this for a little while, with the two men weaving a

tapestry of Cherokee life, pulling together the threads of kinship and community with bits of gossip thrown in for color.

Bobby nudges the sleepy anthropologist at his side. "Hey, Circe, you're catching all of this aren't you?" he says in a half-teasing, half-mocking manner. "Cherokees, that's the first thing we always ask when we meet somebody. . . . Who's your mother?"

She comes out of her comfortable daze of warmth and physical exhaustion, reminded that she's not there just to enjoy the rhythm of the scenery but to observe, as an outsider who is supposed to make sense of it all.

"Who's your mother?" she says listlessly. "Oh, yeah. I get it." Taking it in like the punch line of a joke she's slow to understand, she finally grasps the significance of that one statement, how it ties the Cherokee present to the past in so many ways.

For some Cherokees, having a Cherokee mother is the very key to Cherokee identity. In such cases, a mother's blood links her and her children to a complex web of kinship and community relations, to a custom of matrilineal clan membership and matrilocal residence that extends to the furthest known reaches of Cherokee history. So it was that in this context at a Cherokee ceremonial ground on a special day of celebration when the air was thick with "tradition," my Cherokee companions tried to place people through their mothers. If they knew someone's mother, then they might know his or her family, community, and clan. Of course, there are exceptions to this rule. Cherokees are, and always have been, a highly diverse group of people, and what is true for some is not true for others. Not all Cherokees in all places situate one another in terms of matrilineal kinship, and having a Cherokee father can be just as significant. Nonetheless, most Cherokees with whom I spoke during the course of my fieldwork agreed that kinship was a fundamental aspect of Cherokee identity. To them it was plain and simple: people are Cherokee because they have been born to and raised by a Cherokee family. That so many Cherokees speak of their collective identity in terms of kinship is not unusual. People everywhere are socialized within the context of particular families, and kinship still fundamentally shapes who we are in a variety of ways. In this regard, Cherokees are no different. Like all people, their discourses of kinship reflect past meanings as well as more recent ideologies of blood, race, culture, and nation.

Today, Cherokee kinship has come to mean many things, in part because it has become entangled with modern discourses of identity.

Kinship can mean having a clan identity, a common matrilineal blood-line, or it can be about sharing a political identity as a nation, one based on blood descent more generally. For some, it is both. This entanglement of Cherokee kinship ideologies with modern discourses of identity results from a complex historical process in which over the course of several centuries Cherokee belief systems came both to emulate and contest their Euroamerican counterparts. To understand the meaning of Cherokee blood kinship in the present, we have to understand the more restricted sense of blood in the prenational period and how this became conflated with Euroamerican ideas of race, culture, and nation in early Cherokee nationalism. Only then can we comprehend the historical, cultural, and political contexts shaping contemporary expressions of Cherokee identity as a whole. A comprehensive overview of Cherokee history, however, is not the goal of this chapter, for that story has already been told many times in a variety of scholarly contexts.[2] Instead, I offer a selective history of Cherokee identity in the eighteenth century as expressed through the idioms of blood, race, and culture that were prevalent during this period.

"THE TIES THAT BIND": CHEROKEE SOCIAL AND POLITICAL ORGANIZATION

Before Europeans arrived on the North American continent, Cherokee people made their lives on the ruggedly beautiful terrain of the southern Appalachians.[3] Here, they settled where the mountains gave way to land just flat enough to allow for the cultivation of corn along the Savannah, Tennessee, and Hiwassee Rivers, whose waters provided an abundant source of irrigation as well as a site for regular ceremonies. In the centuries just before contact, some 20,000 Cherokees occupied an area of almost 40,000 square miles stretching across parts of what are now known as Virginia, Tennessee, North Carolina, South Carolina, Georgia, and Alabama (Mooney 1900: 14). At that time, the Cherokees referred to themselves as *aniyunwiya*, a term meaning "the real people" in their own language. They maintained a distinct sense of peoplehood, in part because they were speakers of an Iroquoian language, which differed significantly from the surrounding Muskogean and Siouan languages more common to the Native peoples of the Southeast.[4] Cherokees also possessed a unique kinship system, culture, and religious worldview, all of which further served to define them in opposition to the others in their midst.

Cherokees had much in common, but not everything—important differences existed in terms of language and political organization. By the time they encountered Europeans in the mid-sixteenth century, Cherokees spoke three different dialects and lived in five distinct regional settlements, with each settlement representing a loose coalition of towns. These dialectical and regional distinctions arose in large part due to the challenging topography of Cherokee country, which limited interactions between Cherokee communities. The Lower towns, where the *Elati* dialect was spoken, were located in the foothills of western South Carolina, along the banks of the Savannah River. The Middle and Out towns, whose residents spoke the *Keetoowah* dialect, stretched from the headwaters of the Little Tennessee River to the easternmost reaches of the Tuckaseegee River in North Carolina. Occupants of both the Overhill towns and Valley towns shared the *Atali* dialect. The Overhill towns lay south of the Cumberland chain, along the Upper Tennessee River and the lower courses of the Little Tennessee River, while the Valley towns flourished beside the Valley and Hiwassee Rivers in western North Carolina (Gearing 1962: 1, Gilbert 1943: 199, McLoughlin 1986: 9, Mooney 1900: 16–17). Despite these differences of region and dialect, all of these communities were connected to one another through ties of kinship.

KINSHIP

"One can scarcely overemphasize the importance of kinship in the social life of the Southeastern Indians," anthropologist Charles Hudson wrote a quarter-century ago (1976: 185). In the first half of the eighteenth century, Cherokees distinguished themselves from Europeans, Africans, and other Native Americans not by skin color, race, or even language, but by membership in a Cherokee clan, which was theirs by right of birth or adoption (Perdue 1998: 49, Urban 1994: 172–93). For this reason, to be Cherokee in a social, political, and ceremonial sense was to have a clan identity (May 1996: 34). "A clan was a category of individuals who believed themselves to be blood relatives, but who could not [always] actually trace their relationships to each other through known ancestral links" (Hudson 1976: 191).[5] The Cherokees had (and continue to have) seven matrilineal clans: Wolf, Deer, Bird, Paint, Long Hair, Potato, and Blue Clans, though the translations of the last three are subject to some debate. Being matrilineal, the seven clans were regarded as kinship units that were "identical with the mother's blood" (Gilbert 1943: 298). This meant that Cherokees were members of a Cherokee clan, and thus were Cherokee, because they had a Cherokee mother. At the same time, they did not share a common blood bond with their fathers or their grandfathers on either side, according to the logic of the clan system.[6]

In general, clan relations were more enduring than other kinds of kinship bonds, such as those formed in marriage, and "Clans, not marriage, united Cherokees for life" (Hill 1997: 30). A sister and a brother or a mother and a child were of one flesh and blood, but never a husband and a wife (1997: 31). In fact, husbands and wives were not kin at all, because they were not members of the same clan. Husbands and wives could never share the common matrilineal bloodline that made them kin, for marriage within the same clan was strictly forbidden and considered to be incestuous.[7] To marry within one's own clan, or one's father's clan for that matter, was punishable by death, a severe sanction not replaced by whipping until the nineteenth century (Gilbert 1943: 340). With such sanctions, the Cherokee clan system regulated marriage by defining appropriate and inappropriate marriage partners. Forbidden to marry within their own clan or their father's, Cherokees were encouraged to marry within the clans of their grandparents, and an ideal mate would be a member of the maternal or paternal grandfather's clan (Gilbert 1943: 208).

Although the Cherokee ideal was to find a mate from either grandfathers' clan, this preference was not always reflected in practice, especially after the intrusion of Europeans. In the latter half of the eighteenth century, Cherokees began to marry non-Indians with greater frequency, a practice that had the potential to disrupt the traditional ways in which Cherokees socially classified one another.[8] However, when Cherokee women married European men, their marriages did not threaten the continuity of the tribe. The matrilineal clan system ensured that the child of a Cherokee woman and European man would be identified as Cherokee. As ethnohistorian Sarah Hill writes, "The mother's identity took precedence over all other ancestry, even for one who had 'lost himself' among white people, or whose fathers and grandfathers were white. Identity and a complex of clan possessions, which ranged from land and insignia to customs and prayers, descended from mothers" (1997: 27). Because of the enduring stability of the Cherokee clan system, there was no such thing as a "half-breed," even in the late eighteenth century.

Matrilineal kinship provided the blood substance of identity, and a child's identity was determined solely by the mother, whether she be Cherokee or of another tribe, African, or European (Perdue 1998: 82).[9]

The strong matrilineal bonds of the clan system also meant that when Cherokee women married European men and produced Cherokee children, they did not always form lasting relationships with their husbands. Cherokee women had considerable autonomy and sexual freedom, rights that differed considerably from those of European and other Native-American women in the Southeast.[10] Cherokee women were free to choose when and if they wanted to be with a man, what type of man, and for how long (Fogelson 1990: 170). A Cherokee woman could expect to exercise a great deal of personal freedom over the course of her lifetime, and that freedom stemmed directly from the matrilineal clan, which offered her social and economic security. A woman could expect to reside with her kinswomen, to own her own home, and to share in the agricultural products of her clan. She also could have sex with whomever she pleased, then marry and separate at will.

Cherokee women were not the only ones who reaped the benefits of a matrilineal clan system. All clan members, including men, had certain obligations to one another. A member of the Deer Clan, for instance, was morally bound to protect and provide for any other clan member in need, even those he or she had never met. If a Deer man should be traveling far from home in an unfamiliar part of Cherokee territory, he need only "to ask for the house of his clan in order to be given food, shelter, protection, and hospitality as a member of the family" (Champagne 1992: 38). This form of hospitality was always available, since every Cherokee town had representatives from all seven Cherokee clans (Gearing 1962: 21). As a result, the Cherokee clan system not only ordered social relations among known relatives on a daily basis but also established obligations and a common basis of identity among unknown kin in distant Cherokee communities (Champagne 1992: 38).

One of the clan members' most important obligations to one another was to respect and maintain the law of blood revenge. This "law of blood" meant that if a member of the Paint Clan were killed by someone of the Wolf Clan, even if by accident, then all Paints were morally bound to avenge the death of their kinsman. If they did not, then the deceased Paint's restless spirit and "crying blood" would come to haunt them (Perdue 1998: 52). The clan of the victim would usually exact vengeance by taking the life of the original killer, at which point "both clans involved would consider the matter settled because harmony had been restored" (Perdue 1998: 52). However, if the killer should flee or seek refuge, then the offended clan would be perfectly within in its rights to take the life of any other member of the killer's clan, preferably someone with a similar status to the original victim. Thus, the law of blood served symbolically to unite Cherokee clan members, whose spilt blood was functionally equivalent, whose lives might be substituted one for the other.

BLOOD

Blood ties among Cherokee kin were not merely symbolic. Cherokee clan members believed that they literally shared a common blood, a blood they were morally obligated to protect and defend. As Raymond Fogelson, one of the few anthropologists to have studied Cherokee beliefs about blood and kinship, states:

> For the Cherokees, kinship is literally defined as a relationship of blood. Blood is not, as it is for us, the metaphor for kinship that is indicated by such terms as "consanguineal" or such phrases as "blood is thicker than water." The Cherokee theory of procreation holds, in common with the beliefs of other Iroquoians, that the female contributes blood and flesh to the fetus, while the father provides the skeleton through the agency of sperm, which can be considered a form of uncongealed bone. The blood tie of an individual to a mother is thus regarded as a bond of living, procreative substance, not a metaphoric figure of speech. (Fogelson 1990: 173–74)

Fogelson makes an important point about the literal rather than symbolic meanings of blood kinship among Cherokees. While this distinction holds true for eighteenth-century Cherokee beliefs, that is not the case for other blood ideologies held by Cherokees during this same period. For instance, in Cherokee mythology, blood is repeatedly used as a symbolic metaphor for life, as I will discuss shortly.[11] In general, however, a symbolic rather than a literal understanding of blood and blood kinship became much more common among the Cherokees over time. In the chapters to come, I demonstrate that over the past two centuries Cherokees began to incorporate more and more metaphoric interpretations of blood into their kinship ideologies and their competing definitions of Cherokee identity. Literal interpretations do not disappear, but the addition of metaphoric understandings of blood kinship complicates the picture.

Throughout the Cherokees' history, their beliefs about blood have been central to their interpretations and attributions of Cherokee identity. We have already examined how "the idea of the blood connection of the clan . . . allie[d] with the blood revenge principle" (Gilbert 1943: 207), and how blood was literally the shared substance of matrilineal kinship, but what other meanings did Cherokees attach to blood during the eighteenth century?[12] Like many tribal peoples around the world, Cherokees believed that a woman's menstrual blood was a powerful substance. It was not dirty or polluting, but it was a destructive force and a source of feminine strength (Fogelson 1990: 172–73). The Stone-clad story from James Mooney's *Myths of the Cherokee* (1900) is tell-ing in this regard. Stoneclad was a cannibalistic monster who was vir-tually indestructible because of his impenetrable stone skin. But Stoneclad had one weakness—he could not bear the sight of a menstru-ating woman. Although no Cherokee warrior could stop him, Stone-clad finally met his demise in the presence of seven menstruating vir-gins. One by one, they stood naked in his path, sapping his strength, until Stoneclad finally crumbled into a heap (Mooney 1900: 319–20). In addition to having such symbolic power in Cherokee mythology, menstrual blood was also a force to be contended with in everyday Cherokee affairs. For example, the destructive power of menstrual blood could be channeled against an enemy and thus was often evoked in sorcery, at war, and in ball game rituals (Fogelson 1990: 173). In recognition of this power, Cherokee women were isolated in menstrual huts, far away from family and friends, during their menstrual periods (Fogelson 1990: 173).

Menstruation, childbirth, war, hunting—any activity that involved blood—required strict rules of behavior on the part of Cherokees (Per-due 1998: 35). Always a powerful substance, blood took various forms, and Cherokees made distinctions between its different types, or "states." Blood could be fresh and healthy with a bright crimson color—*gigagé*—or it might become "spoiled" or "exhausted," at which point it would be described as *wodí*, meaning it was a dull brownish red, the color of clay (Fogelson 1990: 173, Shoemaker 1997: 638).[13] To keep their blood from becoming exhausted, Cherokees would engage in pe-riodic rites of bloodletting as a prophylactic measure against illness (Fo-gelson 1990: 173). For example, a young ball player before a game or a warrior before battle would be subjected to ritualized scratching over much of his body. This rite not only purified and strengthened the re-cipients, it also provided a deeply symbolic means by which Cherokee men could appropriate the fearsome power of menstruating women (Fogelson 1990: 175–76). Through episodic bleeding, Cherokee men became like menstruating women, and thus filled with destructive potential.

The power of blood could also have a positive role. For instance, in the "Origin of Corn and Game," one of the most sacred stories from Cherokee mythology, blood is a central metaphor for life. The story begins with Selu (corn) down by a river, washing and preparing meat that her husband, Kanati (the lucky hunter), has brought back from the hunt. The couple has a little boy who loves to play by the river during the day. One morning, the couple overhears their son talking and playing as if he were with another child. When questioned about it, the little boy tells his parents that he has an elder brother who came out of the river saying his mother had cruelly thrown him in the water. The parents then realize that the strange "Wild Boy" had "sprung from the blood of the game which Selu had washed off at the river's edge" (Mooney 1900: 242). Sarah Hill offers a valuable interpretation of this story. She argues that the Wild Boy's emergence is, in part, "a cautionary tale about the power of blood," in which the mother is cruel because she "discards living matter, blood, in the flowing water. Shed blood with care, the story warns, for blood is life itself. Death and birth wind around each other, creating a pattern from woman's labor. Life emerges from her cast off blood, taking form, shape, identity" (1997: 77).

Other events in the story of Kanati and Selu reveal the power of blood as a life-giving force. For instance, later in the narrative, Selu's children wonder how she is always able to provide them with enough corn and beans. Spying on her with curiosity, the two boys see Selu rubbing and shaking her body as beans and corn magically fall to the ground, filling the baskets at her feet. This frightens the boys, who decide their mother is a witch and should be killed. Selu, realizing full well her children's plan, has enough foresight to tell her sons how to produce corn long after she is dead. So, with little struggle, they slay her, chopping off her head. Just as Selu has predicted, when the boys drag her broken body over the ground, wherever her blood falls, corn springs forth to life (Mooney 1900: 244–45). Selu has become not only "corn" but also the "corn mother." Her blood becomes the metaphorical source of Cherokee life, for as she sheds blood for her children, new life comes into being. Thus, as a powerful force in the Cherokee universe, blood was a vital element of Cherokee identity, for it defined who was and was not a Cherokee in both literal and symbolic terms.

TOWNS

Blood, kinship, language, and culture: these fundamental aspects of eighteenth-century Cherokee identity not only bound Cherokees to one another but also defined them as distinct individuals. However, to better understand the complexities of Cherokee identity, we also need to examine the changing forms of Cherokee sociopolitical organization during the eighteenth century, for it was in the realm of politics that Cherokee identity was further created, expressed, and manipulated.

In the first half of the eighteenth century, Cherokees lived as members of a "jural community," a system of sovereign towns related to one another through ties of kinship and culture that provided a framework for regulating hostilities among town residents (Gearing 1962: 109). During the 1700s, the number of Cherokee towns increased from somewhere around thirty to nearly sixty-five and then contracted again toward the end of the century.[14] In each of these towns lived approximately 350 Cherokee individuals who functioned as a single social, religious, and political unit (Fogelson 1977: 191, Gearing 1962: 3). However, as anthropologist Gerald Sider points out, Cherokee towns were not necessarily residential communities: "Among the Cherokee in the early to mid-eighteenth century, for example, several towns' councils—the meetings of collective self-governance—were in fact attended by members of physically distinct residential communities, who regarded themselves as members of a common 'town.' Some residential communities had two distinct and separate town councils meeting separately and independently, each governing the affairs of its own members" (Sider 1993: 233). This distinction between Cherokee residential and political units is often overlooked in the ethnohistorical literature, where terms such as *village* and *town* are used almost interchangeably. To my mind, *village* more accurately describes a Cherokee residential community, while *town* refers to a more coherent sociopolitical entity.

Where a Cherokee lived, worshipped, and weighed in on political matters was a fundamental aspect of his or her identity. For this reason, we need to understand how Cherokee towns and their associated villages functioned and how they organized Cherokee social interactions. Most Cherokee towns were comprised of only thirty to sixty dwellings, but the largest were reported to have nearly one hundred (Woodward 1963: 48). Each Cherokee household consisted of "an extended family linked by women, typically an elderly woman, her daughters and their children, the women's husbands, and any unmarried sons" (Perdue 1998: 24).

Married sons lived with their wives' families, since Cherokees practiced a pattern of matrilocal residence.[15] During the warmer months, Cherokee families lived together in long, rectangular houses, some fifteen by sixty feet in size, constructed of various types of hewn timber and smoothed over with wattle and daub (Hill 1997: 69). The winter hot houses were of a similar construction but were considerably smaller and round, with much thicker walls to hold in heat while the family slept through the long, cold winter nights.

   Individual family dwellings were not the only structures in Cherokee communities. At the heart of community life, each town had a ceremonial and political center that consisted of a town house, square ground, and ball court. The first of these, the town house, was "built on a cleared and level square of ground, often on the summit of an ancient mound," and being a "huge, windowless rotunda . . . covered with earth and thatch," looked like a small mountain from a distance (Hill 1997: 72). Here, as many as 500 townspeople would meet on a regular basis to discuss social, political, and religious matters. The second structure at the center of Cherokee life was the square ground, where Cherokees gathered when the summer heat or windless days made the town house too stuffy and uncomfortable. The square ground, like the town house, was built around a large clearing, surrounded by several wooden arbors where town inhabitants could sit and take advantage of the cool breeze while conducting rituals, dancing, or deciding on community affairs. The third structure was the ball ground, a large rectangular clearing that had a long wooden pole with a fish-shaped carving on top, erected somewhere in the vicinity. Here, Cherokees would compete with other Cherokee towns or with members of other southeastern tribes in a game similar to lacrosse. Known as "the little brother of war," this game provided an outlet for hostilities and was taken quite seriously by the participants. In addition to these three sites, each Cherokee town had its own communal gardens and a public granary, which helped to ensure the welfare of all community members, since items from both were used to provide aid to the elderly, the needy, or those who had suffered unexpected misfortune.

   As the "physical and spiritual center of Cherokee life," each town had a complex political structure (Fogelson and Kutsche 1961: 89). Depending on whether a town was at peace or at war, two distinct "structural poses," as anthropologist Fred Gearing describes them, orchestrated Cherokee community life (1962: 8–9). A "White" organization operated during times of peace, while a "Red" one emerged in response to the stresses of war. If a white flag of peace were flying over the town council house, everyone in the community immediately would assume a certain set of hierarchical relations with one another, but if the red flag of war were flying, then another social strategy would ensue (Gearing 1962: 13). Under conditions of peace, a set of priestly officials presided over the town council, where they consulted with a respected body of elders. These gray-haired, "beloved" old men represented each of the seven matrilineal clans that organized the Cherokee kinship system.[16] The priestly officials, along with the body of elders, counseled with the younger Cherokee men—all of whom were heavily influenced by their female kin. Remarkably, the group managed to forge community consensus in nearly all political decisions. Political unanimity was a necessary outcome of the Cherokee ethic, in which any direct coercion or abuse of power was strongly discouraged (Fogelson 1977: 186). Instead, Cherokees sought to promote harmony with one another and to keep disruptions to a minimum (Gearing 1962: 35).

The desire for harmonious relations extended to trade, with the White organization taking the lead in maintaining diplomatic trade relations. However, when those relationships disintegrated, such as in a military emergency or when there was a need to maintain internal control, the Red organization would assume leadership of the Cherokee community. In place of the priestly officials and the beloved old men of the White organization, a set of war priests and war officials would rise to prominence. As a whole, the body of men who consulted with these leaders were much younger, though the highest ranking men were middle-aged warriors who had earned great respect for heroic feats in battle. The shift from a White stance to a Red one was accompanied by a shift in male identity, with men changing their roles and relative status based on their age and ability as warriors. Under conditions of war, a man's clan identity became somewhat less important in defining his social relations.[17]

Though at first glance, the Red organization seems primarily to have been the province of men, women could also play a significant role in this political formation. Exceptional women who had shown great bravery—usually by choosing to fight on the battlefield in the place of their male family members—had an important voice in the Red organization (Fogelson and Kutsche 1961: 93, Fogelson 1990: 167–68, Perdue 1998: 39). Also, postmenopausal women were a powerful mediating category between men in the Red pose and those in the White pose (Fogelson 1977: 192–93). This Red and White dichotomy played out in every

Cherokee town and later in broader Cherokee political organizations that encompassed the entire tribe. Still, it was not technically a political moiety system: unlike many other tribes in the Southeast, the Cherokees were not divided into Red and White towns, but all Cherokee towns were capable of assuming either a Red or White stance as needed (Urban 1994: 178, Fogelson and Kutsche 1961: 93).

Although this common form of organization existed at the town level, we have to keep in mind that eighteenth-century Cherokee towns were autonomous, self-sufficient units with a highly developed sense of their own identity (Fogelson and Kutsche 1961: 97). Each town valued its independence. This fact, coupled with the differences of dialect and the four regional settlements shaping the parameters of Cherokee social interaction, seems to suggest a lack of political cohesion among the tribe as a whole (Gilbert 1943: 180–81). Although Cherokees were capable of mobilizing larger coalitions of towns under conditions of duress, in the early decades of the eighteenth century they cannot properly be viewed as a unified "nation," at least in a modern political sense. They had no centralized state structure with coercive power, no formalized bureaucracy, and no political officers for the tribe at large (Champagne 1992: 25, Gearing 1962: 82).[18] Still, Cherokee towns, like those of other tribes in the Southeast, were connected to one another through ties of blood, kinship, culture, religion, language, trade, and military alliances (Sider 1993: 231–32).

STEPS TOWARD NATIONHOOD:
CHEROKEE POLITICAL CENTRALIZATION

With no national political structure representing the tribe as a whole, Cherokees made most decisions at the local level, using independent town councils and regional coalitions. Political decisions were typically made by consensus, a practice that continued well into the nineteenth century, though exceptions became increasingly common after 1730. However, as a result of sustained interaction with European colonial powers, the political organization of the tribe changed considerably. In the latter half of the eighteenth century, as Cherokees increasingly identified their common interests and concerns, they became a more cohesive sociopolitical unit and shifted toward a more centralized form of government. These were the Cherokee people's first steps toward political nationhood and a more explicitly unified tribal identity.

Cherokees took these steps only under conditions of duress. When

Europeans failed to differentiate between Cherokee towns and treated them as representatives of a single sociopolitical unit, Cherokees realized that "persons in any village [read 'town'] had no control over the behavior of other villages, and could be made to suffer because of that behavior" (Gearing 1962: 109). Aware of this risk, Cherokees first tried to centralize their political authority in an effort to control the practice of blood revenge (Champagne 1992: 94). When warriors and angry clansmen lost loved ones on the battlefield or in the heated exchanges of the colonial frontier, they often sought revenge among the colonists because they applied the law of blood equally to non-Cherokees. Europeans did not appreciate the logic of the Cherokee position and usually failed to understand these acts of revenge as a product of duty and honor, of kinsmen seeking to right a wrong and restore harmony in the world. As a result, European colonists showed no mercy as they lashed back against Cherokee communities, often treating them as if they were one and the same, punishing those with no relationship to the original offense.

In the wake of conflicts that became common during the mid-1700s, Cherokee towns voluntarily decided to relinquish some of their autonomy in order to create "a single tribal sovereignty" (Gearing 1962: 84). Between 1730 and 1775, the Cherokees created a new, more centralized form of tribal government, though many of the old ways were retained. Since town politics were its only precedent, the tribal government went through successive stages in which it replicated the political structures of local Cherokee towns, in particular the Red and White structural poses of war and peace (Gearing 1962: 85–105). This meant that the tribal government would fall under the leadership of either warriors or beloved old men, depending on which political structure was currently in place to fit the particular context.

At first, the Red political structure of Cherokee towns was adopted in the early attempts at centralization in 1730, when some of the larger Cherokee towns developed a "quasi-government" modeled after the town war organization (Gearing 1962: 85). With warriors at the helm, this new form of tribal government persisted for over two decades and enabled Cherokees to navigate their way through a rapidly changing political environment rife with hazards. Remaining in the Red mode, however, had certain limitations, especially when it came to gauging public sentiment and garnering popular support. Without a regular forum for debate among the tribe at large, the new Cherokee government was limited in its ability to create public policies and to communicate them among the general populace (Gearing 1962: 88). All of this was to change, however, when the beloved old men, who traditionally led the town councils of the White organization, entered politics on the tribal level (Gearing 1962: 89). Under their leadership, a new version of the Cherokee tribal government that overcame many of the last one's limitations emerged in the late 1750s. It included both "a tribal structure for implementing policy, modeled after the village [town] structure for war" and a means for forming public policy "similar to the village [town] structures for councils" (Gearing 1962: 89). Finally, the Cherokee people had a political forum for creating and expressing a single tribal sentiment.

The new tribal government that emerged in the mid-eighteenth century was important to Cherokee identity for several reasons. It not only provided a means by which Cherokees could forge consensus and generate public policy, but it also provided a new tribal polity, one that was increasingly separated from the Cherokee kinship system. This was a dramatic change for Cherokees, who up until this point had decided their political affairs at the local level in individual Cherokee towns, with various kinsmen and women representing the social and political interests of their individual clans. Cherokee politics had always been a matter of Cherokee kinship, but this was changing with the shift toward a more centralized form of government. By the mid-eighteenth century, the Cherokee kinship system was no longer the primary basis of Cherokee political organization, at least at the tribal level. In fact, in his book, *Social Order and Political Change,* sociologist Duane Champagne takes this argument a step further. He writes, "The national [read 'tribal'] council was composed of village delegations that represented the views and interests of their local town councils, not the views of the seven clans or local clan segments. Consequently, the national council was differentiated from the clan system, and clan prerogatives and organization were not the basis of political decision making or of the principles of organization of the national government" (1992: 43). According to Champagne, then, the new Cherokee polity was actually separate and distinct from the Cherokee kinship system, largely because local clan segments did not have official recognition within the tribal council.

Although Champagne makes a good case, some evidence contradicts his argument. For instance, in 1818 Charles Hicks, the Cherokee second chief, stated, "The national council is composed of persons from each clan; some clans sending more, some less, according to their population, though the number is not very definitely fixed."[19] Moreover, Gearing maintains that the tribal council was led in part by village headmen, each of whom represented one of the seven clans (1962: 93). Even town delegates, who were expected to prioritize town interests over those of their local clan segment, remained clansmen and thus were present on the tribal council as such. As I see it, the evidence for the differentiation of political and clan roles in Cherokee society is not as clear as Champagne suggests. Even if we acknowledge that Cherokee kinship was less critical to the working of the tribal council, clan identity continued to be an important organizational principle of Cherokee political life in local town councils, where it defined who Cherokees were and influenced their political behavior. Because town politics were deeply influenced by clan interests and those collective interests were then represented in the tribal council, I suggest that the separation of the Cherokee polity from the Cherokee kinship system was not so neat or definitive. Although the influence of kinship on tribal politics did diminish during this period, it never completely disappeared and may have continued to be an important subtext even in the workings of the tribal council. With this in mind, the political organization of the Cherokees in the mid-eighteenth century can be characterized in terms of both continuity and change. Kinship continued to be a primary force behind local town politics, which were still a priority for most Cherokees, but it also became a secondary influence on the emerging tribal government.

Despite the diversity of Cherokee political forms, the eighteenth century was dominated by a pattern of increased political centralization in which Cherokees began to identify and act as a unified polity in response to the increased pressures of external domination and incorporation. The balance between old and new, between local traditions and centralization, characterized the new Cherokee political structure. Though Cherokees had not created a state in the modern sense of the word, they had built a confederacy.[20] A confederacy is a loose coalition of political entities—in this case, towns—that generate leadership from within. This leadership, then, has authority to deal with external agents but has no coercive power over local political affairs. A confederacy represents an intermediate structural position between the strictly autonomous politics of Cherokee towns and regions that existed prior to 1730 and the more highly centralized and coercive state politics that emerged later in Cherokee history.

Though many Cherokees continued to identify themselves on the basis of clan and community rather than by tribe, the process of political centralization was simultaneously a process of creation in which Cherokees began to see themselves as a more unified entity (Sider 1993: 230–31). Cherokees had long shared a sense of distinct peoplehood, based on their ties of blood, kinship, culture, and community, but by the latter half of the eighteenth century, these ties had begun to coalesce into a new confederation, one with nationalistic overtones. Cherokees had used those cultural ties and understandings to build a government that seems to have had a fairly high degree of social and political solidarity, despite the variance in its structural forms. Because of their increased social and political solidarity, the Cherokees were well positioned to accept further changes in their tribal political structure. This may explain why they created a national government—a "state"—in the early part of the nineteenth century, long before any other native society in the Southeast, a development that would have important ramifications on Cherokee identity for years to come.[21]

FROM "RED" TO "INDIAN": THE ORIGINS OF RACIAL THOUGHT AMONG CHEROKEES

In the latter half of the eighteenth century, as Cherokees became more politically centralized and began to conceive of themselves as a more unified polity, another important change occurred in their self-perception. Cherokees continued to define themselves in their own cultural terms as a people who were unified by kinship, language, and religious worldview and who differed according to their individual dialects, clans, roles, and town political allegiances. However, as a result of their ongoing interactions with Euroamericans, Cherokees also began to define themselves as a wholly different people in opposition to whites. At first, they heard European explanations of difference and offered their own in response, but by the end of the century, Cherokees were beginning to define themselves in terms of race as well as culture. This appropriation and internalization of Euroamerican notions of racial identity, in addition to concurrent changes in political organization, helped set the stage for the emergence of Cherokee nationalism in the early nineteenth century.

To understand the context in which these shifts in Cherokee identity took place, we need to examine that broader field of public opinion and the various explanations of Native-American difference that Europeans and Cherokees employed during this period. The scholarly literature that treats how "white men" imagined Native Americans is quite extensive.[22] Unfortunately, a comparable literature on Native-American perceptions of Europeans does not exist, though the topic is often briefly addressed in specific tribal ethnographies and ethnohistories. Because of the scattered and fragmentary nature of this research, I will provide a brief overview of European perceptions of Native-American difference as they pertain to eighteenth-century Cherokees. Then, I will focus on Cherokee conceptions of human difference, showing how, as they began to define themselves in opposition to the European and African "others" in their midsts, they actively engaged with a broader discursive field of European and indigenous thought. This "field of opinion," to use Bourdieu's term, provided both context and content as Cherokees began to incorporate ideas of race and nation into their own cultural frameworks and identities (Bourdieu 1977: 168).

EUROPEAN PERCEPTIONS OF RACIAL DIFFERENCE

On the matter of racial difference, European contributions to the realm of public opinion were significant. In the first decades after contact, Europeans thought that Native Americans were basically white like themselves and that any differences in appearance could be explained in cultural terms (Vaughan 1982: 921). Europeans believed that Native Americans' skin color was a result of prolonged exposure to sun and smoke and their preference for adorning their bodies with red clay, vermilion, berry juice, or bear grease. Theology bolstered such thinking, since early European writings on Native Americans were also committed to the theory of monogenesis, the idea that all human beings descended from a common ancestor. Pope Paul III gave papal authority to this interpretation when he declared in 1537 that Native Americans were actually human and not animals and that they were worthy of salvation (McLoughlin and Conser 1989: 249).

Paul III's pronouncement had a significant impact on European conceptions of Indianness. It was gradually challenged, however, as Europeans encroached further into North America and met with frequent resistance, both subtle and overt. By the late seventeenth century, with their thinking colored by a century and a half of increasing conflict, Europeans began to espouse new ideas of racial difference. For the first time, they began to describe and classify Native Americans as a red people. Historian Alden Vaughan offers three explanations for why this occurred. First, the term *redskin* emerged as a logical description of enemies who wore red paint on the warpath (Vaughn 1982: 942). Second, when Native Americans refused the trappings of "civilization," preferring their own cultural practices to those of whites, some Europeans began to understand this tendency as the product of innate difference and imagined a connection between dark skins and "dark" ways (1982: 943–944). A third major influence was the work of eighteenth-century naturalists like Carolus Linnaeus, who classified the world's people using color categories, with Europeans as white, Asians as yellow, Africans as black, and Native Americans as red (1982: 944–946). As a result of these influences, most eighteenth-century Europeans began to describe Native Americans as red and to think of them as fundamentally different from themselves.

The perceptual shift from Native Americans as white to red was neither sudden nor universally accepted. Throughout the eighteenth century, Europeans debated back and forth about the specific origins of Native-American people and how these origins might account for their perceived differences. New theories emerged, suggesting separate origins for the different "races" of humankind, but these did not take hold at a broad level since most Christians considered them heretical. Working from the Christian perspective, even in the late 1700s some European and Euroamerican authors continued to maintain that Native Americans were inherently white (Vaughan 1982: 930). Usually, these writers were proponents of monogenesis seeking a biblical explanation for the origin of Native Americans. A popular book in this tradition that made specific reference to the Cherokees is James Adair's *The History of the American Indian* (1775). In this work, Adair argues that the Cherokees and other Native Americans are descended from the ten lost tribes of Israel. Though his thesis implies that Cherokees are Semitic, other writers from this period argue that Cherokees are the descendants of Meshek, the grandson of Noah, and thus are white Europeans (McLoughlin and Conser 1989: 245–48).

It was not until the science of ethnology assumed legitimate stature in the early nineteenth century that there was any "real competition against the belief that all human beings were descended from one ancestor" (McLoughlin and Conser 1989: 249). In the early nineteenth century, Euroamerican ethnologists offered new polygenetic theories of human origins that were finally accepted by a broader public because they were cloaked in the mantle of "science." These pseudo-scientific explanations of racial difference took root among Euroamericans at a time when a new wave of American nationalism was seeking rational justifications for ongoing racial exploitation and the continued expansion of the republic (McLoughlin and Conser 1989: 244).

CHEROKEE PERCEPTIONS OF RACIAL DIFFERENCE

Of course, while Europeans were deciding that Native Americans were innately different, Native Americans were forming their own opinions. But was this opinion based on the emerging racial logic of Euroamericans? Did Native Americans begin to think of themselves as a separate race during the eighteenth century? Historian Nancy Shoemaker points to the fact that long before Europeans began to classify Native Americans as a red people, indigenous people in the Southeast were using *red* as a term of self-reference because it was meaningful within their own cultural categories (1997: 627). In the case of the Cherokees, they were a red people not only when they assumed a structural position of war but also when they hinted of their mythical origins in red clay (1997: 641). Yet, we should not make too much of this redness and certainly should not conflate it with a Euroamerican conception of race. In most cases, Cherokees began to refer to themselves as red in response to Europeans calling themselves white (1997: 629).

Using color terms had some practical benefits in the ongoing dialogue with Europeans. In much the same way that they had used kinship terms, Cherokees also adopted color categories as a strategy to inform Europeans about social obligations (Shoemaker 1997: 638). When Cherokees referred to the English as "elder brother," they did so within the context of their own kinship system, where elder brothers were responsible for the welfare of their younger siblings. In a similar fashion, color-based categories also implied certain social roles. For instance, when a group of seven Cherokees visited London in 1730 to seal their diplomatic and trade relations with the British, one of them said to the English king, "We look upon the Great King George as the Sun and as our Father and upon ourselves as his children[.] For tho' we are red and you white yet our hands and hearts are joined together" (Williams 1928: 140). In referring to the English king as a white father and to the Cherokees as his red children, this speaker invoked metaphors of both Cherokee kinship and town politics to assume certain social relationships with the British. The British would be the white peacemakers, the diplomats, the fatherly providers, while the Cherokees would be the red warriors in need of material goods.

Cherokees used *red* as a term of self-reference in a variety of contexts, so that it appears to have had no fixed meaning (Shoemaker 1997: 641). For instance, they may have used *red* and *white* as metaphors for social obligations and hierarchical differences, without intending them as ra-

Figure 3.   Hand-colored, wood engraving of three Cherokees and their interpreter on a diplomatic mission to London, 1762. Courtesy of the Gilcrease Museum, Tulsa, Oklahoma.

cial categories rooted in biology (1997: 637). Or, if Cherokees had a precontact identity as red based on their own beliefs about their origins, then they may have believed the different color terms "designated innate, divinely ordained differences between peoples" (1997: 637). Although it is difficult to ascertain which of these scenarios held true for much of the eighteenth century, we can be relatively certain that by the end of the century Cherokees had begun to internalize some ideas of race as fundamental to their own identity. In the late eighteenth century, we see Cherokees struggling with the Euroamerican concept of race and its sociopolitical implications, even trying to invert the racial hierarchy and use ideas of racial difference to serve their own purposes. For instance, in 1785 during the council for the Treaty of Hopewell, the Cherokee chief, Old Tassel, said, "I am made of this earth, on which the great

man above placed me, to possess it. . . . You must know the red people
are the aborigines of this land, and that it is but a few years since the
white people found it out. I am of the first stock, as the commissioners
know, and a native of this land; and the white people are now living on
it as our friends."[23] This quote suggests that after the American Revolution, Cherokees began to "abandon the mutually agreed upon racial
hierarchy that had granted whites a higher status in exchange for trade
goods" (Shoemaker 1997: 642). Instead, they emphasized "their age and
precedence as a people," and defined themselves differently, "to neu-
tralize the hierarchy Americans thought they had inherited from the
British" (1997: 642). So, while Euroamericans continued to use racial
difference as a justification for economic exploitation and territorial expansion, Cherokees increasingly used race to legitimate their own political and economic claims.

IDEAS OF RACE IN PRACTICE: THE ORIGINS
OF BLACK SLAVERY AMONG THE CHEROKEES

In the late eighteenth century, ideas about racial difference served Cherokee political and economic interests in another matter: the African slave
trade. Cherokee involvement with black slavery came about as a gradual
and uneven response to the various forms of social, political, and economic change that were taking place in the colonial context. At the time
of European contact in the sixteenth century, Cherokees probably had
not viewed other human beings as commodities. An indigenous form of
human bondage did exist among the Cherokees, but it differed significantly from the chattel slavery of Europeans. In *Slavery and the Evolution of Cherokee Society, 1540–1866,* Theda Perdue argues that before contact Cherokees referred to unfree people as *atsi nahsa'i,* or "ones
who are owned" (1979: 4).[24] This class of people arose from captives
taken during intertribal warfare, who suffered a number of fates including bondage, torture, or even death. However, a Cherokee clan could
adopt a captive, who would then be fully incorporated within the tribe
because the mantle of kinship had been extended over them, offering its
status and protection. Only the clanless and marginal *atsi nahsa'i* were
considered to be less than human (Perdue 1979: 16).[25]

Extended contact with Europeans transformed Cherokee slavery in
more ways than one. Once Europeans began to arrive in force and establish extensive trade networks with Native Americans, the economic
value of war captives rose tremendously. With a growing dependence

on European manufactured goods, Cherokees increased the frequency of slave raids on neighboring communities. Though Cherokees did not value war captives as laborers, they had become valuable assets in an economic market where European goods were exchanged for human captives (Perdue 1979: 35). A large-scale Indian slave trade soon developed in the Southeast, and by 1708 the colony of South Carolina included 2,900 African slaves and 1,400 Native-American slaves out of a total population of 9,850 (Nash 1974: 113). Despite the willingness of some southeastern tribes to participate in the business of selling Indians, the Native-American slave trade slowly started to decline around 1720, in part because Africans began to replace Native Americans as the preferred human commodity. This shift occurred largely because Native Americans were able to resist bondage more effectively through the help of adjacent kinsmen, who guided their escapes through an already familiar terrain. Those who did not flee had a greater susceptibility to disease, making Native Americans a poor long-term investment for Europeans (Kolchin 1993: 8). On the other hand, Africans possessed greater immunities to European germs and seemed less likely to escape, given their lack of knowledge about the surrounding terrain. Still, many African slaves braved these unknown regions in an attempt to find freedom, sometimes with the help of friendly Native-American communities.

Other Native Americans quickly discovered the highly profitable nature of capturing runaway black slaves. As a consequence, by 1776 most Cherokees traded almost exclusively in African slaves rather than Native-American bondsmen (Perdue 1979: 34). This change in the relationship between African and Native Americans suited the European colonists, who lived in growing fear of an alliance between the two groups. To undermine this possibility, Euroamericans began to play Native-American and African-American people against one another, sowing the seeds of hostility, hatred, and suspicion. They did this in a variety of fashions. While southeastern tribes were encouraged to round up runaway black slaves, African Americans were used in military campaigns against Indian nations in the Carolinas and Georgia (Perdue 1979: 41, Nash 1974: 292). At the same time, colonists waged an ideological campaign to persuade Native Americans that their only hope of economic and political survival was to adopt Euroamerican cultural values and practices, which precluded any alliance with African Americans. Motivated by an intense greed for Native-American land, the colonists sought to "persuade the Indian that his interests coincided with those of the whites and that Native Americans only needed to be 'civilized' in order to become equivalent to Europeans" (Perdue 1979: 46). At the same time, Euroamericans insisted that Africans fell into a separate racial category, even going so far as to suggest that the adoption of black slavery was a necessary and beneficial step on the southeastern tribes' road to progress.

By the late eighteenth century, in response to these various maneuvers on the part of European colonists, Cherokees had internalized an understanding of racial difference and racial prejudice that articulated with Western views. At the same time, however, Cherokees manipulated the existing racial hierarchy, aggressively placing themselves on top. For instance, in 1775 James Adair observed that the Cherokees and Choctaws were "so strongly attached to, and prejudiced in favour of their own colour, that they think as meanly of the whites, as we possibly can do of them" (Williams 1930: 1, 3). Another expression of racial hostility was heard in 1793, when Cherokee chief Little Turkey sent a letter to the governor of Tennessee, William Blount, in which he described the Spaniards as, "a lying, deceitful, treacherous people . . . not real white people, and what few I have seen of them looked like mulattos, and I would never have anything to say to them."[26] Thus, by the end of the eighteenth century, human differences that Cherokees had once understood in terms of color symbolism, culture, politics, and kinship were now also understood in terms of race. Red, white, and black had become racial categories "because the Cherokees described the origins of difference as innate, the product of separate creations, and they spoke of skin color as if it were a meaningful index of difference" (Shoemaker 1997: 643). Yet, as these two examples suggest, even as Cherokees internalized Western notions of race as a fundamental aspect of their identity and expressed their own versions of racial prejudice and hierarchy, they also continued to use race in creative and, at times, subversive ways.

One of the most important ways in which Cherokees used race was in the process of nation building. Up until the latter decades of the eighteenth century, Cherokees, like most Native Americans, "had not traditionally understood nations as the West came to define them. Nor did race play much of a role in their thinking" (Walker 1997: 4–5). Instead, as this chapter has demonstrated, their sense of political community was based on ties of culture, kinship, language, and religious worldview, similar to Western notions of ethnic nationalism. But even from this vantage, they were not a political nation in the modern, Western sense of the word. Even ethnic nationalism may be a misnomer because the

term *ethnic* implies a conflation of race and culture that was not reflected
in Cherokee self-perceptions until much later. However, because ideas
of race have persistently reinforced Euroamerican ideas of nation, Cherokees realized by the early 1800s that for their claims to nationhood to
be considered legitimate within the Euroamerican context they would
have to racially codify their distinct sense of peoplehood. The Cherokees
were in the midst of two complementary processes: political centralization and the internalization of Western notions of race and nation.
These shifts in Cherokee social and political organization during the
latter half of the eighteenth century set the stage for the birth of a modern
Cherokee nation in the early decades of the nineteenth century. A child
of Cherokee and Euroamerican politics, the Cherokee nation of the nineteenth century would embody newly developed expressions of Cherokee
nationalism and racism.

CHAPTER THREE

Race as Nation, Race as Blood Quantum

*The Racial Politics of Cherokee
Nationalism in the Nineteenth Century*

The activities of Euroamericans in the early nineteenth century ensured that Cherokee nationalism—and, by extension, racialism—would take hold. Between 1808 and 1835, Cherokees were increasingly confronted with U.S. expansion into their territory in the Southeast (McLoughlin 1986: 146–67). Historian William McLoughlin argues that as they "wrestled with the question of their own identity and future," the Cherokees concluded "with unerring logic . . . that national identity rested upon a cultural heritage imbedded in history, language and culture and a distinct and identifiable 'homeland'" (McLoughlin 1986: xvii). For the first time, Cherokees also came to believe that their national identity rested on a distinct racial identity (McLoughlin and Conser 1989: 258). McLoughlin suggests that Cherokees emulated the evolving model of nationhood before them and soon realized that they had a seemingly better claim to ethnic identity and nationhood than the diverse European peoples who had come to the New World (McLoughlin 1986: xvii). Turning the Euroamerican racial ideologies of the day to their advantage, Cherokees became romantic nationalists with a developed sense of racial identity in the early decades of the nineteenth century (1986: 337–49, 376).

The idea that race was a cornerstone of national identity was apparent in the Cherokees' emerging political organization. As they took steps to establish their own republic, Cherokee leaders modeled their national ideology and structure on the new nation around them. In the first three decades of the nineteenth century, these leaders established a bicameral legislature, a national police force, a supreme court, an elective system of representation based on new geographic districts rather than towns, and in 1828, a written constitution patterned after that of the U.S. federal government (Hill 1997: 95). They also developed a concept of tribal sovereignty that "shared much of the ideology of the individual sovereign states of the Union" (McLoughlin 1986: xvii). Culturally, these actions were in keeping with the Cherokees' long history of political, economic, and cultural syncretism.[1] Politically, it was a case of fighting fire with fire, of building a state to resist a state, of consolidating their power in order to resist further encroachments on their right to independence.[2] Of course, the Cherokee state "did not mean the same thing to all Cherokees, nor did they participate in it equally" (Bender 1996: 67). Town leaders and political organizations continued to operate on an informal basis well into the period of removal (Fogelson and Kutsche 1961: 99).[3] Nonetheless, the new Cherokee state gradually displaced town politics, becoming the official administrative, bureaucratic, and political center of the Cherokees' newly emerging national community.

In this context of nation building, two competing definitions of race came to shape Cherokee politics and identity in profound ways. The first ideology—race as nation—suggested that race, or racial metaphors of blood and kinship, could be used to define a nation "as a collective subject, as a superorganism with a unique biological-cultural essence" (Alonso 1994: 384). The second ideology—race as blood quantum— was buttressed by nineteenth-century scientific thought. It held that blood quantum was a rational measure of racial identity and that the social and biological "fitness" of Native-American mixed-bloods could be calculated according to their degree and type of racial admixture.[4] In this chapter, I show how in the first half of the nineteenth century the Cherokee Nation used the first ideology to define and build its own national body. However, by the end of the century, the federal government was using the second ideology both to define Cherokees and to undermine their political and economic autonomy, particularly when it came to land allotments.[5] I also argue that the complex interaction between these ideologies and other aspects of Cherokee identity produced a racialized sociopolitical formation that is evident in intratribal race relations and the legislation enacted by both the federal government and the Cherokee Nation during this period.

RACE, CLASS, AND GENDER RELATIONS
IN THE NEW CHEROKEE STATE

The creation of a Cherokee state had important consequences for Cherokee ideas about race, class, and gender. For example, we can see the
reproduction of Euroamerican ideologies of race and nation in the Cherokee Nation's own legal structure. By 1800, after more than a century
of intimate contact with whites, Euroamerican racial ideologies had
taken hold among the Cherokees, but they had not been codified in any
formal way. Though the tribe had no law regarding blood or racial
identity, in some measure due to the difficulties of systematic enforce-
ment in a prestate era, once the Cherokee state began to develop in the
early nineteenth century, race became a standard measure of social and
political belonging.[6] Not surprisingly, the new Cherokee state would
increasingly replicate the racial ideologies and practices of the U.S. federal and state governments.

This tendency is evident in the Southeast prior to removal, when the
Cherokee Nation passed a series of antimiscegenation laws to discourage
intermarriage between Cherokees and their African-American slaves.
For instance, in 1824 the Cherokee Council passed an act stating:

> Intermarriages between negro slaves, and Indians, or whites, shall not be
> lawful, and any person or persons permitting and approbating his, her or
> their negro slaves, to intermarry with Indians or whites, he, she, or they, so
> offending, shall pay a fine of fifty dollars, one half for the benefit of the
> Cherokee Nation, and . . . any male Indian or white man marrying a negro
> woman slave, he or they shall be punished with fifty-nine stripes on the bare
> back, and any Indian or white woman, marrying a negro man slave, shall be
> punished with twenty-five stripes. (Halliburton 1977: 37)

Similarly, the 1827 Constitution forbade anyone of African descent
from holding public office (Halliburton 1977: 50–51). These laws were
political maneuvers on the part of Cherokees to increase the social distance between themselves and African Americans.[7] As citizens of a new
multiracial nation, Cherokees were willing to accept intermarriages between themselves and whites but not with African-American slaves. Although, many Cherokees had a strong sense of their racial distinctiveness
apart from African Americans, they also understood that the racial hierarchy in the United States placed them somewhere between African
Americans and whites in status. They realized that they too were racial
"others" in the new American nation-state, and if they were not careful
to establish their own social and political uniqueness, then they might

be subjected to the same harsh treatment as African Americans.[8] This realization may have come to individual Cherokees at a much earlier date, but only with the emergence of a Cherokee state did they have the means, both political and ideological, to enforce it.

The Cherokees followed the Euroamerican racial pattern in more than legal codes. Prior to contact, matrilineal clan membership had been the marker of social belonging, and Cherokees in their own minds were as distinct from other Native Americans as they were from Europeans and Africans. However, as Euroamericans pushed their program to "civilize" the Indians, they attacked the matrilineal clan system as a "savage" practice that needed to be abandoned, and by 1808 the Cherokees began to adopt the European system of patrilineal inheritance (Perdue 1979: 51, Perdue 1998: 41). Two years later, in 1810, the Cherokee Nation centralized control over the practice of blood revenge, so that murder was treated not so much as a crime against the clan as one against the national body (Champagne 1992: 93, Perdue 1998: 142). With this move, Cherokee blood itself became the possession of a single national body rather than of the distinct matrilineal clan bodies to which it had belonged previously.

As the clan system eroded, Cherokee women retained certain property rights but lost much of their economic power and status. In the mid-1820s, even as the Cherokee council extended citizenship to the children of Cherokee men and white women, Cherokee women were denied the right to vote (McLoughlin 1986: 398, Perdue 1998: 145–47). Cherokee gender relations went through other transformations as well. The United States government encouraged the Cherokees to adopt Euroamerican farming techniques and implements, causing Cherokee men and African slaves to replace Cherokee women as agricultural laborers and upsetting the sexual division of labor. Plantation slavery followed these changes in the three decades before the Civil War but developed slowly among the Cherokees and only after enormous social and political upheaval (McLoughlin 1986: 62, Perdue 1979: 50).

The growth of a plantation economy brought new forms of inequality to Cherokee society, which suffered not only from changes in race and gender relations but from a growing class antagonism between slave-holding and non-slaveholding Cherokees. Just as in Euroamerican society, class divisions between Cherokees tended to fall along racial lines. However, with Cherokee classes these divisions occurred not so much according to separate racial groupings (white vs. Indian) but according to degree of Cherokee racial ancestry ("fuller blood" vs. "lesser blood").

For instance, according to an 1835 census, only 17 percent of Cherokee citizens had any degree of white ancestry. But of the wealthier slave-owning class, 78 percent claimed white descent (Perdue 1979: 60). Indeed, only one percent of all full-bloods owned slaves (Thornton 1990: 53). Although we can discern some correlation between white racial ancestry, a higher class standing, and slave ownership, there were also significant exceptions. For this reason, we should not make too much of this correlation, as if it provided a simple road map of the various social and cultural options available to Cherokees. The Cherokee population was, and continues to be, far more complex than such a neat division between wealthy mixed-bloods and poor full-bloods allows.

This reductivist tendency has shaped too much of the debate about Cherokee identity. Running throughout much of the scholarly literature is an assumption that the racial ancestry of Cherokees correlates not just with their class standing but with certain social values. Full-bloods are often understood as cultural conservatives, as bearers of "tradition," whereas mixed-bloods are expected to be oriented toward progress and change. This assumption harkens back to an earlier era when agents of the Indian Service linked the white ancestry of mixed-blood Cherokees to their "civilization" and progress. For example, the federal agent to the Cherokees, Return J. Meigs wrote in an 1805 letter to Benjamin Hawkins, "It seems as if the Graver of time had fixed the savage character so deeply in the native Indians, I mean those that have arrived at manhood, that it cannot be effaced: but where the blood is mixed white, in every grade of it, there is an apparent disposition leaning towards civilization, and this disposition is in proportion to its distance from the original stock" (in McLoughlin 1986: 69). To someone like Meigs, adult Cherokees without white ancestry would never be "civilized" because they were innately savage, by virtue of their race. But for Cherokees with white ancestry, their degree of white blood provided a quantifiable measure of their predilection for civilization. Because civilization was a virtue that Meigs attributed to whiteness, he actively encouraged marriages between Cherokee women and white men in hopes that the practice would soon make "the real Indian disappear" (letter to Henry Dearborn 1805, quoted in McLoughlin 1986: 70). His efforts to eradicate Cherokee culture and identity were guided by his belief in white racial superiority, the common Euroamerican ideology of his day.[9]

Racist assumptions like these run throughout much of the United States' historical record, and contemporary scholars have to be careful not to reproduce the idea that racial identity provides a simple gloss for

cultural orientation and social values (i.e., that mixed blood equals progressive or that full blood equals traditional). Social divisions did exist
among the Cherokees in terms of race, class, and political orientation,
all of which intersected with one another in powerful ways, much as
they do today. However, if we universalize this association between
white racial ancestry and a progressive sociocultural/political orientation, then we miss important elements of Cherokee life. Different Cherokee individuals, whether they had white ancestry or not, might have
tried their hand at plow agriculture, monogamy, reading, and writing,
or supported changes in the tribal government. But to advocate "progress" in any one of these areas did "not necessarily go hand in hand
with the adoption of Christianity or the abandonment of Cherokee traditionalism" (Bender 1996: 79–80). Thus, the standard dichotomies of
mixed-blood vs. full-blood and traditional vs. progressive are sometimes
misleading and when universalized tend to obscure the diversity of the
Cherokee community, both historically and at present.

COMPETING EXPRESSIONS
OF CHEROKEE NATIONAL IDENTITY

During the early national period, Cherokees' identity took many possible forms, since the old ways of doing things continued to exist side
by side with the new. Some Cherokees became Christian but retained
their communal ethic of landholding. Others worshipped as their grandparents did but learned English in order to gain advantage in the market
place. This common blend of attitudes and practices reflected the increasing complexity of Cherokee identity, as well as the diversity of the
Cherokee people. As members of a national body, Cherokees differed
from one another in myriad ways, and these differences were sometimes
a source of contradiction and tension.

We can see these tensions in the practices of the Cherokee state, itself
an arm of the Cherokee people. Though the Cherokee government had
used the concept of race to establish who was a Cherokee citizen, other
preexisting definitions of Cherokee identity continued to operate on
both the national and local levels. Consider the case of Molly, an
African-American slave who had been adopted as a member of the Deer
Clan, shortly before the American Revolution. Her adoption came about
in the context of clan revenge: a white man had killed his Cherokee wife
by beating her to death, and her clan sought his death in revenge, according to the law of blood. To save his own skin, the man purchased

Molly and offered her to the grieving Deer Clan in his place. When the clan accepted his offer, Molly was adopted as a Deer, given a new name, *Chickaune,* and became Cherokee. Because she had been adopted into the Cherokee kinship system, Molly's identity as a Cherokee would never have been contested. However, several decades later, descendents of the white man's family sent agents to reclaim Molly and her son and return them to a life of slavery. The case was brought before the Cherokee supreme court, which ruled that Molly had become Cherokee by virtue of her adoption into a Cherokee clan and that she and her son were Cherokee regardless of their racial ancestry (McLoughlin 1986: 347, Perdue 1998: 151). The case of Molly reveals an ongoing commitment to the matrilineal clan system, despite legislation eroding the rights of Cherokee women. It also demonstrates that in the early national period clan kinship could still occasionally take precedence over race, since legislative decisions at the national level were subject to the contradictory discourses and practices of Cherokee identity at the time. Yet multiple forces were at work in the continuing evolution of what it might mean to be Cherokee, and other cases of Cherokee identity were so complex that they defy even the label of *contradictory.*

A cloud of cigarette smoke from the lunchtime crowd wafts over their corner booth, the scent of Winston and Marlboro clinging to the tiny droplets of bacon grease and perspiration that coated their hair, clothes, and skin from the minute they walked in. Most folks are willing to endure the stickiness of Scott's Café in downtown Tahlequah for the giant plates of biscuits and homey food, all cheaper than the overcooked hamburgers in the chains down the street. Finishing their meal, the anthropologist and her friend, a Cherokee man in his mid-thirties, relax with yet another glass of iced tea. Their conversation has been pleasant and lighthearted, but then she begins to broach a more serious topic, something that makes her nervous and uncomfortable.

"I don't know exactly how to say this," she hesitates, "but I've been having a lot of trouble trying to figure out the status of blacks in the Cherokee Nation. I mean . . . historically. There seems to be a lot of racism, but I keep digging around in the archives and everything is so confusing and contradictory, and no one seems to want to talk about it." She feels more like a journalist pressing for a scoop than a scholar, and she isn't sure if she likes it. Did anthropology always need an "informant?" Was it realistic to avoid not just the term but the relationship it implied?

She takes a sip of tea and continues, "I was just wondering if you had a strong opinion one way or another, or if you could point me in some direction that might help me clarify what was going on."

Well acquainted with the nuances of Cherokee history, her friend doesn't seem to mind the question. "Do you mean if they were citizens?" he asks calmly.

"Well, yes and no," she hedges. Social science sounded precise in the abstract, but in practice it was often a messy business. "I guess I'm asking if they were accepted as Cherokees by the broader Cherokee population."

After a thoughtful pause, he begins, "You know, that's not an easy question to answer because it really depends on the situation. Who, when, what, where: you have to take all that into consideration. Yeah, there was racism. I mean, we were southerners; we had slaves. But we also had a lot of tolerance and openness, and you can see that if you look back at the history, look at the stories themselves."

He thought a minute and continued, "You need to go to the library at Northeastern and look up the story of Shoe Boots. I can't tell you where you'll find it but I'm sure you'll figure it out. . . . Shoe Boots. His story will tell you what you need to know."

Shoe Boots. She couldn't forget the name. Grateful, she sat with her friend a while longer before they were both claimed by the obligations of the workday. She always tried to follow up on the leads she got in town and especially from this friend, who knew a little bit about a lot of things and a lot about more than a few. Shoe Boots. She seemed to remember reading something about him in one of McLoughlin's books. An hour later, she pulled the book from a shelf and found what she was looking for.

Shoe Boots (Chulio) was a full-blood warrior who married three different women, Cherokee, white, and black, in that order.[10] In 1792, while still living with his Cherokee wife, Shoe Boots went raiding and captured an eleven-year-old white girl named Clarinda Ellington, whom he and his wife kept as a slave. When his Cherokee wife died some years later, Shoe Boots persuaded Clarinda to marry him, and they soon had several children. Clarinda's white family tried several times to get her to return, but she refused unless she could take her children with her. Shoe Boots said no. The thought of losing his children was unbearable, and he said, "If my children are taken away, I shall look on it the same as if they were dead."[11] Yet he trusted his wife and eventually let her take the children to visit their white relatives. He purchased new clothes for them and provided a good horse and even a slave to attend to their needs. They left for Kentucky in 1804, but he never saw any of them again.

Distraught, he found some solace three years later when he began to have a relationship with one of his African slaves, a woman by the name of Daull. Over time, they grew closer, married, and had three children together, who were slaves like their mother because they had inherited her status. By 1824, Shoe Boots worried about their black-Cherokee children and feared that after his death they might be sold away from the family. A prominent man, a member of the Cherokee National Council, he realized that the status of blacks in the Cherokee Nation was changing, and he wanted to protect his children. With this in mind, Shoe Boots wrote to the National Council, pleading the case of his children.

"My desire is to have them as free Sitizens of this Nation. How can I think of them, having boan of my bone and flesh of my flesh, to be called property, and this by my imprudent Conduck. And for them and their offspring to suffer for Generations yet unborn is a thought of to great magnitude for me to remain Silent longer."[12] Moved by his words, the Cherokee National Council gave his children their freedom, though it ordered him to "cease begetting any more children by this said slave woman."

The final statement was harsh and explicit, but Shoe Boots obviously did not comply, for he and Daull had two more children, twin sons, before his death in 1829. When Shoe Boots's estate was settled, his twin sons were treated as slaves and inherited as property by his sisters. Though the law seemed to require this, because the children were blood kin the sisters petitioned the National Council to grant the twins freedom and citizenship, but not their mother. The Cherokee government was divided over the issue, and the boys officially remained the slaves of their aunts. Eventually, a white man who claimed Shoe Boots's estate as his own took them away from their Cherokee family, just as Shoe Boots had feared.

The complexities of the story of Shoe Boots and his kin do not end there, for his other children by Daull, the two daughters who had been granted their freedom by the Cherokee National Council in 1824, had their own children. Though these granddaughters were part black, they had inherited the status of their mothers and thus were free. This did not keep them from suffering racial harassment, however, and some time later white slave hunters illegally captured them. Yet because they were Cherokee citizens, the Cherokee National Council stepped in and sent two Cherokee men to obtain their freedom, reimbursing them for their expenses.

Christ. No wonder being Cherokee was no simple matter, then or now. This is the sort of thing the anthropologist's friend wanted her to think about, and she was beginning to see why.

THE RACISM OF REMOVAL

When the Moravian missionary Albert Steiner returned to the Cherokee Nation in 1820 after his initial visit in 1801, he noted with delight the progress Cherokees had made according to white standards of civilization. In a letter to John Calhoun, he deemed them "the most advanced in civilization of any of the Indian tribes without exception" (McLoughlin 1986: 299). Steiner witnessed orderly farms and orchards, an overall growth in animal husbandry, and a number of well-tended plantations. If economic growth were a primary measure of white civilization, then the Cherokees would be well on their way to meeting, if not exceeding, the expectations of their white neighbors. Steiner's impressions were fairly superficial, however, since the majority of Cherokees were culturally conservative, valuing their traditional lifestyle and resisting sudden social and economic change. Nonetheless, his words contributed to an overall perception among Euroamericans that the southeastern tribes were civilized. Although these tribes seemed to meet many of the standards of white civilization, in one of the great paradoxes of U.S. history, President Andrew Jackson would nonetheless engineer their violent removal. To the Cherokees and the other southeastern Indian nations, the message was clear: the United States would not accept sovereign entities within its own border unless they were white. Because of this deep-seated racism in Euroamerican culture, the Cherokees would soon face the crisis of forced removal to the West in 1838.

Ten years before, several events exacerbated the political tension between the Cherokees and their white neighbors. When the Cherokees established their rights to national sovereignty in 1828 through the creation of their own constitution modeled on that of the U.S. government, the state of Georgia contested this move and proclaimed its own rights of sovereignty. Because much of the Cherokee national homeland fell

within its geographic boundaries, the state of Georgia sought to incorporate the Cherokee Nation and its people under its jurisdiction. Thus,
that same year, the state of Georgia made Cherokees second-class citizens against their will. Cherokees were placed in the same category as
freed slaves, without the right to vote, hold office, attend school, or
testify against whites in court (McLoughlin 1993: 6). U.S. national leaders were faced with a perplexing question—whose rights to sovereignty
should take precedence, those of states guaranteed by the U.S. Constitution, or those of Indians guaranteed by treaty? With the election of
Andrew Jackson to the presidency in 1828, the answer came all too
quickly. Jackson, who had been elected in part because of his reputation
as an "Indian killer," sided with the state of Georgia, and Cherokee
fortunes took a turn for the worse.

When gold was discovered on Cherokee land soon thereafter, Congress had the necessary incentive to quickly pass the Indian Removal
Act in 1830. The Cherokees resisted this act, taking their case all the
way to the Supreme Court, where in two landmark decisions, Chief
Justice John Marshall laid out the terms under which the independence
of the Cherokee Nation would be constructed (Walker 1997: 115). In
the first of these cases, *Cherokee Nation v. Georgia,* Justice Marshall
sought a compromise that would shield the Cherokee Nation from removal. He decided that the Cherokees were a "domestic dependent nation" whose "relationship to the United States resemble[d] that of a
ward to his guardian" (5 Pet. 1 [1831]). Unfortunately, this decision
undermined the Cherokees' ability to pursue their rights in the U.S. Supreme Court, which was open to direct appeal only by foreign nations
(Sider 1993: 281–82). For this reason, in 1832 Samuel Worcester, a
longtime missionary to the Cherokees, brought a similar case before the
Supreme Court, this time on behalf of the Cherokees. In what seemed
like an about-face, Justice Marshall declared that the Cherokee Nation
was a distinct community and that the state of Georgia had no right to
enter the boundaries of the nation without the Cherokees' express permission (*Worcester v. Georgia,* 6 Pet. 515 [1832]). The Cherokee Nation, the state of Georgia, and the executive and judicial branches of the
federal government were each vying for control. Ultimately, executive
and state powers won out when President Jackson refused to uphold the
Supreme Court's decision and reportedly said, "John Marshall has made
his decision. Now let him try to enforce it" (Jennings 1975: 332).

In response to these legislative and administrative maneuvers, a group
of wealthy, slaveholding Cherokees began to coalesce around the lead-

ership of Major Ridge, a prominent Cherokee war hero. Convinced that the efforts of Chief John Ross and his political supporters (the National Party) to resist the president and the populace of Georgia would eventually prove futile, this relatively small group of Cherokees believed that their only hope for autonomy was to sign a treaty of removal. On December 29, 1835, Major Ridge and several hundred Cherokees later known as the Treaty Party, met at the Cherokee capital of New Echota, Georgia. They signed a treaty relinquishing their homeland for $5 million and agreed to move west of the Mississippi to lands already occupied by earlier Cherokee emigrants known as the Old Settlers. The Treaty Party left almost immediately, taking their slaves with them, and were thus spared the forced removal of 1838.

For the Cherokees who were left behind, the pending crisis of removal exacerbated already existing class divisions that had come about from the development of plantation slavery. Slaveholding and non-slaveholding Cherokees were increasingly divided "not only in an economic sense but also in terms of values and world views" (Perdue 1979: 68). Culturally conservative Cherokees now associated slavery with the white southerners trying to force them from their homes and with those slaveholding Cherokees who had signed the fraudulent removal treaty at New Echota.[13] While members of both the Treaty Party and the National Party held slaves, only the Treaty Party had adopted the values and lifestyle of white southern plantation owners enough to give up their traditional homeland (Perdue 1979: 68). Chief Ross and the National Party clung tenaciously to Cherokee values, waging battle after battle in the U.S. courts to protect the tribe's communal landholdings and autonomy.[14] In spite of Ross's wealth and European ancestry, the majority of Cherokees supported him and believed that at his core he retained a "traditional" Cherokee worldview.[15] But Ross was unable to unify the tribe—the lines of division had been drawn too deeply. Black slavery had created lasting boundaries of cultural and class difference between Cherokee tribal citizens.

Though Chief Ross collected the signatures of 15,665 Cherokees on a petition protesting the actions of the 500 Cherokees at New Echota, nothing could stop "the removal," as this tragedy is euphemistically known to this day. At bayonet point, the Cherokees were forced from their homes and rounded up into stockades. In the winter of 1838, about 16,000 Cherokees began their deadly trek west on the "trail where they cried." They lost at least a quarter of their population and in a wake of grief struggled to rebuild their lives in the unfamiliar country of Indian

Territory.[16] Removal was an act of greed undergirded by racism, "a rejection of all Indians as Indians, not simply a rejection of unassimilated Indians who would not accept the American life-style" (Horsman 1981: 192). This trauma of racial and national exclusion left a psychic wound and exacerbated the existing divisions among Cherokees that had evolved from the development of plantation slavery. Once in Indian Territory, growing social and political factionalism brought chaos and violence to the Cherokee Nation.

POLITICAL AND RACIAL FACTIONALISM AFTER THE TRAIL OF TEARS

"I have signed my own death warrant," said Major Ridge after signing the Treaty of New Echota (McLoughlin 1993: 15). Ridge was aware that the Cherokee Nation permitted capital punishment in only a handful of circumstances, one of which was for selling any portion of the national homeland without the permission of the tribe as a whole—an act of treason. When the rest of the tribe arrived in Indian Territory, clan representatives and other culturally conservative political leaders made the decision to execute several of the leaders of the Treaty Party. At the top of the list were Major Ridge, John Ridge, Elias Boudinot, and Stand Watie. All of these men were violently killed on the same day in the summer of 1839, most in front of their families, with the exception of Stand Watie, who either by a stroke of good fortune or because someone had warned him, was not home when the executioners arrived.

The killings caused widespread panic and ushered in one of the bloodiest eras in Cherokee history. Although the clan leaders had agreed that the executions would not invoke the Cherokee law of blood, the victims' close kin and political allies still sought revenge (McLoughlin 1993: 16). In 1845 and 1846 alone, thirty-three deaths were attributed to the dispute, and surrounding whites began to spread the rumor that the Cherokees had reverted to barbarism (McLoughlin 1993: 42, 48). Federal authorities, failing to understand Cherokee law, considered the executions to be a posse style of political justice. Along with a minority of tribal citizens who were allied with the Treaty Party, the federal government held Chief John Ross accountable, despite his claims of innocence (McLoughlin 1993: 54). Most Cherokees questioned the government's accusations, but otherwise reached no consensus. They argued among themselves about how it all began and whether the fighting and bloodshed stemmed from the original betrayal of the Treaty Party or from the murders of the Ridges and Boudinot (McLoughlin 1993: 55).

In the turbulent years immediately following the executions, the majority of Cherokees continued to support John Ross and to reelect him as principal chief. Part of Ross's popularity as a leader stemmed from the fact that he recognized the diversity of the Cherokee people and often sought political compromise. Holding the Cherokee's national sovereignty in the highest regard, Ross helped reestablish their constitutional government in 1839 and held a national convention in the hopes that he could clear the air with regards to the murders (McLoughlin 1993: 18–19). But his efforts were of little use, and the violence and tension continued to mount.

One of the biggest obstacles to peace was that, with the arrival of John Ross and his followers, there were now three distinct Cherokee polities coexisting side by side within Indian Territory. The Old Settlers, the Treaty Party, and the National Party all claimed rights of sovereignty and autonomy. As many as 3,000 Old Settlers had left their homeland for independence in the West beginning in 1794, though most arrived in 1810–11 and 1819. They were living under their own government in well-established communities when the Treaty Party arrived with Major Ridge in 1835. Most of the individuals who comprised this second wave of immigrants chose to take advantage of the stability that the Old Settlers offered and moved in alongside them in the eastern part of present-day Arkansas, forming a sizeable population of over 5,000 Cherokees living in the West. However, what originally had seemed like a sizeable group quickly became a minority when the 14,000 Eastern Cherokees arrived at the terminus of the Trail of Tears. Though the Old Settlers and members of the Treaty Party sided with one another, creating a distinct "western" faction, the vast majority of the tribe had arrived under their own leadership and were not about to give up their autonomy. These competing interest groups, each of which had its own legitimate claims to independence, ripped at the seams that held together the Cherokee Nation as they fought for their rights of self-governance. Though the lines of division were new, they reflected an ongoing political diversity that had long been a fundamental part of Cherokee life.

Because the Treaty of New Echota had exacted such a terrible price, John Ross and the National Party initially refused to recognize it. More importantly, they believed that it would fundamentally undermine Cherokee sovereignty and forever separate them from their original home-

Figure 4.   Principal Chief John Ross. Courtesy of the
Western History Collections, University of Oklahoma
Libraries, Norman, Oklahoma.

land. However, because of the threats dividing the nation, Ross was
forced to compromise with Washington; he accepted the Treaty of New
Echota in 1846 in order to maintain peace (McLoughlin 1993: 56). Yet
even in the most trying of circumstances, Ross could be a skillful and
dignified leader. Soon after he endorsed the treaty, Ross called a national
meeting. Before the assembled crowd, with representatives from all three
factions present, he urged peace and reconciliation, stating, "We are all
of the household of the Cherokee family and of one blood . . . embracing
each other as Countrymen, friends and relatives" (Moulton 1985, 1:
712–13). When, in closing, Ross shook hands with Stand Watie, his
sworn enemy and the defiant leader of the Treaty Party, the symbolism
was powerful. Both sides had decided to compromise, to uphold unity

Figure 5. Bust of Stand Watie. Courtesy of the
Western History Collections, University of Oklahoma
Libraries, Norman, Oklahoma.

and sovereignty at all costs. Yet for each side the toll was heavy. The
outnumbered Western Cherokees had to give up their autonomy and
concede to Ross's leadership, while the Eastern Cherokees had to endorse the fateful Treaty of New Echota and accept its terms. Nonetheless, the Cherokee people had decided to put their differences behind
them in the name of nationhood, and when the two great rivals shook
hands, their act marked the end of the removal crisis at long last (Mc-
Loughlin 1993: 58).

Though Cherokees on both sides had gone to great lengths to establish some semblance of political unity, they could do little to overcome
the growing social and cultural divisions within their nation. Despite
rapid social upheaval and cultural change, Cherokees maintained many
of the old ways. Most Cherokee families, whether multiracial or not,
still honored the law of blood, though they did so within a new patri-

lineal framework (McLoughlin 1993: 75). Most went to their *adonisgi,* their medicine men and women, though they attended both Christian and non-Christian religious ceremonies (McLoughlin 1993: 74). A few Cherokees owned large plantations that were cultivated by black slaves, but most were small-scale farmers and hunters. However, by 1846, a distinct group of approximately 300 families began to coalesce and came to constitute an elite social class of multiracial Cherokees (McLoughlin 1993: 77). The majority of these individuals, though far from all, were proslavery, English-speaking Christians who sometimes were known locally as "white Indians" (Wardell 1977: 122). In this particular context, the terms *mixed-blood* and *white Indian* became more socially salient among Cherokees. Of course, these categories of identity were social constructions that had only a loose correspondence with racial ancestry, since Cherokees with white ancestry could also be poor, non-Christian, or against black slavery. Nonetheless, during this period, the idiom of race began to shape the discourses of Cherokee social and political identity in distinct ways that help to explain its meanings among Cherokees today.

CHEROKEE AND AFRICAN-AMERICAN RACE RELATIONS IN INDIAN TERRITORY

In the mid-nineteenth century, the Cherokee Nation was a multiracial entity, not simply because it had different types of citizens, some with white and black ancestry, but because it had long condoned the practice of black slavery. Some scholars and many contemporary Cherokees argue that Cherokee masters were more lenient to their black slaves in Indian Territory than were white southerners to theirs. One reason for this interpretation is that Cherokees did not indulge in mob violence, as southern whites often did. The Cherokee Nation has no record of mass lynching, and one historian has suggested that Cherokee slaves did not fear for their personal safety as much as their bonded counterparts in Alabama or Mississippi (Littlefield 1978: 68). Such generalizations, however, are often in conflict with individual cases. The leniency of these relationships often depended on the individuals involved. More significantly, any conclusion about Cherokee leniency toward black slaves must be viewed in a larger social and historical context. The fact remains that "the Cherokees held a greater number of slaves than any other tribe in Indian Territory" (Littlefield 1978: 8). Further, despite claims to the contrary, many historians agree that "slavery among the Cherokee was little different from that in the white South" (Littlefield 1978: 9).

Like white southern slave owners, most Cherokee slave owners had only one or two slaves, who often shared the same household. With this proximity came an exchange of food, medicine, clothing, religion, and language.[17] Also following the pattern of white slavery, the growing numbers of black-Cherokee offspring are evidence of biological exchange between black slaves and their Cherokee masters. In 1835 there were only 60 "mixed-Negroes," or black-Cherokees, enumerated within the national census (Thornton 1990: 53). But by 1870, a census taken by agent John N. Craig listed 1,545 Cherokees of African descent (Thornton 1990: 102).[18]

Cherokee slavery mirrored that of the white South in another revealing way, the efforts of black slaves to escape or rebel. With the social, political, and economic upheaval of removal all around them, Cherokee slaves saw their masters' weakness in full relief and began to run away in increasing numbers, many trying to make it to the northern states or to Mexico. At least two small, armed slave rebellions occurred during this period, one in 1842 and another in 1846 (Perdue 1979: 82–83). These uprisings instilled fear in wealthy and powerful Cherokees, who responded by enacting a series of harsh slave codes (see the accompanying list).[19] With these new laws, Cherokee slavery could hardly be distinguished from the peculiar institution of white southerners.

1840   Slaves were forbidden to own property.

1841   Patrol companies were appointed to police slave areas; no slave was allowed to carry firearms, knives, or other weapons; education of blacks was made illegal.

1842   Any free black or slave aiding another slave to escape received 100 lashes and was removed from the Cherokee Nation.

1848   Anyone teaching blacks to read or write was removed from the Cherokee Nation.

1855   No public school teacher favoring abolition was allowed in the Cherokee Nation.

The clearest example of this growing similarity is evident in the Cherokee Constitution of 1839, which reaffirmed the inferior status of residents with African ancestry. "No person who is of Negro or mulatto

Figure 6.   Rare photograph of Cherokee slave cabin. Near Fort Gibson, Oklahoma. Photograph by A. L. Aylesworth, secretary to the Dawes Commission. Courtesy of the Oklahoma Historical Society, Oklahoma City, Oklahoma.

parentage either by the father or mother's side shall be eligible to hold any office of profit, honor, or trust under this government" (McLoughlin 1974: 381). Further the first law passed by the National Council after removal was "An Act to Prevent Amalgamation with Colored Persons . . . providing that intermarriage shall not be lawful between a free male or female citizen and any slave or person of color" (Perdue 1979: 84). Like the earlier Cherokee antimiscegenation act from 1824, these laws demonstrated beyond a shadow of a doubt that the Cherokees' own matrilineal system of descent had fallen prey to the prevalent racial ideologies of nineteenth-century Euroamericans, who held that race was an inherent biological factor and that "one drop" of African ancestry from either parent was sufficient to color one's social standing.

By excluding African Americans from the body politic, the Cherokee state was reproducing nineteenth-century Euroamerican racial ideologies in its own legislation, including the idea that national identity was linked to racial identity and the notion that "race-mixing" with African Americans was polluting. Efforts to police Cherokee national boundaries on the basis of race continued, and the next step was the use of blood to codify racial identity in Cherokee law. In 1840, the Cherokee National Council made it unlawful for "any free negro or mulatto, *not of Cherokee blood* [emphasis mine], to hold or own any improvements within the limits of this Nation" (Halliburton 1977: 69). The wording of this legislation is significant because it marks the time when Cherokees officially began to conflate ideas of race and blood in their own political discourse and practices. Though it had been common for Europeans and Euroamericans to equate these two concepts, Cherokees do not seem to have made this connection in their own ideology before this point.[20]

INTERNAL DIVISIONS OVER AFRICAN-AMERICAN SLAVERY: CIVIL WAR IN THE CHEROKEE NATION

The growing hostility in the United States between the North and the South would bring many of these issues of race and nation to a new level of upheaval. At the beginning of the Civil War, the Confederate Indian commissioner tried to lure Chief John Ross into joining the southern struggle, arguing that slaveholding peoples shared common interests. However, Ross saw advantages in loyalty to the U.S. government, with which he had signed numerous treaties, so he resisted the Confederate overtures and sought to keep Cherokee people out of the hostilities. Ross's efforts were undermined by the old factionalism between his National Party and the Treaty Party. Some years before, Stand Watie had organized the Knights of the Golden Circle or, as they later became known, the Southern Rights Party (Perdue 1979: 129).[21] Using southern proslavery rhetoric, the group struggled to bring the Cherokee Nation within the Confederate fold and to oust Ross and the National Party. Opposing the pro-Confederate Cherokees was a smaller group of culturally and politically conservative Cherokees known as the Keetoowahs, who "protested the Cherokees' acceptance of slavery as well as other aspects of white man's 'civilization' and favored Ross' policy of neutrality" (Perdue 1979: 130).

The Keetoowahs were members of a secret religious organization that had been revived and strengthened between 1858 and 1859. During that period, conservative Cherokee leaders had joined forces with Evan

Jones—a devoted abolitionist and longtime Northern Baptist minister among the Cherokees (Champagne 1992: 182). Because of his popularity, Jones was well positioned to stir up antislavery sentiments among a broader population of culturally conservative Cherokees (McLoughlin 1993: 155). Jones and other Cherokee leaders worked together to revitalize the Keetoowah society as a response to the newly emerging proslavery societies among the Cherokees, such as the Blue Lodges and the Knights of the Golden Circle.

As it grew in membership, the Keetoowah society began to rival the Christian churches as a unifying force and an organization for mutual assistance, with possibly as many as 3,500 Cherokees joining its ranks (Woodward 1963: 7). Yet in keeping with their history of cultural and religious syncretism, many Cherokees simultaneously held membership in both a Christian church and the Keetoowah Society (McLoughlin 1993: 244). Though the Keetoowah Society was open to Christian Cherokees, it did not admit members of mixed racial ancestry, and even educated full-bloods were suspect (McLoughlin 1993: 158).[22] Keetoowah meetings were conducted in Cherokee and the proceedings recorded in the syllabary, which provided a modicum of protection from curious outsiders. However, this "anti-mixed blood sentiment among Keetoowahs was strange, because several important leaders had mixed racial ancestry, such as Oochalata, Red Bird Smith, and Ned Christie. The categories of full and mixed were much more complex than mixed biological parentage" (May 1996: 83). Again, we see how full-blood and mixed-blood were social, cultural, and political constructs. "Politically speaking, the terms served as shorthand. Mixed stood for accommodation with whites, a willingness to negotiate. Full bloods were uncompromising and religiously insistent" (83).

Mixed-blood also designated the elite class of slaveholding Cherokees, who used their wealth and influence to lobby the tribal government to support slavery, even at the expense of national sovereignty. Culturally conservative Cherokees, such as the Keetoowahs, questioned the loyalty of this Cherokee elite, who seemed to be undermining national unity by placing their own self-interest before that of the Cherokee Nation. Also, since proslavery Cherokees wanted to expel any abolitionists, their desire threatened the religious freedom of those who supported missionaries like Evan Jones (McLoughlin 1993: 151). Thus, in the Cherokee Nation, unlike the white South, non-slaveholders and slaveholders were not allied with one another (McLoughlin 1993: 152). Instead, their loyalties and political interests were divided between Chief

Figure 7.   The antebellum home of George M. Murrell. Park Hill, Oklahoma, Cherokee Nation. Photograph by Sammy Still (Cherokee).

John Ross's National Party, which represented approximately 11,000 Cherokees, and the Southern Rights Party of about 6,000, associated with Stand Watie (McLoughlin 1993: 224). Though the language of blood and race was often used to describe these conflicting pressure groups, slaveholding and non-slaveholding Cherokees, as well as those with mixed racial ancestry and those without it, were on both sides (May 1996: 64).

After a series of Confederate victories, Chief Ross signed a treaty with the Confederacy in October of 1861, but he repudiated this alliance two years later in 1863 (McLoughlin 1974: 383). Ross's shifting loyalties reflected his confused response to the growing division among his own people. Even the Cherokee national leadership was divided between pro-Confederate and pro-Union factions. When federal forces captured Ross in 1862, Thomas Pegg became acting principal chief. As a pro-Union Cherokee leader, Pegg decided to follow the precedent of President

Abraham Lincoln's Emancipation Proclamation by calling "an extraordinary session of the Cherokee National Council. . . . On February 19, 1863 the body passed an act to become effective on June 25, 1863, emancipating all slaves within the limits of the Cherokee Nation" (Littlefield 1978: 16). Although this was two years before the United States formally ended slavery with the Thirteenth Amendment, most of these "freed" Cherokee slaves belonged to masters who were still loyal to the Confederacy, and in the end they had to fight their way to freedom (McLoughlin 1974: 383).

After 1863, slavery no longer existed as a legal institution within the Cherokee Nation, yet its legacy of social and economic inequality endured (Perdue 1979: 140). After the end of the Civil War in 1865, federal officials ignored the factionalism that existed among Cherokees and treated Union and Confederate Cherokees alike in the reconstruction process. In negotiations, the southern faction "thought the United States government should remove the freedmen from the Cherokee Country at its own expense. The northern Cherokees . . . wanted them adopted into the tribe and given an area of land for their exclusive use" (Wilson 1971: 233). But federal officials went even further: they offered a plan for the adoption of the former Cherokee slaves into the tribe, granting them citizenship, land, and annuities in the same amount as Indian tribal members (Halliburton 1977: 134). On July 19, 1866, the Cherokee Nation signed a treaty with the United States extending Cherokee citizenship to the freedmen and their descendants. Article 4 of the treaty set aside the Canadian District, a large tract of land extending southwest of the Cherokee Nation proper, for those freedmen who desired to settle there. Article 5 entitled them to citizenship, to elect their own officials, and to enact their own laws as long as they were not inconsistent with those of the Cherokee Nation. But Article 9 was crucial, for it stated, "They [Cherokee Indians] further agree that all freedmen . . . and their descendants, shall have all the rights of native Cherokees" (Wardell 1977: 225). This clause would become the source of much legal, political, and social controversy for many years to come.

QUESTIONS OF CITIZENSHIP
IN A MULTIRACIAL CHEROKEE NATION

Despite the promises of the 1866 treaty, the freedmen were never fully accepted as citizens of the Cherokee Nation. In his annual address to the Cherokee Nation in 1876, Cherokee Chief Oochalata, also known as the Reverend Charles Thompson (principal chief, 1875–1879), identified the status of freedmen as a pressing concern requiring prompt resolution. The National Council struggled with the issue and eventually decided to create a citizenship court in 1877 to hear claims on a case-by-case basis (Wardell 1977: 228). John Q. Tufts, the federal agent who negotiated in 1880 with Cherokee officials on the status of blacks in their nation, revealed the political atmosphere in which this occurred. Tufts stated that the question of citizenship eluded resolution and was so unpopular that no Cherokee politician was willing to jeopardize his position by advocating equal rights for the Cherokee freedmen (Wardell 1977: 229–30).

The Cherokee Nation's resistance to incorporating the freedmen was motivated largely by economic factors. In the 1870s, the Cherokee Nation had sold a large tract of land in the Cherokee Outlet, an area extending west from the northern perimeter of the Cherokee Nation.[23] In 1880 the Nation compiled a census for making a per capita distribution of the communal funds received from the sale (Sampson 1972: 125). In that same year, the Cherokee senate voted to deny citizenship to freedmen who had failed to return to the Cherokee Nation within a six-month period specified by the 1866 treaty (Wardell 1977: 229–31). Yet even those freedmen who had always resided within the Cherokee Nation were passed over for citizenship. The resulting Cherokee census of 1880 did not include a single Cherokee freedman, "it being the position of those of Cherokee blood that the Treaty of 1866 had granted freedmen civil and political rights but not the right to share in tribal assets" (Sampson 1972: 125–26).

This denial of citizenship to freedmen reflected a broader controversy over who had legitimate claims to Cherokee citizenship, a question that was increasingly raised as the Cherokee Nation became more and more culturally and racially diverse. In the late nineteenth century, several distinct classes of people resided within the Cherokee Nation. Besides the Cherokees themselves, other Native Americans had claims to Cherokee citizenship, including a sizeable group of Delawares and Shawnees who were adopted as citizens of the Cherokee Nation between 1860 and 1870. Because each of these tribes purchased land from the Cherokee Nation, they retained some rights to self-governance and sent their own representatives to meetings of the Cherokee tribal council (McLoughlin 1993: 259–60). A few Creeks had also broken away and become Cherokee citizens, but there were other Creeks with no rights to citizenship at all and a small group of Natchez who had been absorbed into the tribe through intermarriage (Littlefield 1971: 405).

In addition to these various groups of Native Americans, a number of intermarried whites had become Cherokee citizens through ties of kinship. However, whites and blacks without kinship claims were rejected as Cherokee citizens and often referred to as intruders. In the latter half of the nineteenth century, both African-American and white intruders destabilized the Cherokee Nation in their grab for Cherokee land and resources, but the whites were far more destructive because of their large numbers. Though their overall impact was negative, the intruders did prove helpful to some wealthy Cherokees who needed poor whites and freed blacks to work as laborers on their land (Perdue 1998: 125). Yet as the numbers of intruders grew, they began to threaten Cherokee sovereignty by agitating for more land and a political voice. When the Cherokee Nation could no longer exercise control over the situation, the U.S. Cavalry stepped in and removed almost 1,500 intruders in an effort to uphold the Cherokees' sovereignty. Though this marked a small victory for the Cherokee Nation, the intruders continued to be a problem, and within six years they had returned in equal numbers (McLoughlin 1993: 287).

Whether white, black, or Indian, the increasing diversity of the Cherokee Nation brought new legal problems, particularly in defining rights to tribal citizenship (McLoughlin 1993: 304). For instance, an ongoing concern was the status of the Cherokee freedmen who had been adopted under the treaty of 1866 and of those who were not adopted but not removed because of their pending claims to citizenship (1993: 405). Cherokee Chief Dennis Wolf Bushyhead (principal chief, 1879–1887) believed that omitting the Cherokee freedmen from the tribal roll in 1880 violated the Treaty of 1866, and he protested vigorously on the freedmen's behalf in the early 1880s. However, in 1883 the Cherokee Tribal Council overrode his veto to pass an act authorizing per capita payments only to citizens of the Cherokee Nation "by blood" (Wardell 1977: 233). Once again, when faced with conflicting political interests, the Cherokee Nation defined tribal citizenship on the basis of blood, just as it had done in the wake of removal. In addition to excluding the Cherokee freedmen and intermarried whites, the act also excluded the approximately 1,000 Delawares and a smaller band of Shawnees who had been adopted into the tribe. By the latter half of the nineteenth century, the Cherokee state was using blood not only as a basis for racial, cultural, and national identification but also as a mechanism for controlling access to economic resources. This policy alienated most of the non-Cherokee citizens of the tribe and contributed to a general sense of unrest in the nation.

Because of the tense political atmosphere in the Cherokee Nation, the federal government once again became involved in the citizenship controversy. In 1888, Congress passed a bill mandating that the freedmen and other adopted citizens share equally in tribal assets (25 Stat. at L. 608–9). To identify the freedmen, Congress sent federal agent John W. Wallace to Tahlequah in the summer of 1889 to create a roll listing all the individuals who could share in the per capita distribution of federal monies to the tribe (Littlefield 1978: 148). Known as the Wallace Roll, this document listed 3,524 enrolled freedmen by 1889 (Sampson 1972: 126; 25 Stat. at L. 980, 994 [1889]). This was not the first tribal roll nor the last, but federal enrollment had taken on greater significance since removal: those persons who were "accepted as Cherokee received federal money, and those disputed as Cherokee did not" (Hill 1997: 160).

While the Wallace Roll made it plain that the federal government believed that the 3,524 freedmen deserved these benefits, the Cherokee Nation continued to contest the freedmen's legitimacy. Because of the continued foot-dragging, Congress passed a jurisdictional act in 1890 authorizing the Federal Court of Claims to hear and determine once and for all "the just rights of the Cherokee freedmen . . ." (26 Stat. at L. 636). In the case that followed, *Whitmire v. Cherokee Nation and United States,* the court decided in favor of the freedmen. It held that the sovereign power of the Cherokee Nation could not be exercised in a way that breached the treaty obligations of the Cherokee Nation to the United States (30 Ct. Clms. 138 [1895]). When the tribal council liquidated the common property of the tribe, as in the case of the Cherokee Outlet, the monetary payments could not be restricted to a particular class of Cherokee citizens, such as those by blood (*R. H. Nero, et al. v. Cherokee Nation of Oklahoma, et al.*). The court also held that freedmen as a whole had the right to recover $903,365, as their portion of the $7,240,000 in question.

The freedmen's sense of victory was short-lived: the Cherokee Nation had already distributed the money to Cherokees by blood, leaving its codefendant, the U.S. government, standing with the bill (Sampson 1972: 126). The U.S. government, for its part, demanded another roll before it would pay the freedmen, and the Federal Court of Claims decreed that the secretary of the interior must compile a list of eligible freedmen. For reasons that are vague at best, the court made no mention of the previous Wallace Roll, and a new freedmen roll was not completed until 1896. Why this new roll was initiated without any reference to the prior roll is a perplexing question (Sampson 1972: 126). The Kern-Clifton Roll, as the second one came to be known, was named for Robert H. Kern and William Clifton, the bureaucrats in charge of compiling it (Littlefield 1978: 148). It listed 5,600 freedmen who received their portion of the tribal funds in the following decade (10 Ind. Cl. Comm. 117–18 [1961]).[24] Finally, the freedmen were temporarily able to secure their treaty rights as citizens of the Cherokee Nation (Littlefield 1978: 250–51).

RACISM, ALLOTMENT, AND THE DISSOLUTION OF THE CHEROKEE NATION

As early as the Sauk and Fox Treaty of 1830, the federal government had used blood as a basis for racially identifying Native Americans and distinguishing them from the national body. However, in the late nineteenth century, it began to impose a different racial ideology on Native Americans—the eugenic notion that Native-American identity was tied to Indian blood quantum. Beginning with the General Allotment Act of 1887, commonly known as the Dawes Act, the federal government used this ideology mostly to control access to economic resources. The Dawes Act was designed to break up the communally held Native-American land base by allotting parcels of 160 acres to individual Indians. Blood quantum was crucial to its implementation: Native Americans living on reservations who were documentably of one-half or more Indian blood received allotments, while those who did not meet this standard were simply excluded.

This new quantification of Indian blood was as much a disaster for Native Americans as a boon for Euroamericans. Because the federal government had imposed a strict new definition of Indianness based not only on blood but on a particular blood *quantum,* there were not enough Native Americans who met this criteria to absorb all of the existing reservation acreage. The remaining land was immediately made available for non-Indian use, an important factor in the massive reduction of tribally held lands, not to mention tribal power generally. Much tribal land was alienated and, according to Commissioner of Indian Affairs John Collier, "between 1887 and 1934, the aggregate Indian land base within the United States was 'legally' reduced from about 138 million acres to about 48 million" (Collier 1934: 16–18).

For a variety of legal and political reasons, the Five Tribes in Indian Territory were exempt from the provisions of the Dawes Act for six years, but by 1893 the legislation had been extended to include them. In 1899, the Dawes Commission began compiling the final rolls of the Cherokee Nation, and by 1906 its work was complete. The resulting Dawes Rolls were divided along racial lines—Cherokees by blood, Cherokee freedmen, and intermarried whites—but everyone listed was eligible to receive an allotment.[25] For the Cherokees and the other tribes in the territory, Indian blood quantum came to serve another purpose, one implemented by the federal government. It was used not to determine eligibility for allotments but the trust status of allotments—in essence, who was in control of the land. For example, Congress held in 1908 that if a Native-American allottee was of one-half degree Indian blood or more, his or her allotment was held in federal trust and restricted from sale and taxation. If an allottee were less than half Indian, which included the freedmen and intermarried whites, then he or she had to pay taxes but was free to sell his or her allotment if so desired, a mixed blessing that created both greater autonomy and the possibility of land loss. The justification for this division between fuller bloods and lesser bloods was based on the eugenic notion that "competency," the ability to understand the complex and shifting system of land tenure in Oklahoma, somehow correlated with degree of race mixture.[26]

What motivated the federal government to introduce a more restrictive definition of Indianness based on blood quantum? Native American scholar M. Annette Jaimes argues that because of its historic treaty-based obligations to provide ongoing economic assistance to Native Americans in exchange for land, the federal government had to find a way to minimize or avoid these payments altogether while appearing to honor its commitments (Jaimes 1992a: 116). Obvious noncompliance with Native-American treaties on the part of the federal government would negate not only the legitimacy of its own acquisition and occupation of much of North America but also "the useful and carefully nurtured image . . . of itself as a country of progressive laws rather than raw force" (1992a: 116). To negotiate this difficult political terrain, Jaimes suggests that the federal government, through the Dawes Act, devised the blood quantum standard of identification specifically to delimit the Native-American population. Western historian Patricia Nelson Limerick explains the apparent cynicism of this move: "[S]et the

Figure 8.   Students at the entrance of the Cherokee Nation Female Seminary.
Tahlequah, Oklahoma, Cherokee Nation, 1898. Courtesy of the Western
History Collections, University of Oklahoma Libraries, Norman, Oklahoma.

blood quantum at one-quarter, hold it as a rigid definition of Indians,
let intermarriage proceed as it has for centuries, and eventually Indians
will be defined out of existence. When that happens, the federal government will be freed of its persistent 'Indian problem' " (Limerick 1987:
338). However, both Jaimes and Limerick seem to confuse effect with
intent. Cynical manipulation was not the only force at work in the adoption of blood quantum. Blood quantum was widely embraced by nineteenth-century scientific thought as a rational measure of racial identity
and racial "purity." Thus, the racial logic behind this move lies at a
much deeper hegemonic level. In fact, blood quantum could just as easily
have been introduced by naively well-meaning bureaucrats and liberal
supporters who wanted to help "deserving Indians" but had no effective
way of identifying them except through the crude contours of genealogy.
Whatever its original intent, the effects of this legislation were clearly

advantageous to the federal government, which gained access to millions of acres of land for white settlement.

The racialization of property rights that occurred under the Dawes Act had a serious impact on Native-American communities that went beyond land loss. Ethnohistorian Sarah Hill points out that "a nearly obsessive preoccupation with the biological fiction called 'race' had infected Indian policy" since the beginning (1997: 160). As "federal agents asked and recorded the quantum of 'Cherokee blood' of each person, [they set] up a division that has persisted for more than a century. A more divisive and destructive policy for Native Americans can hardly be imagined" (1997: 160). These actions on the part of the U.S. government constituted a more subtle exercise of power, a type that Michel Foucault calls "disciplinary." (Foucault 1979: 308). As Pauline Strong and Barrik Van Winkle assert, bureaucratic activities that "disciplined" Native Americans according to white standards "were probably of even greater importance than military action in reigning in Indian sovereignty and replacing it with dependency" (1993: 15). As a result, many tribes, having lost much of their land base and their communal system of land tenure, went into economic, social, and political decline in the first several decades of the twentieth century.

The Cherokee Nation faced these same difficulties and others. Not only did the Dawes Act pave the way for Oklahoma statehood, but it did so at the expense of the Cherokee Nation. In 1907 when Oklahoma became a state, Congress formally dissolved the Cherokee Nation as a governing body. Euroamerican ideologies that had helped give birth to Cherokee nationalism now worked to destroy it. The Dawes Act also helped cement the various racial ideologies from earlier in the century. By the turn of the century, these racial ideologies had been reproduced not only in the Dawes Act itself, but in various forms of blood legislation in the state structures of both the Cherokee Nation and the federal government. As we shall see in the next chapter, these ideologies continued to interact and racialize Cherokee national identity in contradictory ways throughout the twentieth century. When the Cherokee Nation finally began to reemerge in the 1940s after three decades of quiescence, the stage had already been set for it to reproduce these contradictions, once again, in its own state structure.

CHAPTER FOUR

Law of Blood, Politics of Nation

The Political Foundations of Racial Rule
in the Cherokee Nation, 1907–2000

Turning onto Muskogee Avenue, the narrow main street running through downtown Tahlequah, she begins her journey from the old Cherokee capital to the new. As she drives by Cherokee square, she is impressed, as always, by the elegant lines of the two-story red brick building at its center. Built in 1870, the former Cherokee capitol is one of many old Cherokee buildings dotting the landscape. The 1845 Cherokee supreme court building, the oldest governmental structure in the state of Oklahoma, lies just to the south of the capitol, across from a modern bank with Cherokee script etched into its windows. Only a block later, she passes the old Cherokee national prison, with its grim stone walls, iron bars, and courtyard gallows dating back to 1874. Even though she is distracted by the stop-and-go traffic of the noon hour and the billboards promising affordable antiques and hefty cheeseburgers, these old buildings pull history into the present and remind her that this was Indian Territory long before it became Oklahoma.

She continues on the hectic commercial strip, driving south past the fire station, the post office, a Christian bookstore, two pawn shops, several convenience stores, a slew of fast food restaurants, and of course, a Wal-Mart, the ubiquitous center of small-town consumption. A mile or so later, she reaches the outskirts of this town of 10,000, and the traffic begins to clear a little. On her left, she passes a winding road leading to Park Hill less than a mile away, where the Cherokee

Figure 9.   The old Cherokee Nation capital that currently serves as the tribal
courthouse. Downtown Tahlequah, Oklahoma. Photograph by Sammy Still
(Cherokee).

Historical Society runs an "ancient village," a "pioneer village," a
Trail of Tears drama, and a Cherokee museum, all for the benefit of
tourists from as close as Tulsa or as far as Germany and Japan. She
drives on, past the tour-bus trail, and just as she reaches the crest
of the next hill, she can see the countryside, the golden and green hills
rolling gently across the horizon to the east. They are dappled with
light and shadow, as the occasional dark clouds play in the blue sky
overhead, forming a mosaic of color and texture.

But the pastoral beauty is fleeting, for only a few miles down the
road, more businesses appear—massive GMC car dealerships and
a large plastic cowboy towering over a burger joint. The traffic begins
to thicken again as she nears the new capital of the Cherokee
Nation. After a stoplight, she passes an outcrop of buildings with a
gas station and what was once a motel run by the tribe. Turning

left across the rutted highway into the tribal complex, she tries to make out the shape of the main building, a low-slung, angular, brown-brick giant that seems to sprawl across the ground with limbs akimbo. Different parts of the building jut forward, others recede, but there is no distinct pattern to its architectural movement.

Parking her dusty black truck in a visitor space, she walks toward the main entrance and notices for the first time the noise of three flags blowing in the wind overhead, one for the United States, another for the state of Oklahoma, and still another for the Cherokee Nation. Avoiding the heat, she walks quickly across the parking lot and into the building through the heavy glass double doors, where she confronts someone who appears to be a security guard at a podium. The Cherokee marshal, with brown uniform, gun in holster, glances her direction and nods. She returns the gesture and moves down the long white hall. The place is clean, modern, and has an institutional feel, with buzzing fluorescent lights and the click of heeled shoes across linoleum. Doors on the left and right open into various administrative offices housing the five main divisions of the Cherokee Nation— tribal operations, law and justice, marshal services, health services, and social services. She walks past each door, until at the end of another corridor, she rounds a corner and finally arrives at the registration department.

She heads to the front counter to sign in, hoping to get a packet of materials and some specific statistical information. As she waits in the reception area, she marvels at the cool efficiency of the Cherokee people behind the blue counter. Almost expressionless, they move quickly from one file, one station, one person to the next. She also notices the steady stream of people coming through the front door. One after another, they ask for assistance: "My daughter, Joanna, can you believe it, she's now nearly three months old. We kept puttin' it off but we figure it's about time we got her CDIB," says a young woman with long, tightly permed, light brown hair and black eyes ringed with purple shadow. She has two young children in tow and an infant slung across the front of her pink and lavender cotton T-shirt.

Another young woman in her late twenties walks delicately to the counter with what appears to be her elderly mother. They speak quietly in Cherokee to each other, and then the younger one turns and translates to the man behind the counter. "Our old auntie, we're worried about her and she don't have no papers, but the rest of us do." She turns to her mother again, who nods her head for her to

Figure 10.   The current headquarters of the Cherokee Nation, also known as the tribal complex. Tahlequah, Oklahoma. Photograph by Sammy Still (Cherokee).

continue. "She doesn't have a birth certificate, but grandpa, her father, is on the rolls. We need her CDIB so she can go to the Indian Hospital."

After them, a man approaches with a short, scraggly beard, thick oily hair and olive skin. He's wearing faded blue jeans, dusty work boots, and a dark green T-shirt from a 1989 bluegrass festival in nearby Fayetteville, Arkansas. He says as far as he knows, no one in his immediate family was ever registered as a tribal member, but he has been doing some research into his family history. His great-great-grandma is on the tribal rolls and he wants to know what he needs to do to get registered. The Cherokee man behind the counter, with the same bored efficiency, explains for the umpteenth time that day how to apply for tribal membership, saying among other things that, "You must first make application for a certificate degree of Indian blood."

As she sits in her chair in the reception area, taking mental field notes, overhearing these different people seeking a CDIB from the tribal registrar, her mind wanders back in time. She imagines the first

Cherokees who intermarried with Europeans centuries ago. How could they have known that the commingling of their blood would result in such bureaucratization, such a Euroamerican standard of measuring Indianness? Would they be disturbed to find that being Cherokee was no longer a simple question of community and clan belonging? How would they feel if they had to apply for a permit to be Cherokee, to prove that they had Cherokee blood? How could they have known that their mixed-blood children, born of love, violence, or necessity, would find themselves caught in a tangled web of race, law, culture, and nation?

During the course of my fieldwork, I saw the subtle repercussions of an obvious fact—Cherokee citizenship is based on blood, on the ability of individuals to prove that they are Cherokee in some measure. In this chapter, I explore how this came to be, how blood became central to Cherokee identity in the twentieth century, not just as a racial, social, and cultural metaphor but as a documented biological possession.[1] This historical process has involved two competing notions of race: first, a Euroamerican sense of ethnonationalism linking blood, race, and nation, which was borrowed early on by Cherokees in their efforts to forge their own national identity; and second, another Euroamerican notion based on nineteenth-century science that racial identity was tied to blood quantum, which signified the nature of one's racial ancestry and degree of race mixture. Over time, the interactions between these two competing ideologies of race gave rise to an overarching racial formation that came to be expressed in the blood legislation of both the Cherokee Nation and the U.S. federal government.[2] Each used this blood legislation at different points in time for different political purposes—but usually with the same underlying motivations: either to control access to economic resources or to maintain racial purity as the basis of a national identity.

Today in Native North America, we see the legacy of these racial ideologies in the institutionalization of what anthropologists Pauline Strong and Barrik Van Winkle refer to as "blood reckoning," a process in which blood remains "central to individuals' and communities' struggles for existence, resources and recognition" (1996: 554). Strong and Van Winkle point out that among federally recognized tribes in the United States, Indian blood quantum continues to be the most common criterion of membership. In the past century and a half, the federal government, usually through the Bureau of Indian Affairs (BIA), has used blood quantum in the administration of Native-American boarding schools and land allotments and in census reports (Strong and Van Winkle 1996: 555). Consequently, the significance of blood quantum was internalized and then codified by tribes themselves in many tribal constitutions written in the wake of the 1934 Indian Reorganization Act (Strong and Van Winkle 1996: 555).

Given this history, it is not surprising that blood legislation continues to determine and shape the boundaries of the Cherokee Nation and that Cherokee national citizenship is based on proof of blood belonging. Just as with most other Indian nations, to register as a citizen of the Cherokee Nation an individual must first have a certificate degree of Indian blood (CDIB) issued by the U.S. Department of the Interior's Bureau of Indian Affairs. This small white card, so critical to an individual's legal and political recognition as a Cherokee tribal member, provides some "essential" information: the individual's name and degree of Indian blood, in fractions according to tribe. For instance, a fairly typical CDIB in Oklahoma might describe someone with multitribal Indian and Euroamerican ancestry in the following manner: seven thirty-seconds Cherokee, two thirty-seconds Kiowa, and two thirty-seconds Choctaw. While the various tribal connections are stated with mathematical precision, the remaining non-Indian blood quantum is not provided.

Obtaining a CDIB is a complicated process that requires a journey down a bureaucratic paper trail. First, individuals must apply to the Cherokee Nation's registration department, which processes applications for the BIA. Then they have to procure legal documents, usually in the form of state-certified vital statistics records, which establish them as lineal descendents of Cherokee ancestors. However, not just any Cherokee ancestors will do. They must be listed on the Cherokee Nation section of what is commonly referred to as the Dawes Rolls, the Final Rolls of Citizens and Freedmen of the Five Civilized Tribes. As mentioned in the previous chapter, the Dawes Rolls were authorized by the Indian Appropriations Act of 1893 that extended the General Allotment Act of 1887 to include the Five Tribes in Indian Territory. The rolls were compiled between 1899 and 1906 for the purpose of breaking up the communal landholdings of Indian nations.[3] Today, their primary use is genealogical. If an individual can find a copy of the Dawes Rolls at a local library or federal repository, such as the National Archives, and his or her ancestor is listed with a roll number and a Cherokee blood degree, then he or she has the necessary information to apply for a CDIB. The Cherokee Nation will then calculate that person's Cherokee blood quantum according to the Indian blood degree of his or her nearest direct ancestor listed on the final rolls.

Even though the Cherokee Nation requires some blood connection to an ancestor listed on the Dawes Rolls, it sets no minimum blood quantum for tribal membership, unlike most other Native-American nations. Once someone has a CDIB, Cherokee tribal citizenship is virtually automatic, requiring only that he or she file a simple form. As a result of this more inclusive enrollment policy, the Cherokee Nation is now the second largest tribe in the United States, with well over 200,000 enrolled citizens.[4] According to the blood standards set by the federal government, it is also one of the most diverse tribes, as I mentioned in the introduction, since the degree of Cherokee blood among citizens ranges from full-blood to 1/2,048. Of course, there is no calculus for identity, and social scientists acknowledge that blood quantum analytically has no causal link with cultural belonging or racial self-identification. However, the common sense understanding of the general public in the United States and the Cherokee Nation is quite different. Most people think that blood matters, both socially and politically. To better understand how this plays out on the ground, let us take a closer look at the discourse of belonging in the Cherokee Nation, particularly the way in which the Cherokee Nation documents its own population in terms of blood fractions.

According to the Cherokee Nation's Department of Registration, 21 percent of the tribe has 1/4 or more degree of Cherokee blood, or at least one full-blood Cherokee grandparent.[5] Twenty-nine percent of the tribe has 1/4 to 1/16 degree of Cherokee blood, or at least one Cherokee great-great grandparent. And 21 percent has between 1/16 and 1/64 degree of Cherokee blood, or at least one Cherokee great-great-great-great-grandparent. That leaves 29 percent, over 50,000 members, close to one third of the tribe, with a Cherokee blood quantum somewhere between 1/64 and 1/2,048. Hypothetically, this is as many as ten generations removed from a full-blood Cherokee ancestor who would have lived sometime during the eighteenth century.

Many people, Cherokees included, wonder how someone can document his or her lineal descent back to an ancestor in the eighteenth century, given the paucity of records from that period. This is possible because Cherokee citizens have to prove descent back only to the Dawes Rolls of 1899–1906, where Cherokee blood degree varied from full-blood to 1/256. Today, tribal citizens have even smaller fractions of Cherokee blood. For example, if we consider a generation to be about

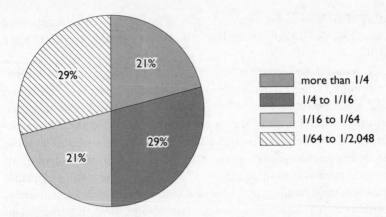

Figure 11. Percent of total 1996 Cherokee population by degree of Cherokee ancestry (N = 175,326).

twenty years, then it would take only three generations of exogamy beginning with an ancestor having 1/256 degree of Cherokee blood to reach a descendent with 1/2,048. If the trend continues, we can expect to see more Cherokee citizens with even lower blood quanta on their CDIBs in the coming decades. In approximately one hundred years, or five generations from now, the Cherokee Nation is likely to contain a sizeable number of citizens with 1/4,096, 1/8,192, 1/16,384, or even 1/32,768 degree of Cherokee blood.

Among Native-American tribes, the Cherokee Nation is not unusual in requiring some Cherokee blood for membership, but it is remarkable for having no minimum biogenetic standard, no minimum degree of blood, for citizenship. In this sense, Cherokee Nation citizenship requirements both reproduce and challenge racial hegemony, particularly what Gerald Vizenor calls the "perverse arithmetics" of blood set forth by the federal government (Vizenor 1990: 12). Federal legislation regarding Native-American identity is complex and contradictory. At times, the federal government imposes a minimum blood quantum standard, usually one-quarter degree Indian blood, to determine eligibility for social services. At other times, it requires only verification of lineal descent and tribal recognition. At still others, it asks only for self-identification. Because of the intricacy of the U.S. federal state, different agencies identify Native Americans in different ways for different purposes.[6] The Cherokee Nation reproduces federal standards, in general, when it requires that all citizens document their Cherokee blood as a basis of tribal belonging. However, it also challenges the hegemonic notion that Native-American identity is based on blood degree—an ironic fact since it is degree of blood that is so carefully certified by the CDIB.

So, how did the Cherokee Nation come to be this way? In the following sections, I begin to answer this question by exploring how competing racial ideologies continued to interact and shape Cherokee political history and national identity throughout the twentieth century. In particular, I examine the racial politics behind the resurgence of the Cherokee state in the period between 1946 and 1976. I show how the ideology of race as nation was manipulated by "white-Cherokee" elites to justify their national belonging on the basis of blood, even the smallest amount, and their right to political power. At the same time, however, their claims to power were increasingly contested by fuller-blood Cherokees, who used the ideology of race as blood quantum to argue that racial identity and national belonging centered on a specific degree of Indian blood. Understanding this political and ideological tension between these competing definitions of race provides a framework for the final sections of this chapter, where I explore contemporary expressions of Cherokee nationalism. Here, I show how Cherokees conflate blood, culture, race, and nation, and how they manipulate this race-culture continuum in their political acts of national representation.

CREATING A STATE WITHIN A STATE: THE RACIAL POLITICS BEHIND CHEROKEE NATIONAL RESURGENCE IN THE TWENTIETH CENTURY

Following Oklahoma statehood in 1907, the Cherokee people had no legal government recognized under U.S. law (Wahrhaftig 1975: 53). In fact, their political situation was so dire that for the next sixty years their principal chief was "appointed by the president of the United States without the advice, consent or ballot of the Cherokees themselves" (Strickland and Strickland 1991: 130). Beginning in the late 1940s, however, the rudiments of a Cherokee government were slowly reorganized. After the passage of the Indian Claims Act of 1946, a Cherokee government was created as a legal fiction for the purpose of bringing lawsuits before the Indian Claims Commission and as a device for participating in federal programs (Wahrhaftig 1975: 55–57).[7] The first step in this process occurred in 1948 when Bartley Milam, the federally appointed principal chief, called a tribal convention in Tahlequah. The primary purpose was to select an executive committee that would attend to tribal political matters and select attorneys to prosecute a case before the Indian Claims Commission (Wahrhaftig 1975: 55). When Milam died shortly thereafter, the secretary of the interior assigned the office of principal chief to W. W. Keeler, a Texas oilman, who had served a brief stint as one of the members of the executive committee.

From the late 1940s to the early 1970s, Chief Keeler was a powerful and controversial tribal leader (Strickland and Strickland 1991: 130). Keeler had a significant power base, not only as chief of the Cherokees but also as president and CEO of the Phillips Petroleum Corporation. Operating out of the Phillips headquarters in Bartlesville, Oklahoma, Keeler "knew how to manipulate the federal structure, and the tribe benefited from his power and position" (Strickland and Strickland 1991: 130). However, Wahrhaftig argues that because Keeler was only minimally Cherokee in both a biological and a cultural sense, he failed to understand and meet the needs of the more traditional Cherokees living in rural communities (1975: 64). His tenure was controversial but effective from the perspective of the Cherokee Nation, if not always the Cherokee people. "Although considerable hostility and agitation marked his final years, there is no question that when Keeler finally retired from office as chief, the Cherokee Nation had become a vital force once again" (Strickland and Strickland 1991: 130).

Under Keeler's leadership, Cherokee political organization went through several stages, each marking the rise of what Wahrhaftig calls the Cherokee establishment, or what I refer to as the Cherokee state (Wahrhaftig 1975: 52). In the late 1940s Chief Keeler began his political activities by handpicking a group of individuals from old Cherokee families to serve on his new executive committee (1975: 55–56). Members of what was essentially a white-Cherokee elite, these individuals dominated the political and business life of northeastern Oklahoma.[8] As the executive committee came increasingly to control Cherokee political affairs, they organized with other tribes in the area and created the Five Civilized Tribes Intertribal Council, which "controlled early policies of the National Congress of American Indians;" and in 1952 they established the Cherokee Foundation, Incorporated (Wahrhaftig 1975: 56). With more than a hint of paternalism, the foundation operated much like a charity organization and exercised its sense of social responsibility by helping needy Cherokees on an individual basis for nearly a decade (Wahrhaftig 1975: 57). This was the extent of social services provided by the Cherokee tribal government. Cherokees seeking further economic assistance had to turn to the BIA.

Figure 12.   Principal Chief W. W. Keeler (1949–75).
Courtesy of the University Archives, John Vaughn
Library, Northeastern State University, Tahlequah,
Oklahoma.

In the early sixties, political developments took a dramatic turn when
the Indian Claims Commission awarded the Cherokee tribe nearly $15
million as an additional payment for tribal land (Wahrhaftig 1975: 58).
Because the distribution of large sums of money was at stake, suddenly
the tribal government had to operate in an effective administrative ca-
pacity. Again, blood became a critical factor in determining tribal identity and rights to economic resources. Just as under Chief William P.
Ross in the late nineteenth century, the money was divided only among
enrolled Cherokees by blood. Once the distribution was complete in
October 1964, less than $2 million remained in the tribal coffer (Wahr-
haftig 1975: 58). Now that they had working capital, tribal leaders invested the money in various projects, the most notable of which was the
Cherokee National Historical Society (CNHS) (Wahrhaftig 1975: 58).
The executive committee provided the CNHS with start-up funds in the

hopes that its planned tribal museum, "ancient village," and theater would attract tourism to the area. Such projects served to strengthen the economy in northeastern Oklahoma in general, but they had little direct impact on the poor rural Cherokees who were most in need.

This shortcoming was revealed most dramatically in the mid-1960s, when the Cherokee political elite used the Indian Claims Commission settlement funds to make some dubious investments, whose failure they attempted to hide from public scrutiny (Wahrhaftig 1975: 59). In response, Cherokees living in traditional communities grew suspicious and began to protest the tribe's programs and policies. They demanded a voice not only in how the tribal government operated but also in how tribal money was spent (Wahrhaftig 1975: 60–61). Several community organizations formed and put forth their own agendas, but the tribal government's response was "to either compete with or to absorb projects that had been initiated in Cherokee settlements" (Wahrhaftig 1975: 62). What had been initially spontaneous, autonomous political organizations began to come under the increasing supervision and control of tribal authorities, those nonelected white-Cherokee businessmen headed by Chief Keeler.

At the same time, Cherokee leaders tried to quell dissent by instilling a nationalistic sense of unity in the Cherokee populace. For example, the Cherokee government launched its own newspaper. As Benedict Anderson suggests in another context, the development of print media lays the base for a national consciousness (1983: 44). Anderson argues that it creates a "unified field of exchange and communication" where readers become aware of others to whom they are connected through language and print. This process, he contends, helps to nurture "the embryo of the nationally imagined community" (Anderson 1983: 44). Just as they had in the nineteenth century, Cherokee leaders used the tribal newspaper as one tool among many to carefully manipulate a developing sense of nationalism and to lend legitimacy to a Cherokee government that had been little more than a legal fiction only twenty years earlier. By 1967, that government had become the principle entity through which federal funds were channeled into northeastern Oklahoma (Wahrhaftig 1975: 54). Bombarded by a well-established public relations department and "a bewildering assortment of tribal programs" and faced with no other more viable, democratic option, most Cherokee people began to accept the Cherokee Nation as their legitimate tribal government, if only by default (Wahrhaftig 1975: 62–63).

To bolster its position of power, the Cherokee Nation decided to create its own institutional identity apart from the BIA (Wahrhaftig 1975: 65). It did so by constructing an impressive office complex and by taking over some administrative duties from the BIA. Once this was accomplished, the Cherokee Nation "began to function like a small centralized state, with the Cherokee population and much of eastern Oklahoma under its jurisdiction" (Wahrhaftig 1975: 65). However, "as forces from outside the region became interested in Cherokees, began to point out that Cherokee settlements existed there as viable and oppressed little communities, and began to publicize the fact that Cherokees had no voice in the selection of their federally-appointed chief," the Cherokee political machinery "moved to present an appearance of democracy by promoting 'grass roots' organization[s] within Cherokee settlements" (Wahrhaftig 1975: 64).[9] To maintain stability and to "expand the extent of its control over its population," the Cherokee Nation encouraged local communities to select representatives, who by 1970 were attending meetings of the executive committee and voting in the proceedings (Wahrhaftig 1975: 64–67).

As the system of community representatives developed, Cherokee tribal leaders also sought new federal legislation authorizing a Cherokee election that would presumably legitimate their power and validate their leadership (Wahrhaftig 1975: 67). This legislation was soon passed, and on August 14, 1971, W. W. Keeler was elected by popular vote as principal chief of the Cherokee Nation, the first elected chief since 1907 (Wahrhaftig 1975: 68). But why would the Cherokee people, newly invigorated with autonomous political power, choose to elect the same man who had been an appointee of the federal government? In spite of surface appearances, the vote being about seven to one in his favor, the election of Chief Keeler was not truly a popular election. Less than half the tribe, only about 10,000 enrolled Cherokees, participated in the election (Wahrhaftig 1975: 68). Of that number, the vast majority were culturally assimilated Cherokees who supported the white-Cherokee political elite in order to maintain the status quo. At the same time, more culturally conservative Cherokees, who might have altered the course of the election, expressed their political disapproval in a traditional way honoring the harmony ethic, by withdrawing from the election and refusing to participate (Wahrhaftig 1975: 68). Most did not even register to vote. With this, the racialized pattern of electoral politics in the Cherokee Nation would be established for some years to come.

REACTIONS TO WHITE-CHEROKEE ELITE POWER IN CONTEMPORARY EXPRESSIONS OF CHEROKEE ETHNONATIONALISM

The 1971 election was a landmark event, marking the return of some degree of tribal sovereignty. As the Stricklands describe, "the popular election of Chief Keeler, who had previously been named by every president from Harry Truman to Richard Nixon, brought an end to the era of colonial appointment of the Cherokee tribal leadership" (Strickland and Strickland 1991: 130–31). Then, only a few years later in 1976, the Cherokee Nation took another significant step toward tribal sovereignty when it adopted a new constitution (Strickland and Strickland 1991: 131). Tribal leaders called "a constitutional convention, revised their old governance documents in light of new circumstances, and submitted it to popular referendum" (Strickland and Strickland 1991: 131). Although initiated under Keeler, the new Cherokee constitution was finally approved under Keeler's successor, Chief Ross Swimmer.

Like Keeler before him, Chief Swimmer (1975–85), had minimal Cherokee ancestry and was socially and culturally oriented toward white society. For the most part, both Cherokee chiefs were regarded as white men by the populations they governed (Wahrhaftig 1975: 65). Even at a more general level, this perception seemed to be associated with the Cherokee national leadership. For instance, in the early 1970s, the business manager of the Cherokee Nation, referring to the executive committee said, "the Cherokee Nation is controlled essentially by non-Indians" (Wahrhaftig 1975: 59). Wahrhaftig argues that because of this perception and the controversy surrounding it, Cherokee Nation administrators had to maintain their credibility and right to leadership in the eyes of the larger Cherokee and U.S. society. They had to control the legal definition of Cherokee identity as the very key to the maintenance of their economic and political power (Wahrhaftig 1975: 65). Therefore, it comes as no surprise that although the legal definition of a Cherokee citizen has shifted over time, rarely has it disenfranchised those with minimal Cherokee blood, who have become a powerful majority in the tribal population. This is a significant reason why the Cherokee Nation requires no minimum blood quantum requirement for tribal membership and why degree of blood has rarely mattered in Cherokee national law.

However, blood quantum did become a critical factor in the federal government's policies toward Native Americans after the Dawes Act,

Figure 13.   Principal Chief Ross Swimmer (1975–85).
Courtesy of the University Archives, John Vaughn
Library, Northeastern State University, Tahlequah,
Oklahoma.

particularly in determining eligibility for federal social services. The
most notable of these is the Indian Health Service (IHS). For decades,
the IHS set the standard of eligibility at one-quarter degree of Indian
blood or more. But in 1977, the Cherokee Nation successfully challenged the one-quarter blood quantum limitation. As one tribal member
described the situation to me:

> The Cherokee Nation originally used the one-quarter blood cutoff for IHS.
> But Hastings [the local Indian Hospital] was overloaded with just the one-
> quarter people. The old facilities were a joke. Everyone was overworked and
> it was just a mess. So, they opened up the rolls and soon there was a flood
> on the hospital. This forced the hand of the IHS. Now, we have a brand new
> hospital facility. . . . So, it was a local political thing, although I remember
> at the time it being argued as an issue of sovereignty.

When I asked a Cherokee Nation employee about this statement, she
agreed but added that it was also a question of economic power, a num-

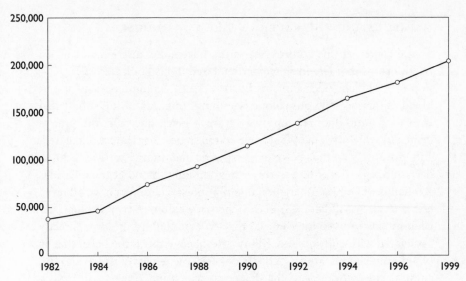

Figure 14.   Overall Cherokee Nation enrollment pattern, 1982–99.

bers game. As she put it, "more tribal members means more federal money." The flip side of the coin is that more federal money attracted more tribal members. New economic incentives, such as free health care, lured many people to return to the tribal fold, particularly those who through a gradual process of acculturation and intermarriage had long since passed into the surrounding communities of Oklahoma. As a result, throughout the 1970s and continuing to this day, the Cherokee Nation has become progressively "whiter."

It has also become substantially larger. The Cherokees' more open policy regarding blood has helped create the second largest tribe in the United States, one that quintupled in size between 1982 and 2000, from a population of less than 40,000 to well over 200,000. At present, the tribe continues to grow at a rapid pace, with approximately 1,500 applications for tribal membership arriving every month. Of that number, approximately 85 percent are newborns and 10 percent are adults, commonly elders who need economic assistance in their later years.[10] The remainder, only 5 percent, are ineligible for tribal membership, for any number of reasons having to do with lack of documentation. With each succeeding generation of newborns that join the tribe, blood connections are stretched to an even more controversial level.

MANIPULATING THE RACE-CULTURE CONTINUUM

At the center of this controversy is the hegemonic discourse of blood relationships that David Schneider analyzed in his book *American Kinship* (1980). Schneider explains Euroamerican "common sense" about blood as follows: "Because blood is a 'thing' and because it is subdivided with each reproductive step away from a given ancestor, the precise degree to which two people share a common heredity can be calculated, and 'distance' can thus be stated in specific quantitative terms" (Schneider 1980: 25). According to this line of thought, blood degree provides a calculus of common heredity, one that most Cherokees have adopted as a measure of Indianness. In the Cherokee community, this blood hegemony has been so internalized that race mixing has become directly associated with cultural loss. Many Cherokees express the belief that as blood connections are stretched thin over the generations, so too are cultural connections, and the degree to which individuals still have a Cherokee culture can be measured by their degree of Cherokee blood.

During numerous interviews, I asked various Cherokee citizens whether they thought there was a dividing line according to blood quantum when someone stopped being Cherokee. One tribal leader replied to me with this statement: "I'm hesitant to say that, yes, there is. If they have a tiny amount [of blood], then they really don't have a heritage. They know very little. I'm talking about 1/100 or whatever. . . . They wouldn't know their family or ancestry, and they'd know little about their culture or language." The vast majority of Cherokee people I interviewed wanted a blood quantum to be reinstated, although the exact cutoff was hotly debated, because it would most likely exclude a friend, a spouse, a child, or a grandchild.[11] Many of the fuller-blooded Cherokees argued that the tribe should revert back to the former federal standard of one-quarter, although they feared that future generations of their own families would not "measure up." Others said that the tribe would lose too many people and too much federal funding and that the cutoff should start with blood fractions in the triple digits, making 1/100 the minimum blood quantum for tribal citizenship. Regardless of the specific cutoff suggested, these rationalizations tended to conflate blood with culture. One Cherokee person made this point explicit in an interview with me: "If we continue to mix ourselves, then the blood heritage runs out. The blood of a Cherokee is not just a biological thing, but a lot of heritage. There are a lot of real Cherokee people running through our veins. There's a cultural heritage in there."

The conflation of blood and culture among Cherokees is not surprising if we take a step back and consider the relationship between racial ideologies and nationalism at a broader level. The anthropological literature on race and nationalism suggests that virtually all nations, including the United States, have normative racial ideologies that homogenize cultural diversity and shape discourses of social belonging.[12] The Cherokee Nation is no different. In the nineteenth century, Cherokees adopted the Euroamerican racial ideology linking blood and nation in an effort to forge their own national identity, a strategy that later came into conflict with the federally imposed ideology that racial identity is a question of blood quantum. Because Cherokees are binationals, citizens of both the United States and the Cherokee Nation, they are subject to a complex ideological matrix where mutually embedded sets of racial ideologies associated with two different national identities articulate and compete with one another. If we understand how this matrix works, then we can better understand Cherokee expressions of nationalism, which at different times both reproduce and challenge dominant Western ideologies, conflating blood, race, culture, and nation.

Cherokees appropriated Western ideologies of race and nation at a time when it was politically expedient, but today these same ideologies raise some troubling questions. For instance, if according to these ideologies national sovereignty is based in part on biological purity and cultural homogeneity, then what happens to the Cherokee Nation? Does its own racially mixed and culturally diverse population somehow threaten Cherokee national sovereignty? Many Cherokee people say yes. As one Cherokee told me, "If I had it in my power, I would go back and establish a cutoff at one-sixteenth or one thirty-second for the good of our survival. This situation will be our undoing. The federal government will say these people aren't culturally Indian, and that will be the end of us." Similarly, David Cornsilk, a prominent Cherokee political activist told me:

> One of the greatest dangers to us as a people is that, as a race, if we are simply relegated to a racial category, persons who are more white than they are Indian are in danger of being reclassified as non-Indians. Because I don't think that mathematically you can look at someone who is one sixty-fourth Indian and sixty-three sixty-fourths white and say that they are Indian. . . . We jeopardize ourselves by classifying ourselves as a race in this country. . . .

Such sentiments reflect a growing fear among Cherokees that they might lose their political status as a result of their increasingly phenotypically white population. According to this line if thinking, as the Cherokee

Nation progressively "whitens," it runs the risk of losing its distinct racial and cultural identity, the primordial substance of its national identity. In the eyes of the general public, the Cherokee Nation would no longer be a "real" Indian tribe.

In response to such concerns, over the past few decades Cherokee tribal leaders have often debated whether they should set a minimum blood quantum for tribal membership. However, no specific reforms have ever gotten off the ground, in part because Cherokee leaders fear losing federal funding that is tied to population. Local political concerns play an even greater role. For the Cherokee Nation to set a minimum blood quantum, it would have to revise its own constitution and then submit the revision for popular approval. The primary voting force in the Cherokee Nation—citizens with one-sixteenth or less degree of Cherokee blood—is not likely to support such a revision. Not surprisingly, politicians who have run for office on such a platform have failed to get elected. Only among the more blooded or culturally conservative Cherokees has setting a minimum blood standard received approval. However, many of these Cherokees do not vote in Cherokee elections; they feel it would be an exercise in futility since the Cherokee Nation does not represent them or their needs. This situation has led to one of the great ironies of Cherokee blood politics: the individuals at the cultural and racial margins of the Cherokee Nation have come to define the center. Many culturally conservative Cherokees make this argument, which is no secret in northeastern Oklahoma, but they have gained little support for policy changes from the majority of the tribe.

Many culturally conservative Cherokees and tribal leaders feel that their hands are tied when it comes to the influx of white blood that threatens their national identity as a distinct people. As a result, tribal administrators have turned increasingly to cultural preservation. Through various language programs, cultural centers, tribal museums, and historic preservation projects that have surfaced since the early 1970s, the Cherokee Nation has attempted to preserve its cultural patrimony, its other national substance aside from race and blood. If the Nation cannot remain biologically and racially Cherokee, then it is even more essential that it remain culturally Cherokee.

This same maneuvering along what I describe as a race-culture continuum can even be seen in the composition of the tribal leadership itself. In the past twenty-five years, while the tribe has progressively whitened, elected Cherokee officials have tended to become more phenotypically Native American and to some extent more culturally "authentic." First,

Figure 15. Principal Chief Wilma Mankiller (1985–95). Courtesy of Wilma Mankiller.

there was Ross Swimmer, a phenotypically white and culturally non-Indian banker and lawyer who served as principal chief from 1975 to 1985. Recall that it was under his administration that the one-quarter blood quantum for Indian Health Services was successfully challenged and the tribal rolls began to swell with white-Cherokees. Then Swimmer's former deputy chief, Wilma Mankiller, replaced him. Mankiller, the daughter of a full-blood Cherokee father and a white mother, was phenotypically mixed and not a Cherokee-language speaker. From 1985 to 1995, she was one of the most popular chiefs in Cherokee history, retaining her popularity until the 1995 tribal elections. "[The 1995] election was a revolution, although no one calls it that," one reporter wrote in the local Tahlequah newspaper. The reporter continued, providing one common interpretation, that "after months of mudslinging, shamelessly biased media coverage, and a parade of lawsuits that

Figure 16.   Principal Chief Joe Byrd (1995–99).
Courtesy of Joe Byrd.

marches on, the tribe deposed the Swimmer/Mankiller regime by rejecting their anointed heir, George Bearpaw" (*Tahlequah Daily Press,* April,
28, 1996).

   The newly elected leadership was Principal Chief Joe Byrd and Deputy Chief Garland Eagle (1995–99), who differed from their predeces-
sors in some significant ways. For the first time in well over a century,
both the Cherokee Nation principal chief and deputy chief were full-
blood Cherokees and fluent Cherokee-language speakers.[13] Because of
this, many Cherokees were hopeful that their new leadership would re-
integrate culturally conservative Cherokees who had withdrawn from
the tribal political process. However, these hopes were dashed in early
1997 when a major crisis erupted that would dominate the remaining
years of Byrd and Eagle's administration.

The turmoil began in February 1997 when Cherokee Nation marshals raided the headquarters of Chief Byrd. The marshals, operating under a search warrant issued by a Cherokee supreme court justice, had reason to believe that they would turn up evidence that the chief had been misappropriating tribal funds. Byrd responded by firing the marshals, and his supporters on the tribal council moved to impeach the Cherokee supreme court. But the marshals believed the chief's actions were unconstitutional and continued to operate under the auspices of the Cherokee supreme court. When Byrd ignored the court's order to reinstate the marshals and hired a new set of marshals in their place, battle lines were drawn and allegiances torn throughout the executive, judicial, and legislative branches of the Cherokee government. It was a painful moment in Cherokee history. The tensions culminated in June 1997 when Byrd's administration forcibly closed the Cherokee courthouse, locking out the "fired" marshals and "impeached" justices. A month later, fighting erupted as two sets of Cherokee marshals clashed on the steps of the historic Cherokee courthouse in downtown Tahlequah, vying for control of the symbolic and historical center of Cherokee national government.

When things settled down, the Cherokee courthouse was reopened to the public, but the damage had been done. Even in the summer of 2000, the tribe was still undergoing investigations by the FBI, the Department of the Interior, and other federal agencies, while several lawsuits were pending in tribal, state, and federal courts. Some Cherokees believe that Byrd set himself above the law and undermined the Cherokee constitution in the process. Others believe that he was not prepared for the rigors of such a high profile office and that his actions were more the result of political naiveté and bad advice. Either way, Byrd undermined his credibility enough to lose his bid for reelection in 1999.

Elected instead were current Principal Chief Chadwick "CornTassel" Smith and Deputy Chief Hastings Shade, who ran on a ticket promoting honesty, improved health care, and a return to Cherokee culture. Like the two previous tribal leaders, Deputy Chief Shade is also a Cherokee full-blood and a fluent Cherokee-language speaker. Chief Smith, on the other hand, is only one-half Cherokee and not a fluent Cherokee speaker. Still, their election symbolizes a return to Cherokee culture in other important ways. As the great-grandson of Redbird Smith, the famous Cherokee political and religious leader, and as an occasional participant at the Keetoowah ceremonial grounds, Chad Smith possesses cultural capital that far outweighs any limitations that might be posed

Figure 17.   Principal Chief Chadwick "Corn Tassel"
Smith (1999–present). Courtesy of Chad Smith.
Photograph by Sammy Still (Cherokee).

by his multiracial identity or linguistic shortcomings. Furthermore, because Deputy Chief Shade is an active member of a Cherokee Baptist
Church in Hulbert, Oklahoma, their combined leadership represents
cultural and religious unity among Cherokees.

Despite this symbolic unity, Smith and Shade's political tasks in the
Cherokee Nation have not been made any easier. They have inherited a
host of problems from the previous administrations. Even with the best
of intentions, they are forced to work within the Cherokee Nation's own
state structure—what for many years has been a large bureaucracy that
mimics the state structure of the federal government. Though they aim
to create a new style of Cherokee politics, one that integrates traditional
forms of Cherokee culture into their modern bureaucracy, they will have

to do this as they strive to meet the various needs of an increasingly diverse population. They will also have to weather the storm of local identity politics that results from this diversity.

FRAMING CONTEMPORARY CHEROKEE IDENTITY POLITICS

If we examine these developments more closely, we can see that contemporary Cherokee identity politics revolve around an apparent contradiction. The tension lies between the tribe's national identity as a people who share a common racial and cultural heritage and its sociopolitical reality—a highly diverse society maintained not primarily by social or cultural bonds but by government regulations. I argue, along with Albert Wahrhaftig, that Cherokee blood policies constitute the Cherokee Nation in a legal and political sense but that these legal definitions do not correspond with sociocultural realities at the local level (Wahrhaftig 1975: 65). These blood policies originate in the Cherokee Nation's relationship with the federal government, as I have demonstrated throughout this and the previous chapter. One aspect of this relationship has been the proliferation of two competing racial ideologies in the legislation of both the federal government and the Cherokee Nation. One ideology supports the use of blood as a basis for determining national identity, and the other suggests blood quantum as a basis for policing and delimiting the Cherokee population. The first ideology tends toward racial inclusivity, while the second tends toward racial exclusivity. However, both ideologies have reinforced the racially hegemonic notion that Cherokee identity is based on blood. As a result, Cherokee citizens are confronted daily with questions of national belonging influenced by dominant ideas associated with blood and race.

Even though hegemonic ideas about blood, race, and culture influence and shape most national communities, in the Cherokees' case blood aligns with power in unique ways. In other racially marked communities, the logic of hypodescent has historically been a source of oppression and has been used to assign a single racial identity to multiracial individuals according to their lower-status blood, even if that blood is only "one drop." But in the Cherokee Nation, having a little Indian blood is a valuable commodity, the stuff of power that ensures a political identity, voting rights as a Cherokee citizen, and access to a variety of economic resources. In fact, we can chart the historical trajectory of blood ideologies in the Cherokee Nation and how they have moved back and forth between the realm of political contestation and the realm of uncontested hegemony. What started as blood ideology in the hands of the federal government—that nation was defined by racial substance—became blood hegemony as Cherokee National identity slowly became an unquestionably racialized category. However, this hegemony in turn became an ideology again when white-Cherokee elites began to manipulate the idea of blood as nation in order to secure and legitimate their position of power in the latter half of the nineteenth century. In other words, white-Cherokee leaders began to challenge blood-quantum ideologies in order to secure their right to political rule and to build a larger and more diverse Cherokee national body. They justified this maneuver by arguing that it was blood and not blood degree that was the socially, racially, and culturally cohesive force among the Cherokee people. This same pattern of political manipulation continued through the middle decades of the twentieth century and has only begun to taper off in the past ten years, as fuller-blood Cherokees increasingly invoke another racial ideology in response—that Cherokee identity is a question of blood *quantum*. In other words, to be truly Cherokee means that someone has to have a certain degree of Cherokee blood.

In spite of these recent efforts by fuller-blood Cherokees, Cherokee citizenship remains a question of blood and not degree of blood, and this has had some unexpected political consequences. As the Cherokee Nation has become larger and more diverse, traditional Cherokees living in rural communities have been increasingly marginalized. As a result, the Cherokee state apparatus has become an even more powerful force in the administration of Cherokee identity and citizenship, conforming to the model set forth by Anthony Giddens (1987). Giddens argues that all states act as "power containers" through the concentration of allocative and administrative resources. As states generate power, they create systems of surveillance and authority that influence the formation of ideology (Giddens 1987: 13–16). If we apply this model to the Cherokee case, then the Cherokees' state-like bureaucracy "monitors aspects of the reproduction of the social systems subject to [its] rule" through the administration of blood legislation (Giddens 1987: 17). This reifies ideologies of blood that legitimate political power and Cherokee national identity. As the Cherokee Nation experiences demographic shifts in its national substance, the Cherokee political bureaucracy becomes a powerful ideological center, knitting together an increasingly diverse Cherokee population.

Today, the Cherokee Nation continues its efforts to instill a sense of national unity around blood belonging. However, there are many dissenters who resist the incorporation of minimally blooded Cherokees into the tribal body, at least at a discursive level. They do so not only because of political and economic concerns regarding the balance of power in their nation, but also because they too have internalized hegemonic notions conflating blood, color, race, and nation. Cherokee citizens have also resisted the erosion of their national substance in practice by electing tribal leaders who are increasingly Cherokee in a cultural and phenotypic sense. As a result, the public face of the Cherokee Nation reflects not the tribe's demographic reality but its imagined center. In the remaining chapters, this tension between national representation and social reality will come into play again and again as I explore the various ways in which Cherokees internalize, manipulate, and resist the racial structure of the Cherokee Nation.

CHAPTER FIVE

Social Classification and Racial Contestation

Local Non-National Interpretations of Cherokee Identity

Henry James said a century ago that it was a complicated fate to be an American. He had no idea, of course, about the future complications of being Native American. Today, whether or not someone is Cherokee has different answers depending on who is being asked and within what context. National and local definitions of Cherokee identity are often in tension, particularly in regard to race. Due to the historic interplay between various racial ideologies and legal codes, the Cherokee Nation has come to define its citizens on the basis of blood ancestry, a policy that fosters a widespread tendency toward hegemonic race-thinking in the tribe. However, even within the social and geographic space of the Cherokee Nation, local systems of social classification are still shaped to a significant extent by criteria other than blood ancestry, causing Cherokees to question the almost exclusively blood-based definition of tribal identity. For example, I recall a long conversation that I had with a full-blood Cherokee woman who had been raised in a traditional community. I asked her how she felt about the numerous minimal-blood Cherokees who were recognized as citizens of the Cherokee Nation. With a smirk on her face, she responded, "Well, if they have their little card, then I guess they are Cherokee, huh? I mean it says so." This ironic comment, like many I heard during the course of my fieldwork, reveals the articulation of local definitions of Cherokeeness with and against Cherokee national hegemony about blood and race.

One of the facets of the tension between local and national definitions of Cherokee identity can be seen in the distinction that many Cherokees make between being Cherokee and being Indian (a distinction that is also made in the Cherokee language). According to local understandings, Cherokee is a more inclusive political category that can include anyone who has an acknowledged political identity as a Cherokee National citizen—from those with "pure blood" and "full culture" to those who are phenotypically and culturally white. On the other hand, the term *Indian* is a more explicitly racial category. In fact, many tribal members consider themselves to be nationally, politically, and socially Cherokee but not racially Indian. Still, there is a racial subtext to both categories, since the national definition of Cherokee identity has a racial component. After all, the CDIB required for national recognition as a Cherokee citizen certifies Indian blood and not some other national substance. Thus, the local definition of a Cherokee slips back and forth from a nonracial category to a racial category as it articulates with blood hegemony.

When I interviewed one Cherokee man about this tension around race, between national and local definitions of Cherokee identity, we had an interesting and pointed exchange:

CS: You talk about Cherokee identity as explicitly racial but in legal and political terms, then you contradict yourself, like right now, when you say there is a racial element too.

CHEROKEE MAN (CM): Right. There is, and it's hard to get away from. It really is.

CS: So, which is it?

CM: Well, I think it can be both in different contexts.

CS: Just like when you say both in different contexts! (laughter) I'm just catching you.

CM: Yeah . . . I understand the contradiction in myself, and that's what makes it so ugly to me. . . . There is this conflict. But I think the difference is that in our relationship with outsiders, with people who would take from us, and in protecting our institution of citizenship and government, that it [the definition of a Cherokee] is legal and political. But in my personal relationships and in my personal interactions with other people, it becomes a racial issue. I can accept legally that someone who is one sixty-fourth is Cherokee, but I cannot accept personally that person as an Indian. But that's me, that's inside of me. So I've got this dichotomy inside of me.

As this exchange suggests, contradictory consciousness around racial hegemony affects Cherokee practices of social classification. At one level, this man recognizes the need for the Cherokee Nation to define its citizens in an inclusive manner, to protect its own political institutions. Thus, he consciously, perhaps reluctantly, accepts the legal definition of a Cherokee citizen as an ideological tool for dealing with the outside world. However, on a more personal level, he believes that Cherokee identity is a matter of racial and social recognition, that it is more than a fluke of genealogy that makes someone Cherokee. His stricter "working definition" of Cherokee identity reveals a deep racial hegemony at work, so that the national, political, and legal definition of a Cherokee is in tension with the local, more explicitly racial and social definitions of a Cherokee Indian.

This same racial hegemony partially accounts for why the term *Cherokee* can refer to phenotypically ambiguous or white mixed-bloods, who are often socially accepted as members of the national body, but never to phenotypically black individuals, even those with Cherokee blood. These men and women, known as Cherokee freedmen, have been progressively rejected as political citizens of the Cherokee Nation, in part because certain aspects of race are privileged in local definitions of Cherokee identity.[1] Whether or not a multiracial individual, like a freedman or a white-Cherokee, will be socially classified as Cherokee and/or Indian depends on how various racial markers intersect with other important indices of identity in a given social context, at a particular moment in time.

In this chapter, I examine how multiracial Cherokees are socially classified at the local level, in the present moment in the early twenty-first century, and how this process articulates with and against racial hegemony from the Cherokee national level. I explore five indexical markers of Cherokee identity other than blood ancestry: phenotype, social behavior, language, religious knowledge and participation, and community residence and participation.[2] In doing so, I try to convey not just general tendencies but also the range of variability in the way different types of Cherokees and Cherokee communities assign social meaning to these categories. (Although all five of these indices are cultural categories, I separate them to avoid reifying the concept of culture.) I also provide specific ethnographic examples of how these categories intersect with each other, and especially with race, to shape Cherokee practices of social classification "on the ground." These various examples of social and racial classification reflect not only individual Cherokee interpretations and manipulations of social meanings, but also how community standards of identity are in tension with those imposed by the Cherokee Nation.

PHENOTYPE

When the two young women walk through the front door of the Cherokee Baptist church, they immediately notice the bare simplicity of the interior—plain wooden pews, a pine podium at the front, and gray-green paneled walls covered with religious calendars and posters. Everything is clean and neat and appears to date from the 1940s or so, though the church is much older. Despite the spartan surroundings, people seem relaxed and comfortable. They lean back in the pews and talk to one another in Cherokee, filling the room with life and laughter. The two women, both outsiders, look for a seat and try to slip unobtrusively into the last pew. Several people take notice of their shy presence but lose interest when the song leader asks, switching between Cherokee and English, if anyone has a special request, if anyone has a particular song they want to share. After some gentle urging, an older Cherokee woman walks to the front of the room. She fidgets with her red windbreaker and her short permed hair and then begins to address the gathering in Cherokee, only announcing the title of the song and its page number in English. With a glance over her shoulder to the singers behind her, she nods her head and begins to sing in Cherokee, in a delicate, low voice. The crowd recognizes the song and suddenly the room is filled with beautiful four-part harmonies, sung in rounds.

Although they are unfamiliar with this Cherokee style of singing, the two visitors catch the English reference, find the song in a hymnal and follow along. Unlike the older hymnals written in the Cherokee syllabary, these newer editions have the Cherokee words written in the English alphabet, so the two women can approximate the sounds even without knowing their meaning. They continue like this for two hours, adding their voices to the others in the room. At first they sit alone, but after a while, two middle-aged Cherokee women who invited them in the first place make their way over to greet them between songs. They join them in the pew and make an effort to introduce them to the others in attendance, proudly announcing that "these girls are trying to learn Cherokee. You should hear them." People seem excited, generous, and helpful, and offer new words and on-the-spot Cherokee lessons. But when the singing finally stops late in the evening, a very old Cherokee woman, a monolingual Cherokee speaker, walks to the pew where they are seated. She greets the two young women, and as people look at them with anticipation, they can only begin to eke out the most basic responses—"Osiyo . . . howa . . . wado."[3] The elder shows no disappointment, but the young women feel like failures.

They stand up to leave and, as they walk out the front of the church toward one of the old buildings in back, their Cherokee friends laugh a little and tell them not to worry. The young women appreciate the kindness and chat with their friends on the short walk across the yard to the impromptu dining hall, where a community potluck supper is about to take place. When they step inside the screen door, the place is a bustle of activity. The hollow floor seems to buckle under the weight of so many bodies crammed into such a small space. A group of Cherokee women has been busy in the side kitchen, and a long row of picnic tables is already laden with fried pork, squirrel stew, deer chili, greens, potatoes, cornbread, and beans. The two outsiders immediately go to help the others. They move back and forth between the kitchen and the dining area, serving the elders first, making them plates and bringing them coffee, cherry Kool-Aid, or Diet Coke. Sitting against the wall, the men and children wait for the deacon's blessing. Then, the elders will begin eating and the men and children will line up for food.

Although the many women in the room will eat last, they seem in control as people wait for their final word that the food is ready. With their laughter and joking louder than any other noise in the two rooms, they dominate the space. As the two young outsiders help in the kitchen, the Cherokee women seem to grow more comfortable with them and begin to ask them personal questions, like where are you from, and where are your parents from? Finally, they get around to asking what people always ask—Are you part Indian? Part Cherokee? Both women answer in the affirmative, though one identifies more as Choctaw. This response is not as interesting to the women in the room, who focus on the one who identifies herself as Cherokee. She has long, straight, dark-brown hair brushing the top of her hips, a round face, dark-brown almond shaped eyes, high cheek bones, and olive skin. As the other women scrutinize the physical appearance of the two outsiders, one with lighter hair and eyes than the other, they seem to differentiate the two young women for the first time.

A Cherokee woman says to the lighter one, "Well, you look like you could have some Indian blood in you, but not much." And then she turns to the other one with long dark hair and says, "But you, how much Cherokee are you? I bet you're about one-quarter, right? Am I right?"

"No," someone else says, "I saw her reading Cherokee in there. She's got to be more than that. I bet you're a third or maybe even a half, more like that."

The young woman laughs nervously and says, "Oh, no. Really, I don't know how much blood I have. My family doesn't have very good records and, well, I'm not even enrolled." Then, sheepishly, she admits that she's maybe one sixty-fourth or so. The Cherokee women raise their eyebrows in surprise, say something to each other in Cherokee, and then tell her that they're pretty sure she's got to be more Indian than that.

As I experienced it that night out at Swimmer's church, physical appearance is a key point of social difference among Cherokees. Initially, my friend and I were treated as a unit. Even though we were outsiders, we were granted some measure of social toleration, if not acceptance, because of our mere presence at a Cherokee function and, to a lesser extent, our participation in the language community, as we "read" and sang Cherokee songs. But later in the evening, when we became a focus of attention as several Cherokee women began to ask us about our respective backgrounds, we were no longer a unit—these women had differentiated us from one another. They did so not just because we had different tribal ancestries and identities but because my friend was physically "read" as being part Indian, while I was not. Despite the protestations of my friend, this group of women seemed to imbue her with a relatively high degree of Cherokee blood and to a lesser extent with racial belonging.

As this experience suggests, Cherokee people often respond differently to individuals who "look Cherokee" than to those who do not. However, there is no universal standard of what a Cherokee should look like, and the criteria vary from person to person. On the one hand, phenotypically darker Cherokees tend to have a more narrow standard of what it means to look Cherokee. These individuals often argue that, in a crowd, they can distinguish a "real" Cherokee from another Native American based on facial features, skin color, and height. On the other hand, phenotypically lighter Cherokees and even some darker ones express a much more fluid and inclusive standard of physical appearance, though they look for the same markers that would make Cherokee identity plausible: high cheekbones, round features, olive or dark skin, black hair, and a certain slant of eye. When trying to figure out whether or not someone is part Cherokee, or even part Native American, Cherokees use these markers to read the physical appearance of others, just as they had read my friend's, just as they often read my own. This subtle interpretation of physiognomy has developed into a fine art in Cherokee country, where the faintest trace of physical Indianness may provide the only clue to the ancestral bond, however thin, between different Cherokee citizens who share a national identity and a social space in northeastern Oklahoma.

Not only do Cherokees read phenotype in different ways, but they also assign varying degrees of social importance to looking Cherokee. Some feel that physical appearance is critical. For instance, a full-blood Cherokee man explained to me that "in the Cherokee Nation, overall, so many people are claiming to be Cherokee that it is very important that someone be identifiable. If there weren't so many, then it wouldn't be as important. But I think you feel closer to people you can identify with, even if they're in other tribes." For this man, phenotypical distinctiveness was a key point of Cherokee identity, as well as pan-tribal unity, and he felt that he had more in common with other Cherokees and Indians who were racialized in the same way.

Other Cherokees whom I interviewed who were not recognizably Indian had a different experience. They argued that not looking Cherokee had a negative impact on their lives. One woman said, "Growing up, the ones that looked Cherokee treated me like a white kid in school, because they didn't know that I was one half. I was shunned, too, after I 'came out' as a Cherokee. Now, it's not so bad in the schools. Kids are proud to be Cherokee."

Another woman echoed this sentiment, saying, "You're frowned on if you're not identifiable. The stigma is that you're *yonega* [white]. Some people have a lot of problems, especially younger kids, if you're not identifiable. That's sad." Similarly, a phenotypically white Cherokee citizen explained to me that her appearance had affected where she was able to work within the Cherokee Nation administration: "It matters, here, at the Cherokee Nation [tribal complex]. If you work in the front offices where people can see you, then you have to look Indian."

At the same time, a few Cherokees with whom I spoke said that looking Cherokee was not essential, that cultural considerations outweighed phenotypic ones. When they decided whether or not someone was Cherokee, they took into consideration other social factors, such as language or residence. For example, one older Cherokee man told me, "The first thing I look for is language. Non-Cherokee features don't matter to me. They just have to have that attitude that we are kin." And a younger Cherokee woman who was also a language speaker said, "Features is not what divides us as to who's Cherokee and who's not. A blue-eyed, blond person can be a Cherokee as much as a brown person. What matters is the way they were raised. What's important is what's inside."

Most Cherokees, however, took a more nuanced stance regarding the importance of phenotype to Cherokee social recognition. They argued that physical appearance mattered little in terms of local community acceptance but was vitally important for social acceptance or discrimination in the outside world. One Cherokee man, a Cherokee speaker who was socially classified as a full-blood, explained that "the community doesn't treat people who look white or Cherokee any different, although they'll be treated different in the larger society. Still, in the communities, people who are whiter feel a need to compensate, to put on a ribbon shirt or weave a basket." Another Cherokee who was more phenotypically ambiguous than the first man said, "looking Cherokee is important, depending on the group of people. . . . If you're outside of the community or in another state, then people will be disappointed if you don't look Indian. But I think you can look at people who are mixed and tell by the hair and the eyes." However, fulfilling the popular conception of Cherokeeness can cut both ways. For instance, a phenotypically white Cherokee described the pros and cons of not looking Cherokee: "If you're recognizable to the community, then you have less explaining to do. But because I don't look Indian, I [can] choose to be Cherokee. It's not chosen for me. . . . and you get a lot of bigots the further out you go [outside the Cherokee Nation's boundaries]. Then, nonrecognizability with racists is a plus." While Cherokees have conflicting arguments about where physical appearance matters and whether or not it matters in terms of community acceptance, they still make meaningful social distinctions between Cherokees who look Cherokee and those who do not, and those distinctions carry over into defining who is Cherokee.

SOCIAL BEHAVIOR

A middle-aged, full-blood Cherokee woman sits behind the wheel, navigating a Cherokee Nation minivan over a narrow gravel road. She and the young female anthropologist in the passenger seat are headed to a community meeting at Big Cabin, a small Cherokee settlement. At first they are quiet, but as the country miles stretch on and on, they settle into the darkness and the older woman begins to talk about her life.

"You know that until I was sixteen I never ate out at a restaurant. We had some fast food every once in a while, on special occasions, but it was nothing like pizza. I had pizza for the first time when I was in high school on a school outing. . . . I grew up in such poverty. My father raised chickens for Tyson and my mother did shift work in factories. I had five brothers and sisters. . . . We all lived in what I guess you would call a matrilineal household. Actually, it was several houses all connected to one another. An extended family—my grandmother, my mother, all my mother's sisters, my cousins, and uncles. I think there were five houses in all. We lived near the border of Arkansas on a Cherokee allotment.

"I was raised very traditional," she continues. "But my family began to treat me differently when I started to place an emphasis on education. My father had always encouraged me to be anything I wanted to be. This gave me high hopes, and these high expectations, these dreams for my life are what ostracized me from my family. . . . I suppose, though, that I really gave up my family when I married my husband. He's one-quarter Cherokee, enrolled and everything, but he doesn't look Indian and he doesn't act Indian. My family felt that I married out, which was a real no-no, and they never have fully accepted him or forgiven me. Our children have made some difference. Still, they're not treated in the same way as my cousin's children, who are full-blood and traditional."

The anthropologist interrupts with a question. "When you say 'traditional,' what do you mean exactly? People always talk about traditionalism, but it seems so slippery."

"Yeah, I guess you're right," the Cherokee woman responds, "It's often a topic of conversation, but sometimes people mean different things by it. I would describe it as living for the present, from moment to moment. Thus, education, job security, these things aren't so important. You don't place a big emphasis on them. It's just a desire to have your basic needs met. Being traditional is being very family and community focused. Because Cherokee families live in extended households, there's a greater sense of security. You have your child care taken care of, and your uncles and cousins are just as significant as your brothers and sisters. You live simply. You use kerosene and propane for cooking, and you eat wild foods—onions, greens. . . . Mostly, traditionalism is a type of reserve. You can talk and be animated with your friends outside, but when you come indoors and are around your parents, then you're careful to stay quiet and not disturb anyone. It's a kind of a strong harmony ethic, don't rock the boat."

The anthropologist asks, "I know your family doesn't consider your husband to be Indian, but do you?"

"Oh, no, not at all. In fact, of our four children, only two seem Indian to me. As for the other two, one is dark, but too outgoing. And the youngest girl, she's too light and too gregarious. There are some people like my husband, with one-quarter blood, who could be Indian. But for me, they would have to look Indian and have Indian values, to have grown up traditional."

Later that evening, when I was looking over my field notes, I remember thinking how remarkable it was that this Cherokee woman racially classified her children in different ways. After all, her children shared the same genetic background and the same household with their parents, and as an anthropologist I expected that they had been "enculturated" and even socialized in the same fashion. But the more I lived among Cherokees, the more I realized that the offspring of multiracial Cherokee marriages often racially identify themselves, and are identified by others, in different ways from their parents and from their siblings. Phenotype and behavior are key factors in this process. For instance, this Cherokee woman's children may actually have been socialized in different ways because of their different physical appearances, and this may have had a bearing on their behavior and their personality formation. On the other hand, she may have simply attributed different personality traits to her children, because of her own expectations regarding behavior and physical appearance. What I find most interesting about this example is the way it captures the subtle manner in which phenotype and behavior intersect in Cherokee social classification. In order for this woman to identify her children and her husband as Cherokee, neither looking Cherokee nor acting Cherokee were sufficient. Both criteria had to be met.

Like this woman, the vast majority of Cherokees believe that they have a unique style of social behavior and interaction, and this difference plays a key role in whether or not they recognize someone as Cherokee. They argue that when Cherokees live with other Cherokees in a community they learn a particular type of culturally appropriate behavior, which they often refer to as traditionalism. For them, being traditional is not just about having specialized cultural knowledge regarding Cherokee medicine, religion, language, and food ways but manifests itself in the more subtle markers of Cherokee identity seen in day-to-day social interactions and ways of behaving.

I heard numerous descriptions of what constitutes Cherokee behavior. For instance, one young Cherokee woman told me that "being Cherokee is about showing respect, showing honor to our elders, and [having] a sense of family." Another middle-aged Cherokee woman said, "It's what's in a Cherokee's heart, the inner self. Cherokees are giving, caring, and sharing. In many ways, they are Christ-like in their purity of actions and emotions. Few [Cherokees] are mean spirited, especially the traditionals. That just doesn't happen." One older Cherokee man suggested to me that "more affluent people [i.e., whites], they're more aggressive. But Cherokees are more congenial and humorous, because they're not after the almighty dollar. That's what's very Cherokee." This man not only equates aggression with materialism, but he also implies that these are prevalent characteristics of Euroamerican society. In doing so, he essentially defines Cherokee "reserve" in opposition to Euroamerican "aggressiveness." I was told many times about the importance of reserve, from the Cherokee woman in the vignette above to the Cherokee man who said, "Cherokees stay in their own groups. They stay in the back. You just don't get involved when it doesn't deal with you."

When I first arrived in Oklahoma, reserved social behavior was not something that I associated with Cherokees in particular, although I had experienced it in other Native-American communities. However, as I spent more time with Cherokees, I began to feel awkward at certain Cherokee social gatherings when I would catch myself being too gregarious. Much as Cherokee children must check their own behavior around their parents, I would try to contain these tendencies so as not to appear so obviously the social outsider. Cherokee people never commented on my behavior, but I felt that I embodied too much whiteness in certain contexts, particularly when I was with traditional Cherokees in large public settings, like church functions or other ceremonial occasions. I am not suggesting, however, that Cherokees are never socially outgoing or gregarious. In fact, to the contrary, Cherokees are usually funny and expressive when they are with smaller groups of friends and family.

Some Cherokees I interviewed implied that Cherokee reserve, indeed Cherokee behavior in general, was innate, that it was carried in Cherokee blood. One elderly woman explained, "I can tell if someone is Cherokee. It's the way they talk and act. I can tell if they have the blood." This conflation of biology and social behavior, however, was often contested. For example, one Cherokee man told me about an exchange he had with a Cherokee woman:

> I had a lady tell me yesterday that this woman acted Cherokee. She said, "she was real polite and she turned her house over to us, and she served us all dinner, and she acted just like we were old friends and neighbors." And my response to that was, "That's not proof she is a Cherokee." And that's what she was trying to say, "Well, she must be a Cherokee." Personally, I don't think gentility is a genetic trait. It's a southern trait.

In this exchange, the Cherokee woman and man are arguing over whether or not they can tell if someone has Cherokee ancestry based on their behavior and whether or not that particular behavior—gentility—belongs to Cherokees alone or to southerners in general. Still, another Cherokee was more definitive about the relationship between biology and behavior. He said:

> I knew this guy. He was white genetically, but he was raised by a Cherokee family. Everything about him was Indian except the color of his skin. I just felt something different about him. . . . It was the way he carried himself. . . . He was never in a hurry. He would stop and really listen to people. He did things slowly, as if he had all the time in the world.

For this Cherokee man, behavior is the litmus test of Cherokee identity. In fact, he privileges social behavior over biology when he recognizes a genetic white man as a social Indian. But for other Cherokees, the distinction is not so clear. Acting Cherokee and being Cherokee may be a question of blood ancestry or it may be a question of community belonging and enculturation. Regardless of the individual interpretation, we see in these various examples how social, biological, and cultural categories intersect with one another in Cherokee practices of racial and social classification.

LANGUAGE

Tired, she leans against the old oak and watches as the people gather
around the ancient fire. It is already well past midnight and the dance
is just getting underway. The first to line up are the song leaders in
their uniform of Wrangler jeans, plain, long-sleeved western styled
shirts, old cowboy boots, and straw hats—each with a single eagle
feather inserted into the brim. They walk leisurely around the fire,
calling the others in Cherokee to join them. On their heels are the
shell shakers, the young Cherokee women wearing long gingham
skirts and heavy layers of stone-filled terrapin shells that rattle
around their ankles when they walk. She hears a spine-tingling, high
pitched "oh hey wey yah," and the stomp dance begins. Cherokees
of all ages begin to wind their way around the fire, shuffling their
feet in unison, arms bent and swaying with every step. As the line
begins to lengthen and spiral in upon itself, she notices that the
dancers in the center have slowed their pace, while the ones at the
perimeter move more quickly, trying to keep up with the person
directly in front of them. As the song speeds up, people join hands,
and a dozen Cherokee children at the end of the line use the opportunity to play crack the whip. She laughs as she watches them running
and shouting with glee, spinning out of control from the centrifugal
force, falling in a tumble when their short legs can no longer keep
pace.

As the adults continue dancing, three little boys pick themselves out
of the tangle of bodies. She notices one with a shock of blond hair,
who stands out at the gathering where the only other towhead is
a shell shaker who has had a recent run-in with a bottle of peroxide.
Spitting dust, the youngster chases the other two boys out of the inner
circle, beyond the Bird and Paint Clan benches. She watches as the
two boys continue running past the next clan arbor, but the blond-
headed little boy hesitates. Sitting in a lawn chair next to the Wolf
Clan benches, an old, heavy-set, Cherokee man calls to the boy, who
breaks into a grin and charges up to where the old man is seated.
With surprising agility for his age, the man grabs the boy and wrestles
him into his lap, where the little boy plays possum until it's too
funny to stay dead any longer. Then, he revives with a giggle and
begins an animated discussion in Cherokee, causing his silent observer
to forget his blond hair. His Cherokeeness, as far as she can see, is
in his words, his ways, his comfort in this place.

This little boy is one of many phenotypically lighter, Cherokee-language speakers whom I encountered during the course of my research. As this ethnographic example suggests, he and others like him are usually accepted as members of a larger Cherokee sociocultural community. In fact, most Cherokees cite language proficiency as the most important and distinctive aspect of Cherokee identity, regardless of whether or not they themselves are Cherokee-language speakers. For example, one Cherokee man, a nonspeaker, told me, "I wouldn't determine to say that someone is less Cherokee because they can't speak. But it is my closely held personal opinion that when the language ceases to exist, then we cease to exist. . . . When Cherokee becomes a dead language, then we may as well throw in the towel. Then, we cease to maintain our identity, and we are only a shadow of ourselves." A fluent Cherokee-speaking woman shared this sentiment, telling me, "For older people, if you can't speak the language, then you're not Cherokee." This intimate association between "speaking Cherokee" and "being Cherokee" stems from the sense of difference the Cherokee language provides. As one young Cherokee man said to me, "Language is a priority, because it separates Cherokees from the rest of the world." The same attitude came from a young Cherokee woman who said, "I would give anything to be able to speak fluently. The language is what sets us apart. No other tribe can understand it."

The connection between language and difference has various nuances. For most Cherokees, speaking the Cherokee language represents a symbolic and practical marker of social connections with and commitment to Cherokee community life. Fluency stands for time shared. After all, to become a fluent Cherokee speaker one has to be raised in a Cherokee-speaking household or community or spend a large portion of time with other Cherokee speakers. The inverse of time shared is time apart from Euroamerican society, a realization of which causes many Cherokees to tie language to a sense of cultural difference. For example, one Cherokee-speaking man, a full-blood, told me, "The language is a main staple of Cherokee identity. I guess you could say I'm a racist, because I think you're not a full Cherokee unless you can speak. The language is very important to the culture, and if you can't speak and read, then you can't do the ceremonies you were brought up with." The connection between language proficiency and maintaining Cherokee religious traditions was also made by another Cherokee-speaking man, who said, "The language is critical, because it is part of a spiritual base. It's a God-given gift to be able to communicate and speak."

Language proficiency is also linked to maintaining a sense of racial distinctiveness that goes beyond the more widespread belief in the social and cultural significance of speaking Cherokee. For instance, one Cherokee tribal official, a light-skinned nonspeaker said, "The Cherokee language is the most important [element of Cherokee identity]. That's why we try and get people to learn. It's not too late. Because what happens if we lose the language? What will separate us from everybody else? The Spanish [Mexican-American] people aren't losing their language. Why is there stuff in Spanish and English, but not in Cherokee? God intended that we speak Cherokee. It's what separates us from the other races." Some Cherokees took this connection between language and racial difference a step further. I remember on several occasions Cherokees who told me that speaking the Cherokee language was an innate ability, something that only Cherokee people were "born with." They swore they had never known a white person who could speak fluent Cherokee. In their opinion all the various pedagogical materials and language classes directed at whites (not white-Cherokees) were a waste of time, and regardless of what outsiders chose to do, it would be better for the Cherokee Nation to focus language retention efforts on those with Cherokee ancestry.

For many Cherokees, race is clearly a central consideration in the debate over what constitutes Cherokee identity. But many other Cherokees assign race a secondary role, and make a clear distinction that language is a social and cultural category, not a racial one. I met one Cherokee man, a full-blood, who understands the Cherokee language but cannot speak it. He told me, "if we don't learn the language and teach it to our young ones, then we're in trouble. Because if you can't speak, then you're just an Indian. And if we lose our language, then we lose our identity." He seems to suggest that Cherokee nonspeakers like himself have no unique cultural identity as Cherokees, only a racial identity as Indians. His views are not uncommon. In fact, other Cherokees argue that in local practices of social classification, speaking Cherokee is more important than race, thereby ignoring the Cherokee Nation's more biogenetic standard of Cherokeeness. One older Cherokee woman claimed, "I would accept a nonidentifiable Cherokee who speaks, more than a pure- or full-blood who doesn't." An older Cherokee man, also a language speaker, said, "If they keep the language, even if they had red hair and blue eyes, then they can go to any community and be accepted. Even non-Indians would be accepted by the community if they spoke." A young, nonspeaking Cherokee man implied the same thing when he stated, contrary to the other Cherokees above, "There are a few white neighbors who speak who are considered to be part of the community. They're more Cherokee than a lot of the actual citizens!" He paused for a moment before adding, "We need to have some real studies that support language retention. We need to pass it down."

Most Cherokees, both speakers and nonspeakers agree that the ability to speak Cherokee is one of the primary attributes that will make them consider a phenotypically white Cherokee citizen to be socially and culturally Cherokee. However, some Cherokees take a slightly different stance, one suggesting that language skills on their own are not enough to warrant complete community acceptance. As one full-blood Cherokee woman, a nonspeaker, said, "I know of blue-eyed children who speak the language. They have an easier time mixing because they have this cultural knowledge, but they are never fully accepted." According to this perspective, phenotypically white Cherokee-language speakers may be socially accepted as Cherokees, but they are not racially accepted as Cherokee Indians. The implication is that for an individual to be socially accepted as Cherokee, in the fullest sense of the word, he or she must be both culturally Cherokee and racially Indian.

As we can see in these various examples of Cherokee social classification, language intersects with race in significant ways to produce numerous individual standards of Cherokee identity. Sometimes, as in the previous example, race is the decisive factor for Cherokee social classification, irrespective of an individual's ability to speak the language. At other times, however, Cherokee language proficiency is so culturally and socially significant that even individuals with no Cherokee ancestry will be socially accepted as members of a Cherokee community because they speak Cherokee. While some Cherokee individuals may privilege either race or culture above all else, this is an extreme position. Most Cherokees socially classify within a highly nuanced race-culture continuum that reflects the hegemonic conflation of race and culture. Thus, language should be understood as one of the most important attributes of identity that shapes Cherokee social classification. It is so important that Cherokee individuals who speak the Cherokee language usually are seen as culturally "full" and usually are classified socially as Cherokee, regardless of their specific blood ancestry.[4]

RELIGION

Everyone told her that she couldn't miss it, and they were right. The house of the Cherokee medicine man stands directly across the road from the ceremonial stomp grounds. It is a beautiful two-story log home, much nicer than any other she has seen in the past months. She pulls into the circular driveway and parks her truck. Grabbing two bags of groceries she has brought as "payment," she starts to walk toward the house, but suddenly it dawns on her that maybe this simple offering isn't enough. On the phone the medicine man had told her to bring whatever she thought was appropriate, which she has done. But now she realizes that he probably gets paid more than two bags of food. Nervous and embarrassed, she takes a quick inventory. It's not much, but at least she has a few special items—jams, pickles, and dressings that her mother has canned. They will have to do because she is already late and the nearest store is a half-hour away. Maybe the jars from her mother will somehow compensate.

She walks slowly to the front porch. No dogs or children come rushing to greet her. No one peeks through the windows or the front door. She knows they are expecting her. After all, she called to set the appointment at his insistence. Still, she is surprised at the lack of reception. Maybe there are so many people coming and going that he and his wife can't be bothered to run and see who's next. Or maybe it's just that whoever is there must have come for a good reason, and that's sufficient.

Last time, she met him at his other home "in town," where he told her that she needed to come see him. To write her project with any truth, he told her, she needed to experience Cherokee "medicine" firsthand. He said he could tell that because she was an outsider, there were a few people at the tribal complex who were threatened by her presence and her many questions. Even now, he could feel this bad energy following her. He wanted to help get these "willies" off of her, so she could navigate through the many words she would hear and understand what was really being said. It sort of spooked her to hear about the willies, because she knew he was right, even though the last thing she wanted to do was upset anybody. Some Cherokee medicine directed her way would probably do her a lot of good.

So, finally, here she is with groceries in hand, knocking at his door. In a moment, he appears, greeting her warmly with a bright smile. "Thanks for coming," he says, ushering her into the front room, relieving her of the groceries. He tells her to have a seat, that he has to finish with another woman and then he will be right with her. First, he's going to drop the groceries off with his wife, who is making lunch in the kitchen. "Do you want to stay?" he asks." 'Cause there's plenty of food."

"Yes, thanks," her voice trails after him as he goes down the hall, leaving her alone. She makes herself comfortable, settling into the old overstuffed couch. She pats the quilt thrown over its sidearm and takes in the surroundings. On the walls are old black-and-white photos of a long line of Cherokee forebears, many of whom were famous medicine men. She even knew of this man's father and grandfather long before she had arrived in Oklahoma, for their names literally run throughout the pages of Cherokee history. This man has built his large house around his father's old log cabin, and he heals in the very same room where his father worked, indeed where his father passed away. He draws from his father's medicine and reputation, both of which loom large in this place.

Her mind wanders a little, back to when she first met him, how he wasn't at all what she expected. Well, in some ways he was. He had a powerful presence, an air of confidence, a rock solid "center." She remembers how he teased her, saying, "So, you've come to learn about real Indians, huh? Gonna write yourself a story about some real Cherokee Indians, huh?" How she had laughed at herself with him. Yet she felt his subtle dig, his uncanny ability to read the situation. He had a bit of the trickster in him, like many great healers, so the jokes at her expense came as no surprise. What had surprised her was his appearance. Everyone had described him as "a real, full-blood Cherokee medicine man." It was the full-blood and the medicine that threw her. The two adjectives together led her to expect some stereotypically Indian-looking man. What had she imagined—Black Elk? This man, however, had greenish eyes, skin only a shade darker than her own, and mixed features. Yes, he had dark, thick, black hair, and he definitely looked Indian. But he also looked partially white. She should have known better. She could almost hear coyote laughing.

Of course, anthropologists are not immune from racial hegemony. As a result, I, too, conflated race and culture in such a manner that it shaped my expectations about this medicine man's appearance. I knew that among Cherokees the term *full-blood* was as much a social and cultural category as a biological one and that it often referred to phenotypically mixed individuals, but somehow I expected this man to look more phenotypically Indian. Like anyone else, I carried hegemonic ideas with me into the field, but strove to become increasingly aware of them. Still, because so many Cherokees around me conflated race and culture on a regular basis, I would occasionally catch myself slipping into thinking (or viewing people) along the same race-culture continuum. Over time, my attention became increasingly focused on this fluid movement between race and culture as I watched Cherokee culture come to stand for, intensify, and even supplant Cherokee racial identity in local practices of social classification.

Religion offers an excellent case in point. As with the Cherokee medicine man I describe above, Cherokees almost always refer to their religious and spiritual leaders as full-bloods, no matter how phenotypically mixed they may look. This fact is significant because of the central role that Cherokee spiritual leaders play in Cherokee society—as deacons at the local Cherokee Baptist church, as Keetoowah song leaders, and as medicine men and women. The role of a Cherokee spiritual leader is highly valued and respected in Cherokee society, and this person is invested with substantial social and cultural capital. To be a religious leader, an individual usually has to possess very specialized cultural knowledge, the ability to speak fluent Cherokee, and strong ties to a particular Cherokee community. A Cherokee religious leader must embody to the fullest extent the values and meanings associated with Cherokee religious life as a whole. In this sense, the medicine man, the Keetoowah song leader, and even the Cherokee Baptist preacher all serve almost implicitly as symbols of Cherokee culture. In fact, Cherokee religious leaders have social identities that represent an intensification of "Cherokeeness," one that is summed up in the usage of the term *full-blood* even when not literally true.

The reason for this intensification of Cherokee identity, this collective imputation of bloodedness, in Cherokee religious leaders lies in the centrality of religion, generally, to Cherokee culture. Most Cherokees perceive religion as a critical aspect not only of Cherokee culture but also of Cherokee identity. For instance, one older Cherokee man told me, "Spirituality is the most important thing in the traditional Cherokee world because we use it to maintain life as we know it and to survive through periods of turmoil." A middle-aged Cherokee woman made a similar statement:

> A Cherokee has to be brought up knowing their culture, the medicine way
> of life. They have to go out into the woods and know roots and foods and

medicine. It's survival. But they also need to be able to survive with European ways. It's about having an appreciation for both. . . . I don't live like I was raised, but I have the knowledge behind me. I can never lose it. I understand the Cherokee ways of thinking, of living day to day, a good life of natural stuff . . . yes.

This woman seems to suggest that because she possesses specialized cultural knowledge about Cherokee medicine, a profoundly spiritual practice that she learned as a child, she has a uniquely Cherokee worldview that she can never lose. Another middle-aged Cherokee man I interviewed also placed great importance on Cherokee religious practices but made a slightly different point. "Cherokee religion is real important to me," he told me. "Me and my family, we visit with the medicine man and the little people. I know the difference between good and bad medicine, even though I have a college degree."[5] In the context of our conversation, this man's statement implied that in spite of his Western education he was as much Cherokee as anyone because he continued to value and engage in Cherokee religious practices.

Although many Cherokees share a common spiritual cosmology, as reflected in these quotes, they tend to diverge between two distinct religious institutions, both of which they consider to be traditionally Cherokee. The first and more common religious institution is the Cherokee Baptist Church, whose services tend to represent a Cherokee variation of the Southern Baptist tradition. The basic difference, as an older, Cherokee-speaking woman explained to me, is that "in Cherokee churches, the people gather together more. They come earlier and stay later, sometimes all day. They have a longer service and they also sing more." Scattered throughout northeastern Oklahoma, there are over forty Cherokee Baptist churches, each associated with a particular Cherokee community. Services are often conducted in the Cherokee language and usually last for hours, with various church-related activities to follow. Besides language and length of service, Cherokee Baptists break with their southern brethren in their preference for being "saved" later in life. Also, unlike their white and black counterparts, Cherokee baptisms involve a "going to water" ceremony that invokes traditional non-Christian Cherokee mythology.

The other traditional Cherokee religious institution is the Keetoowah Society.[6] Keetoowahs are non-Christians who gather together several times a week, as I described in an earlier vignette, for ceremonies that usually include a stomp dance as the highlight of the evening. Anthropologists and historians typically describe the Keetoowah religion as

Figure 18.   Old Cherokee Baptist Mission and Church. North of Westville, Oklahoma. Parts of the building were carried over on the Trail of Tears. Photograph by Sammy Still (Cherokee).

religious syncretism, a blending of Euroamerican and Native-American religious elements.[7] Many of the Keetoowahs with whom I spoke asked me not to reveal any specific information about their religious beliefs and practices because they feared that non-Indians would misappropriate their traditions. Out of respect for their wishes, I have described the Keetoowah religion in only the broadest of terms.

Being a Cherokee Baptist or a Keetoowah are equally valid expressions of Cherokee religious identity in the eyes of the larger Cherokee community. Nevertheless, social relations between members of the two groups can be tense. Many Keetoowahs move back and forth between Cherokee Baptist church services and Keetoowah services without sanctions from the Keetoowah community. But Cherokee Baptists strongly discourage members of their congregations from attending what they consider to be the pagan ceremonies of the Keetoowahs. One Cherokee woman noted how this tension had affected her community when she told me, "From the beginning, Cherokees are taught to know there is a Creator. It doesn't matter if it's church or the stomp ground, we worship and believe in the same God. I participated in the stomp as a child because we had strong ties. In our community, most people went to the stomp. Now, there is more of a break. Some people who used to go to the stomp go to church instead." Another older Cherokee woman also spoke of the religious division in Cherokee society, saying, "I was raised Cherokee Baptist and this was very central to my identity as a Cherokee. In my family, we always said about the Keetoowahs that was theirs and this is ours. They have their own form of worship and we have ours. I've never been to a stomp," she declared with some satisfaction before concluding, "There was always this line dividing us." Another young Cherokee woman elaborated on this conflict even further:

> There are some conflicts around religion. Many Cherokees stay within the traditional stomp religion. They believe in God, but they're kind of like the Jews that don't believe in Jesus. That's why most Cherokee Baptists don't go back and forth between the two [church and stomp dance]. I was raised with the Bible. I believe in Jesus. I look at these traditional Cherokees and I hope they will be saved, that they will come to find Jesus. There's a split right there, but at least everyone believes in God.

However, this tension between Cherokee Baptists and Keetoowahs does not arise from competition to define one religion as more Cherokee than the other. Instead, it is a fairly typical sectarian conflict between Cherokee Christians and non-Christians, who are both vying for the hearts and souls of the same community. But in spite of this conflict, each camp respects the basic Cherokeeness of the other, and both religions are considered to be equally Cherokee and central to Cherokee identity. Because religion is so important to Cherokee identity, "authentic" Cherokees follow one or the other, but either path leads to social acceptance.

While both religions provide a route to "authentic" Cherokeeness, mixed-bloods interested in maintaining their social and cultural roots are more likely to look to the Keetoowahs. As one middle-aged Cherokee woman explained to me:

> There is a real difference between card-carrying Indians and grass-roots Indians. My children are mixed, not full-blood, but they know their culture. They go to the stomp grounds. This is the real key—growing up in a community that retains its cultural practices. There are lots of full-bloods, particularly at the tribal complex, who know very little about their culture. But somebody can be only one-eighth, but grow up in a Cherokee community

Figure 19. This previously unpublished photograph shows religious leaders
at the Keetoowah ceremonial grounds near Vian, Oklahoma, on Redbird
Smith's Birthday, July 19, 1936. From left to right, Stokes Smith, William
Rogers, Jess Locust, and Sam Smith. Photograph by Eva Horner. Courtesy of
the Eva Horner Collection, University Archives, John Vaughn Library,
Northeastern State University, Tahlequah, Oklahoma.

and participate in Cherokee activities and be considered full blood—especially if they know the language.

From this point of view, Cherokee identity is not so much about race as
it is about culture, and one significant way to maintain a Cherokee cultural identity is to participate in a Cherokee religious community. But
even when race seems absent, it is still present, subtly coloring Cherokee
religious thinking, as Cherokees worry about whether whites will misappropriate, misrepresent, or perhaps even eventually overshadow
Cherokee cultural and religious traditions. This concern was expressed
not only by Keetoowahs, who asked me not to describe their religious
traditions in a public forum, but also by Cherokee Baptists. "I think the

powwows that the Cherokee Nation encourages are just horrible, because they are not Cherokee," said one Cherokee Baptist woman. "The wannabes go crazy at the Cherokee Nation's powwow on Labor Day weekend. It's really bad." Throughout northeastern Oklahoma, whites are explicitly and implicitly associated with the distortion of Cherokee cultural traditions. Conversely, full-bloods are associated with cultural purity and with maintaining the purity of Cherokee religious traditions.

Despite the differences between these two religious camps, most Cherokees accept either as a valid expression of authentic Cherokee identity. Membership in one of these Cherokee religious institutions is a significant factor in Cherokee practices of racial and social classification. As I have attempted to show in the previous examples, Cherokees think of themselves as a spiritual people in general and sometimes conflate the religious and racial aspects of their identity. One tribal leader went so far as to say, "you could say we are the most Christian government and race on the face of the earth. . . . Part of being Cherokee is knowing a supreme being." Race is often a salient factor, but it is not a prerequisite for participation in Cherokee religious life. Other attributes may compensate for the absence of Cherokee blood in judging whether an individual is an authentic Cherokee on a spiritual level. For both Baptists and Keetoowahs, these factors include specific cultural knowledge, Cherokee language proficiency, and participation in Cherokee community life. These allow an individual who is Cherokee by religious affiliation to be accepted as Cherokee by blood as well, since the popular assumption is that one follows the other. Religious participation can increase bloodedness in the communal imagination, granting social legitimacy to Cherokee individuals with minimal blood ancestry. Even individuals with higher degrees of blood ancestry will tend to be classified socially as full-bloods because of their religious affiliation. The result is a "full-blood" whose CDIB indicates only one-half or one-quarter Cherokee blood. In this sense, full participation in a Cherokee religious community is, in the eyes of many Cherokees, interdependent with a fullness of Cherokee blood, such that race and faith commingle as primary elements in the social construction of Cherokee identity.

COMMUNITY RESIDENCE/PARTICIPATION

Cherokee discussions of identity that focus on language, behavior, religion, or even phenotype all centered on another social construction—the Cherokee community. As we have seen in the previous four sections,

Cherokees describe these various indices of Cherokee identity as being tied to participation in Cherokee community life. Place is a critical aspect of each. As Cherokees use the term, *community* references their social geography, the actual social interaction among various kinds of Cherokee people as it occurs in particular locations. In the next chapter, I will examine in detail the tension between Cherokee social identity as it is defined around place, kinship, culture, and race, and Cherokee national identity, which is based almost exclusively on a more biological notion of race that ignores social context. But for now, I want to provide a general sense of where Cherokee social life takes place and how residence and/or participation in different Cherokee communities is a significant aspect of Cherokee identity, shaping Cherokee practices of social and racial classification.

The first type of community that shapes Cherokee social and racial identity is nonresidential, coming together in space and time only on an occasional basis. Cherokee Baptist churches and Cherokee stomp grounds are both examples of nonresidential Cherokee communities. More often, however, residency is a salient factor in defining Cherokee social communities, as with the next three types of Cherokee communities I discuss.

The first and largest of these residential communities is comprised of Cherokees living within the historical boundaries of the Cherokee Nation, also known as the Tribal Jurisdictional Service Area or the fourteen-county area (Figure 2). Although these boundaries are not legally recognized as national, many Cherokees share a sense of national belonging with other Cherokees who live in the same geographic and political space. Some make a distinction between Cherokee national citizens who live within "the Nation" and those who do not, and a significant number want various political and economic rights restricted to citizens who are "national" residents. For instance, a middle-aged Cherokee woman told me, "I have a problem with the open blood quantum policy. I'd like to at least see residency [in the Nation] as a requirement for benefits. We have to develop some type of a priority system." This woman uses territorial residence as one way of defining the Cherokee national community, thus challenging Cherokee national identity based strictly on blood ancestry.

A second type of Cherokee residential community is narrower in scope. "Checkerboard" communities, as I have termed them, are Cherokee settlements located within the historical boundaries of the Cherokee Nation. They are commonly known as Cherokee towns, even

Figure 20.   Eastern Baptist Association assembly grounds. Briggs community, north of Tahlequah, Oklahoma. Photograph by Sammy Still (Cherokee).

though they have a large number of non-Cherokees living within their boundaries. Since non-Indians live next door to Cherokee families in these communities, the term *checkerboard* refers to what a map of non-Indian versus Cherokee residency might look like for these particular places. Local political and economic power tends to be held primarily by whites or white-Cherokees. I consider Tahlequah, the Cherokee national capital and the place where I lived during my field stay, to be an example of this type of community.

A third type of Cherokee residential community is what Cherokees themselves usually refer to as a traditional communities. Smaller and less commercially developed than checkerboard towns, traditional communities are more likely to have Cherokee political leadership. Traditional communities, like Kenwood and Bell, are also located within the Cherokee Nation's historical boundaries, but they are even more distinctively Cherokee social and cultural spaces. If a non-Indian lives in a traditional community, it is almost always because he or she has married into a Cherokee family. Most traditional communities are said to look Cherokee because they are filled with phenotypically recognizable Cherokee Indians and even to "sound Cherokee" because Cherokee is spoken as a first language by many community residents. Traditional communities tend to be small, to be less commercially developed, to center on kinship relations, and to actively maintain Cherokee cultural practices.

Many Cherokees who live within the boundaries of the Cherokee Nation believe that childhood residence in a small-scale traditional Cherokee community is central to the development of a distinctly Cherokee cultural outlook and social identity. As one female tribal employee told me, "The most important thing about being Cherokee is being raised in a community. I've been an Indian all my life and it's all about community recognition. You can't be a newcomer. You just have to understand the community and the needs of the Cherokee people." Another Cherokee man told me, "It's important to have a sense of community, a place where you belong. The tribe is a big extended family, anyway. If you're completely removed from the community, in the broader society, then there's no way for things to be handed down. A Cherokee's roots are in his community."

Other Cherokees with whom I spoke echoed this man's sentiments about traditional Cherokee communities as sites where Cherokee children develop a distinct cultural identity and a sense of connectedness to their extended-kin networks. As an older, Cherokee-speaking man explained, "you have to be raised in a Cherokee community. You can't be away from the family group. If you get into the mainstream, then you're fighting an uphill battle. You get away from who you are and you forget the language." This man refers to loss of language and identity, showing the interdependence of these elements in Cherokee social classification. He also refers to the financial and social struggles that many Cherokees face when they leave the support of their kinship networks. A Cherokee man in his seventies described the importance of the community support system: "When I was a boy, families helped each other to survive. The family was really important, and selfishness didn't exist in the community." An elderly Cherokee woman even suggested this communal network was part of the community's racial identity. "It's very important for someone to be raised in a traditional Cherokee community," she said. "We took in people, in the family and in the community, who didn't have as much. We still carry on, helping each other out. This is very Indian."

Figure 21.   A better than typical Cherokee home. Cherokee County,
Oklahoma, c. 1935. Photograph by Eva Horner. Courtesy of the Eva Horner
Collection, University Archives, John Vaughn Library, Northeastern State
University, Tahlequah, Oklahoma.

Some Cherokees, like the woman above, associate residence and participation in a traditional Cherokee community with a distinctly racial
or Indian identity, as if the former creates the latter. Others, however,
suggest that racial identity intersects with Cherokee community life in
a different way. One Cherokee woman described how when she was
very young, before she started school, she thought the world was pop-
ulated entirely by Cherokees. White-Cherokees were a part of her world,
but that part was small and insignificant. For her, the traditional Cherokee community was a place where her racial identity as an Indian was
unmarked and not stigmatized. A Cherokee man shared this point of
view, saying, "How you live is very important. You always have to
remember where you came from. It's a different society, those people
living in Muskogee [a small city]. I couldn't live that way. People gawk
at you, but here nobody notices or cares if you're Indian. Here, everybody expects you to be Cherokee."

Even in checkerboard communities, Cherokees who are socially identified as Indians are relatively free from stigma since they are members of a particular Cherokee-identified residential community. For example, a middle-aged Cherokee man described his early socialization in a checkerboard community. "I was taught from early on that we were Cherokee. There was no sense of being a minority [i.e., racially marked]. It was not a place of privilege. It was a sense of being from a unique lineage. I was expected to think right and do right, because I was Cherokee!" he said authoritatively. "It was a tradition of perseverance and resilience. . . . Our sense of Cherokee culture was not incredibly distinct, because we were a mixed family, my mother Indian, my father white. But I knew my ancestors and I was taught respect for full-bloods." This last sentence implies that full-bloods warranted respect because of their roles as culture bearers. As he put it, "Full-blood elders were put on the highest pedestal, because they were the keepers of the language and the dances." Here, blood quantum and place converge in the person of the full-blood, showing how Cherokee communities, in all their variations, are specific places where ideas about race and culture intersect to shape Cherokee practices of social classification. Cherokee communities are social sites of interaction with different standards of identity than those of the Cherokee Nation. As a consequence, Cherokee social acceptance hinges not just on blood ancestry, as emphasized by the Cherokee Nation, but also on membership in a social body, an extended kin network, and a culturally and racially defined community.

DISCURSIVE STRATEGIES OF LABELING: VARIATIONS OF CHEROKEE IDENTITY

Cherokees use the five indices of identity that I have just discussed—phenotype, social behavior, language, religion, and residence—to define the racial and social boundaries of their community and to socially classify other Cherokees into categories of identity other than just Cherokee or Indian. These variations on Cherokee identity might be read as different degrees of Cherokeeness, with full-blood being the most Cherokee. However, I want to distance myself from this hegemonic reading, in order to avoid the traditional anthropological role in Native-American communities of authenticating one kind of sociocultural group over another. Race shapes local systems of social classification, but as I have already pointed out, it does so in dialogue with other attributes of identity. For instance, in this process of social naming, Cherokees often speak about racial belonging in terms of blood and color. When they use these terms, however, Cherokees use them both literally and metaphorically, and their meanings move back and forth. Let us examine in detail these discursive categories and how they shape and are shaped by the indices of Cherokee identity mentioned above.

FULL-BLOODS

The first case in point is the term *full-blood,* which as with the Cherokee medicine man above, does not necessarily refer to an individual with pure biological Cherokee ancestry but one with full social and cultural acceptance among Cherokees. Usually, full-bloods look "mostly Indian," although some have green eyes and light brown skin. However, those who do have mixed features tend to speak fluent Cherokee and be active participants in Cherokee community life. In these instances of social classification, blood is a racial and cultural metaphor. At other times, though, Cherokees use the term *full-blood* in a more literal sense, for instance to refer to someone with all Indian ancestry. Then, a full-blood might be either a pure Cherokee or a multitribal individual with, say, Cherokee, Choctaw, and Kiowa ancestry.[8] The same Cherokee person could use the term *full-blood* in both a literal and metaphorical sense and have no problem with the apparent contradiction. This discourse of identity is another example of how Cherokee citizens have internalized racial hegemony, because they employ blood terminology while mediating it through local categories of meaning, where full-blood is a social and cultural category as often as it is a biological one.

APPLES AND UNCLE TOMAHAWKS

Cherokees tend to naturalize others with high degrees of Cherokee ancestry as culture bearers, creating certain expectations about what is appropriate social and cultural behavior for full-bloods. If the behavior of more blooded Cherokees does not meet community expectations, then they can face social criticism. Cherokees employ two terms to identify full-bloods who behave in socially or culturally inappropriate fashions—*apple* and *Uncle Tomahawk.* Both terms are used when a Cherokee is identified as being racially Indian and as behaving or thinking in stereotypically white ways. These stereotypes of white behavior might include being self-centered, deceitful, selfish with possessions, or materialistic. Cherokee individuals who fit this description are commonly referred to as apples because they are "red on the outside, white on the inside." Or they are called Uncle Tomahawks (an allusion to the slave in Harriet Beecher Stowe's 1852 novel, *Uncle Tom's Cabin*), because they have "sold out" their Indian identity in order to "better themselves" according to Euroamerican standards.[9] These two labels of identity and their underlying social meanings show how Cherokee behavior can be sanctioned at the local level according to hegemonic ideas conflating race and culture in a manner that essentializes Cherokeeness.

MIXED-BLOODS

The terms *apple* and *Uncle Tomahawk* both are ubiquitous in many Native-American communities. So, too, is the term *mixed-blood*. Since the vast majority of Cherokee tribal citizens have multiracial ancestry, one would expect *mixed-blood* to be an important term of reference in the Cherokee Nation, as well. During the course of my fieldwork, however, the term *mixed-blood* was used infrequently in my presence, and then only to describe an individual who was socially, racially, or culturally ambiguous in some manner. For instance, I heard people use the term to refer to phenotypically white individuals who were fluent Cherokee speakers or to phenotypically mixed individuals who participated in Cherokee social functions on an *occasional* basis. Most of the time, if Cherokees looked phenotypically mixed and were *regular* participants in Cherokee community life, then they were known as full-bloods or simply as Cherokees. I suggest a simple explanation for the less frequent usage of the term *mixed-blood:* because so many Cherokees have multiracial ancestry, this term is too all-encompassing to have any social saliency or to serve as a measure of social differentiation.

CARD-CARRYING INDIANS AND WHITE-CHEROKEES

Cherokees living in traditional communities, many of whom are phenotypically Indian and socially full-blood, subtly resist the incorporation of phenotypically and culturally white individuals into the social body of the tribe. Having lost political power in the Cherokee tribal government due to demographic shifts in the Cherokee Nation's citizenship, these traditional Cherokees have developed the ironic humor of the marginalized and frequently use jokes as one way of commenting upon uncomfortable sociopolitical relations. They often refer to other nonrecognizable Cherokee citizens, particularly those who are not socially or culturally accepted by a Cherokee community, as "card-carrying Indians" or "those Cherokees who'll be needing their white card." Obviously, *white* in this instance is a double entendre, referring both to a certificate degree of Indian blood, which is literally a white card, and also to white-Cherokees who need proof of their Indian identity and status and must document their Indianness through genealogical research. Nonetheless, in spite of the ironic commentary, Cherokees who use these terms generally acknowledge that card-carrying Indians and white-Cherokees have a legal and political identity as Cherokee citizens.

WANNABES AND FREEDMEN

Cherokees with a wide range of phenotypes and ancestries use another label of identity, *wannabe,* to refer to phenotypically white individuals who self-identify as Cherokee. By definition, Cherokee wannabes are non-Cherokee. They are different from white-Cherokees and other card-carrying Indians because they lack a CDIB and are not politically recognized by the tribe. As a whole, Cherokees make the assumption that it is whites who "wannabe" Cherokee, because they are otherwise socially, culturally, and racially "empty," as if white culture were not "real" culture. Most Cherokees make this distinction between wannabes and white-Cherokees even though they are well aware that many wannabes have some degree of Cherokee blood but cannot become tribal citizens because they lack the necessary documentation to procure a CDIB, to become card-carrying. Then, the critical distinction between wannabes and white-Cherokees, or card-carrying Indians, centers not on a racial or social identity but on a political identity—the fact that white-Cherokees are documentably blooded citizens of the Cherokee Nation and wannabes are not.

Cherokees also have another category of identity, freedmen, which refers to phenotypically black individuals who are the descendants of Cherokees and their former African-American slaves.[10] Some freedmen have Cherokee blood and some do not, but both historically have been treated in an almost identical fashion. For freedmen, phenotype was always privileged over ancestry as a basis of racial and social classification, causing them to be racially classified as African American, not Native American, to the present time. The history of the freedmen and their struggle for citizenship within the Cherokee Nation is quite complex, a topic I treat in detail in chapter seven.

THE CULTURAL PRODUCTION OF BLOODEDNESS

Throughout this chapter, I have attempted to demonstrate how multi-racial individuals of Cherokee ancestry are socially classified at the local level and how this process articulates with and against Cherokee National hegemony about blood and race. I have discussed five main in-dexical markers of Cherokee identity other than blood ancestry—phe-notype, social behavior, language, religious knowledge and participation, and community residence and participation. These mark-ers of identity are socially significant at the local level, and Cherokees use them to classify others with varying degrees of Cherokee ancestry into various categories of identity that reflect the distinctions Cherokees make among individuals perceived as being politically, socially, cultur-ally, and/or racially Cherokee. We see these distinctions, and how they often overlap, in the various labels that Cherokees use to identity one another as Cherokees or Cherokee Indians, as full-bloods or apples, and as card-carrying Indians or wannabes.

I have also tried to show the variability in the way different types of Cherokees assign meaning to these categories of identity. None are set in stone. Some Cherokees expect full-bloods to speak the Cherokee lan-guage, live in a Cherokee community, and behave in a recognizably Cherokee fashion, while others expect them only to look Indian. What is clear is the interdependence of these indices. Most Cherokees will not socially recognize others as Cherokee strictly on the basis of their blood ancestry—it takes a social calculation based on the interrelation of these indices to produce Cherokee identity. To be a social Cherokee or a Cher-okee Indian, that individual has to meet one or more of these five in-dexical criteria. All five define cultural categories that intersect with each other and with race to shape Cherokee practices of social classification. In fact, race and culture are conflated in Cherokee social classification, so that each can stand for the other as they move back and forth along what I have termed a race-culture continuum.

One way to conceptualize this process is to think of a Cherokee in-dividual as a metaphorical container, a microcosm of the tribal body as a whole, that can be filled with blood, culture, or both. At the most basic level, it would seem that if individuals had less Cherokee blood, then they would need more cultural capital to achieve social recognition as Cherokee; at the same time, if they possessed less culture, they would require more biological capital. However, the process is not that simple. Since blood stands for culture and culture stands for blood, there is a circular logic behind Cherokee practices of social classification. This circular logic encourages what I refer to as the cultural production of bloodedness among Cherokees. To understand this process, let us return to an earlier ethnographic example—the full-blood Cherokee medicine man with green eyes. Because this man is seen in the eyes of the community as a critical culture bearer, he is assumed to have a high degree of Cherokee blood, and because he is assumed to be full-blood, he must be a culture bearer. His presumed fullness of culture denotes a fullness of blood, which is itself a metaphor for culture. In this case, the Cherokee people, who are often so literal about blood when discussing its quantification, use blood as a loose cultural metaphor. This and other similar examples of the cultural production of bloodedness reveal not only how individual meanings and interpretations of Cherokee identity are shaped by a particular social context but also how Cherokee community standards of identity, the social definitions of Cherokee life, are in dialectical tension with those of the Cherokee national government.

To use blood as a metaphor for culture and culture as a metaphor for blood are ways of constructing local Cherokee identities in a global field of social and political relations where blood and race do matter. Thus, as we have seen throughout this chapter, Cherokees internalize these hegemonic notions so that the very discourse of Cherokee identity takes place almost exclusively in racial terms. But Cherokees also bend the terms of the debate to fit their own needs. Hence, we find the full-blood Cherokee medicine man with green eyes, a full-blood Keetoowah man with a CDIB stating he is only one-eighth Cherokee, and a full-blood Cherokee-speaking woman with a white father.

These local reinterpretations of blood, culture, and biology reveal the tension between the Cherokee Nation as a political structure or a state entity and the Cherokee "nation" as a social community. It is the latter, with its local system of social classification, in which Cherokees sustain a sense of themselves as a culturally, racially, and socially distinct people. Criteria other than blood ancestry shape these systems of classification to a significant extent, though blood is always present at some level. Local, more socially nuanced definitions of Cherokee identity do articulate within Cherokee national and U.S. federal hegemony about blood and race, but these local definitions also work against national and racial hegemony by reinterpreting blood in local terms and by assigning it new meanings. It is a give-and-take process, a complex dialectic between multiple agents that creates the polysemous social classification of Cherokee.

CHAPTER SIX

Blood and Marriage

*The Interplay of Kinship, Race,
and Power in Traditional
Cherokee Communities*

As we have seen in the past several chapters, blood is a polyvalent idiom of Cherokee identity. Blood can stand for shared biological, racial, or cultural substance, as both Cherokee national identity and individual social identities are manipulated along a race-culture continuum. Recall, for instance, the full-blood Cherokee medicine man with the green eyes, or how Cherokee citizens have elected national leaders with increasingly greater degrees of Cherokee blood as the tribal population has become less blooded since the mid-1970s. This trend toward more blooded political, social, and religious leaders shows how Cherokees have internalized various blood hegemonies and how they have become increasingly concerned with blood, both literally and metaphorically, in every day life. More importantly, Cherokee blood has come to represent the national whole, symbolizing the biological, racial, and cultural substance that Cherokees use to define the sociopolitical boundaries of their community.

In addition to delineating the "national family," blood also plays an important role in establishing the numerous individual family networks that comprise the Cherokee nation. In this chapter, I explore this role, in particular the intricate and even contradictory relationship between dominant blood ideologies and Cherokee kinship practices. I begin by examining how Euroamerican blood ideologies influence traditional Cherokees not only to marry Cherokee, but to marry a specific kind of Cherokee, in an effort to maintain their racial, cultural, social, and national distinctiveness. I show how competing blood/kin ideologies—both Cherokee and Euroamerican—have become imbricated with one another and have confused Cherokee kinship practices, making it difficult for traditional Cherokees to find suitable Cherokee marriage partners. Then I trace the influence of blood ideologies on the various alternatives to marrying Cherokee, by exploring the different levels of social acceptability assigned by traditional Cherokees to intermarriage with other Native Americans, whites, Mexican Americans, and African Americans. Exploring these marriage preferences in detail, I demonstrate how they both reproduce and challenge U.S. racial hierarchies. Finally, I tie the kinship ideologies that support these traditional Cherokee marriage preferences back to ideologies of race and nation, revealing how power differentials around racial identity are created and reproduced within traditional Cherokee society.

KINSHIP THEORY AND RACE

Why explore Cherokee identity politics using kinship as a point of departure? On the surface, it would seem that the study of kinship within anthropology has moved from being passé to moribund in recent decades. This superficial impression is misleading. In fact, in an article in the *Annual Review of Anthropology*, Michael Peletz suggests that although the issue of kinship no longer occupies a privileged place within anthropology, kinship theory is very much alive—albeit "reconstituted and partially subsumed under other rubrics" within the field (1995: 345). Peletz credits feminist and Marxist anthropologists with playing a significant role in reshaping and revitalizing kinship studies since the 1970s. He argues that "systems of kinship and gender are 'about' difference and inequality, and, as such, are most usefully analyzed as components of more encompassing systems of distinction and hierarchy that are variably grounded in cosmology and political economy" (1995: 359–60). By viewing kinship as a fundamental component of these more encompassing systems, which reproduce hierarchical distinctions such as race, class, and gender, then we can expect kinship to provide a useful window into the social construction of racial difference and the reproduction of racial hierarchy.

Yet anthropologists have only begun to make the explicit connection between kinship systems and the social construction of race. This connection has become more apparent as anthropologists have "increasingly turned to their own societies to gather data and build comparative and theoretical arguments" (Peletz 1995: 362). Bringing kinship studies back home, as it were, has resulted in some important new research, according to Peletz (1995: 362). As Western anthropologists have begun to examine contemporary kinship systems within the racially diverse nation-states in which they live, their research has "underscore[d] the importance, when studying kinship and marriage in any context, of factoring into our analyses the intersecting variables of race/ethnicity, class, and gender, as well as the ways state policies, nationalist discourses and other understandings of imagined communities shape local experiences and representations of kinship, family and household" (1995: 362). This is a significant contribution, one that can be seen in the pioneering works of Michaela di Leonardo (1984), Carol Stack (1974), and Sylvia Yanagisako (1985), to name but a few. Their collective research has helped us to understand better how racial identity in particular intersects with various kinship systems within the United States.

Still, we need to keep in mind that factoring in racial difference as one variable among many is not the same thing as explicitly examining the relationship between the social construction of kinship and the social construction of race. In other words, when looking at the kinship systems of a racialized group of people, such as African Americans, too few anthropologists examine how kinship constructs race or how race constructs kinship. They may make this explicit connection, but oftentimes insights about race are an almost accidental by-product of such studies. I agree with anthropologist Brackette Williams, who states that "too few conscientious efforts are made to examine the continuities between cultural constructions of kinship and those of other categorical distinctions such as race, nation and caste" (1995: 201).

Doing exactly what Peletz calls for, Williams uses race as a central point of departure when she returns to several classic kinship studies in her essay "Classification Systems Revisited: Kinship, Caste, Race and Nationality as the Flow of Blood and the Spread of Rights" (1995). To explore how people produce their own racial, cultural, and national identities, Williams examines the various ideologies that intersect with kinship. In particular, she is concerned with the "common ideological precepts that permit the production and ranking of persons of mixed descent in caste-stratified and racially divided societies," all of which have a direct bearing on the formation of kinship networks (1995: 203). She seems to suggest that, because these ideological precepts have been highly naturalized, certain combinations of substance, certain mixtures of identity, are seen as more natural than others, and this, in turn, becomes a basis of hierarchy. Thus, Williams pays close attention to "the interpenetration of kinship and U.S. nationalist ideologies in the social- ization of nature and the naturalization of power" (1995: 203). The effect of her analysis is to illuminate the subtle machinations of power in the discursive production of people, races, and nations out of various mixtures of blood, race, kin, nationality, and class. This is a significant contribution to kinship theory because it shows how kinship plays an important role in the naturalization of power and identity and how this naturalization leads to racial hierarchy and other social differences, such as class, culture, and nationality.

Building on the work of Williams, I extend these theoretical concerns into a new context by examining the relationship among kinship, race, and nationalist ideologies as they are manifested within contemporary Cherokee marriage practices. In particular, I reveal how blood ideologies influence traditional Cherokee marriage practices. I use marriage as my point of departure because kinship by marriage usually involves some degree of choice, whereas kinship by blood does not. David Schneider, one of the major figures in kinship theory, explains that in the U.S. context relatives by blood differ from relatives by marriage because "Where blood is both material and natural, marriage is neither. Where blood endures, marriage is terminable. And since there is no such 'thing' as blood of which marriage consists, and since there is no such material which exists free in nature, persons related by marriage are not related 'in nature'" (1968: 25). Cherokees share these same presuppositions, dating back to the eighteenth century, that blood kin relationships are somehow more natural and more permanent than those by marriage. At the same time, for Cherokees as with most people, the distinction between consanguineal and affinal kin is not so neat and definitive. As numerous anthropologists have pointed out, the institution of marriage is often, though not necessarily, connected to the sociopolitical legiti- mization of sexual relations and reproduction.[1] As a result, Cherokee marriage preferences are highly naturalized and linked to ideologies of blood. Cherokees—at least those in traditional communities, as I will explain shortly—choose marriage partners based on their shared no- tions of who has the right kind of blood and what kind of person will produce offspring with an acceptable blood mixture—one that will keep their family, and perhaps the Cherokee nation in general biologically, racially, and culturally distinct. This process of choosing, I believe, brings ideology to the surface, revealing the connections between mar- riage preferences and blood ideologies regarding the "reproduction" of

Cherokee national, cultural, and racial boundaries. As a result, racial hierarchies and their relationship to Cherokee identity formation can be deduced from Cherokee marriage preferences.

I also use marriage as my point of departure to better understand the demographic crisis affecting the Cherokee Nation and, by extension, Native North America in general. As Cherokee demographer Russell Thornton states, Cherokees continue to marry non-Indians at rates as high as 60 percent, which has led to increasingly lower degrees of Cherokee blood and higher degrees of blood mixture among Cherokee tribal citizens (Thornton 1990: 138). It is race mixing, born of Cherokee exogamy, that many traditional Cherokees believe is the greatest threat to their cultural, racial, and to a lesser extent, national survival.[2] For this reason, it would seem that Cherokee marriage practices—the overall trends toward tribal and racial exogamy—are in conflict with traditional Cherokee marriage preferences. In this chapter, I explore why this is so and why exogamy is so common among Cherokees. In particular, I examine the various blood and kinship ideologies that shape this tendency, and I explore how they pattern Cherokee marriage preferences in terms of race.

TRADITIONAL CHEROKEE COMMUNITIES

Rather than looking at all Cherokee marriages, I have decided to focus on marriage preferences within traditional Cherokee communities. I do so because traditional Cherokees see themselves, and are seen by others, as the bearers of an embattled Cherokee racial, cultural, and national essence. As they see it, the reproduction of these essentialized aspects of Cherokee identity has become increasingly threatened as a result of demographic trends in the Cherokee Nation over the past twenty-five years. While all Cherokees are concerned with boundary maintenance, traditional Cherokees claim to feel the social pressure to marry Cherokee more than do other Cherokees. Because of this heightened pressure, traditional Cherokee marriage preferences and practices reveal a more intensified version of the ideological conflict affecting Cherokees in general.

When applied to Native Americans, the term *traditional* is problematic because it tends to reify Native-American culture and history, perhaps even implying that "real Indians" live in the past or are somehow culturally "backward." Although I appreciate these critiques and agree with them, I continue to use the term not only to describe certain Cherokee communities but also to describe certain Cherokee individuals. I do so for several reasons. First, Cherokees themselves use the term with frequency, and notions of traditionalism play an important role in discourses of Cherokee identity. To be labeled by other Cherokees as traditional usually means that someone was raised in a Cherokee-identified community and belongs to a distinctively Cherokee religious institution, such as a Cherokee Baptist church or a Keetoowah society ceremonial ground. I invoke this discourse of traditionalism as it already exists within Cherokee society, although I realize that I may be contributing to it in the process. Second, I use the term because the other options are equally problematic, including *culturally conservative, tribal,* and *social,* all of which could apply to a wide variety of Cherokees in different contexts. Although I have briefly described what Cherokees refer to as traditional communities in chapters 1 and 5, I will now provide more detailed information on these communities to better frame our understanding of where these specific kinship practices take place.

Scattered throughout the northeastern corner of Oklahoma are roughly seventy traditional Cherokee communities, most built alongside various creeks, streams, and rivers running through the foothills of the Ozarks (see Figure 2). Some of these are practically on top of each other, so close that their boundaries overlap. In Adair County, a small county on the Arkansas border, there are nineteen different Cherokee communities. In other counties, the traditional communities are more dispersed, with ten or fifteen miles of dense, isolating forest between them. To reach a traditional Cherokee community from a larger Cherokee town like Tahlequah or Stilwell usually requires a drive of an hour or more on poorly maintained blacktop and gravel roads. Remote and often unwelcoming to outsiders, these small, cohesive communities of relatives can be geographically, economically, and socially isolated from each other, though not so much as from the rest of the state. The state capital may be only three hours away, but in many ways it can seem much further from the vantage of small Cherokee communities like Greasy and Bull Hollow.

On the surface, Cherokee communities look like other small towns in rural Oklahoma, and in many respects they are not unlike non-Indian communities in the same vicinity. The main difference is that Cherokee communities often appear smaller, poorer, and more haphazard; they are also usually more racially and culturally homogeneous. A handful of intermarried whites might reside in the community and be accepted as community members, but for the most part, the residents of a traditional Cherokee community tend to look Indian and act Cherokee, at least as those concepts are understood in northeastern Oklahoma. It is important to keep in mind the size of these communities, often no more than from 100 to 250 individuals comprising from 20 to 50 different households (Wahrhaftig 1975: 101).[3] Small as they may be, these communities form their own social, ceremonial, and economic unit, though some residents may commute to jobs in larger towns, like Tahlequah, if not too far away (Wahrhaftig 1975: 101). To a surprising degree, these small settlements stand on their own, with the focal points of the community usually including a local Cherokee Baptist church, an elementary school, middle school, or high school, and occasionally a ceremonial stomp ground or community building.

Cherokee homes tend to cluster around these local institutions. Although some sit on neatly fenced lots in the middle of town, most houses are tucked up under the trees or on the side of a hill, hidden from view. Many homes are located on old land allotments from the turn of the century, though they have been increasingly subdivided among descendants. Many traditional Cherokees share these allotments with their kin, living only a footpath away from their aunts, uncles, parents, grandparents, siblings, cousins, and other extended family. There are some communal aspects to such arrangements, but even in a multifamily compound of extended kin, the quality of housing varies substantially. The Cherokee Nation conducted a housing study in 1993 and found that roughly 14 percent of Cherokees lived in mobile homes, 73 percent in some sort of detached home, 6 percent in a multifamily dwelling, and another 7 percent in some other type of arrangement.

Some houses seem almost out of place, and these are usually the modest, brick homes built by the Cherokee Nation Housing Authority (CNHA). These cookie-cutter homes are so standardized that after some time I came to recognize certain styles of housing that the CNHA had built in a given year. Each possessing the somber lines that run throughout many government housing projects, these houses pepper the landscape in traditional Cherokee towns and were one of the subtle signs that I had happened upon a Cherokee community. Dull though they may be, CNHA houses tend to provide a higher standard of material comfort than the majority of Cherokee homes, which are typically simple wood-frame structures. Some of these older homes are in good condition, though many are not, with about one-fifth lacking electrical wiring, and almost a third in need of better heating and cooling systems.[4]

Fixing up an aging house is no small matter, given the low income of most residents. Unless the tribe intervenes, Cherokee homes will often stay in this condition for some time because many members of traditional Cherokee communities face distressing conditions of poverty. Their first concern is to get adequate food on the table, and then they might think about repairing the electrical wiring. In general, Cherokees have lower annual incomes than whites in the same region. For example, in 1989, 30.5 percent of Cherokees in the fourteen counties of northeastern Oklahoma had an annual income somewhere between $5,000 and $14,000, as compared with only 20.8 percent of whites.[5] In small, isolated communities, the economic differences between Cherokees and whites is even more pronounced. In 1989, 17.1 percent of Cherokee households in Nowata County had an annual income of less than $5,000. However, of the whites in the area, only 8.1 percent faced the same hardship. Part of the reason for this discrepancy is that Cherokee communities have lost much of their economic self-sufficiency despite attempts to pool their resources. There are fewer Cherokee farmers and ranchers, as compared with whites, and traditional Cherokees almost always have to leave their rural communities to find work, usually in larger checkerboard Cherokee towns or white towns with some degree of commercial and industrial development.

Based on his research from the mid-1960s, Wahrhaftig estimated that approximately 9,500 Cherokees, or one-quarter of the tribe as a whole, lived in traditional Cherokee settlements (1975: 25). However, in the last thirty-five years, tribal demographics have shifted so dramatically that traditional Cherokees have been increasingly outnumbered. Lacking precise demographic data, I can only roughly estimate that a little less than 10 percent of the tribe—perhaps almost 20,000 people—actively resides in a traditional Cherokee community. My estimate is based on Wahrhaftig's population figures from 1964 and Thornton's data regarding Cherokee population growth nationwide (Wahrhaftig 1975: 25; Thornton 1990: 199).[6] Since the number of Cherokee tribal citizens is now near 200,000, this rough estimate implies a more certain demographic trend—while the traditional Cherokee population has increased in number in the past several decades, their overall percentage within the tribe has decreased dramatically.

A minority in their own tribe in many ways, traditional Cherokees have become increasingly concerned with boundary maintenance. They have pulled together, becoming more cohesive and more socially autonomous, placing greater emphasis on their distinct community, cultural, and racial identity rather than their political identity as tribal citizens.

Even when divided by differences of language, religion, and phenotype, most members of traditional Cherokee communities accept one another as real Cherokees and real Indians. This notion of themselves, and each other, as the bearers of an essentialized Cherokee identity is one of the main reasons why traditional Cherokees exert social pressure on one another to marry Cherokee. Their efforts to resist the erosion of Cherokee identity through endogamy are not only a response to demographic changes in the Cherokee Nation but also to the legal and political discourses of Cherokee National identity. However, because they are caught in a more pronounced conflict between Cherokee and Euroamerican blood/kin ideologies, many traditional Cherokees find themselves "looking for love in all the wrong places," at least as their community and relatives would have it.

"NO BRIGHT EYES": PREFERRED MARRIAGES AMONG TRADITIONAL CHEROKEES

TRIBAL ENDOGAMY AND BLOOD DEGREE

"Our elders always gave us counsel that was wise," a well-known and highly respected traditional Cherokee man once said to me. "They said there are many kinds of people in the world. Treat them like you would your family, but remember who you are." This remembering of one's identity has different meanings for different types of Cherokees. For traditional Cherokees, maintaining a distinctly Cherokee identity is intimately connected to ideas about kinship and race, and these associations rise to the surface more explicitly when Cherokee men and women seek what they consider to be suitable marriage partners. One older Cherokee woman suggested that people in traditional Cherokee communities "just don't think of marrying anyone but Cherokees, 'cause that's all you know." Even if they occasionally interacted with and dated non-Cherokees, most traditional Cherokees told me that they preferred to marry Cherokees, in part because of explicit social pressure from their families and communities to marry within the tribe. One young secretary at the Cherokee tribal complex expressed this widespread sentiment, saying, "My grandparents wanted me strongly to marry Cherokee. My dad, too." Another young Cherokee woman claimed, "My dad really wanted me to marry Cherokee, and that's exactly what I did."

Traditional Cherokee families and communities encourage their members to marry Cherokee as a strategy to ensure the survival of what they see as a uniquely Cherokee racial, cultural, and national identity.

One older Cherokee man recalled how his grandmother taught him the importance of marrying Cherokee, not only to the family but also to the survival of the tribe. She would admonish him to avoid Euroamericans with the phrase, "No bright eyes!" Similarly, a Cherokee father explained to me how he encouraged his children to marry within the tribe and why he thought this was so critical:

> I want my children to marry Cherokees. But I try really hard not to force it on them. Every once in a while, I'll make comments about it. We will see a Cherokee couple and we'll say, 'Isn't that beautiful?' Or like two of our friends, you know Jimmy Redbird and Lorette Terrapin [pseudonyms]? Well, they are getting married. We talk about the union of two Cherokees as not just the union of two individuals, but . . . the union of two huge families. And both of those names, isn't that just beautiful? You know, we really try to express it to our children in terms of the beauty of the intermarriage. But when the day comes and one of my daughters brings home a big black man or a big white man, you know I am going to have to say, that's my son-in-law. But I would rather . . .

At this point, he paused and looked away, as if not wanting to say what was on his mind. Then, he continued, carefully choosing his words, "I think it's a matter of the survival of the tribe. In order for us to be a separate people, we have got to be separate in many ways, and one of those ways is [to be] genetically separate." Encouraging his daughters to marry Cherokees rather than blacks or whites reflects a belief that, for the Cherokee tribe to maintain its distinct sense of peoplehood, the Cherokee people need to practice tribal endogamy in order to remain genetically separate.[7] As this quote suggests, Cherokee tribal identity is intertwined with a distinct racial identity that comes into high relief in discussions of Cherokee marriage preferences.

That Cherokees want to marry within the tribe is not unusual. In fact, endogamy is preferred in most tribal societies. What is unusual is how various Euroamerican blood/kin ideologies have come to be associated with Cherokee endogamy and how this has altered the Cherokee kinship system as a whole. The intersection of Euroamerican blood/kin ideologies and Cherokee kin ideologies has profound implications. For instance, conflating blood, race, and culture, one middle-aged traditional Cherokee man expressed the belief that marriages between Cherokees were somehow easier. "It is so much more difficult if you marry across cultures," he told me. "I didn't conscientiously hunt for a Cherokee spouse, but I did marry a full-blood Cherokee woman. That was a big plus to me, even though I had dated white women." Although this man did not actively seek a Cherokee wife, he still internalized blood ideologies that made marriage with another Cherokee his preferred and eventual choice.

Many traditional Cherokees conflate blood with Cherokee racial and cultural identity but claim that it is not sufficient to simply marry another Cherokee—they also need to marry a particular type of Cherokee. For instance, a Cherokee woman in her forties explained how she and her immediate family had a difficult time relating to her first husband. "My family was open to my ex-husband because he was one-quarter Cherokee," she said, "but he didn't look Indian and he wasn't raised the same. He didn't have the same interests." So, in spite of his Cherokee ancestry, his phenotypic and cultural differences made it hard for his wife's family to accept him as kin. "My family knew he wasn't one of them," she explained. "He couldn't be one of us because he didn't want to. They didn't feel comfortable around him. In fact they used to tease him and say, 'Hey, why don't you just turn your [CDIB] card in?' I guess he thought he was better." Part of her family's discomfort may have stemmed from the fact that Cherokee blood is often linked to class identity. In general, Cherokees assume that individuals with lower degrees of Cherokee blood will have a higher class standing than those with higher degrees of Cherokee blood. Decades of mixed-blood and white-Cherokee political and economic power have fostered this belief, and despite numerous exceptions, class and blood associations are still socially salient among Cherokees today. Although his legal identity, on the basis of blood, as a Cherokee tribal citizen played a key role in her family's initial acceptance of her husband, over time his social and cultural identity did not match her and her family's expectations regarding appropriate Cherokee kin-behavior. In more ways than one, his having Cherokee blood was not sufficient for him to be accepted by a traditional Cherokee family.

Like this woman and her family, most traditional Cherokees define appropriate marriage partners through the idiom of blood, even while marking social and cultural differences. Because Cherokee blood continues to be one of the most important aspects of Cherokee national and social identity, most traditional Cherokees believe that marrying someone with Cherokee blood is a minimum requirement for a successful marriage. Marrying Cherokee is also an important social responsibility because it is presumed to ensure tribal, racial, and cultural continuity by keeping high degrees of blood in future Cherokee offspring. For example, one young Cherokee woman, known as a mixed-blood because she is one-quarter Cherokee and a fluent Cherokee-language speaker, said, "I want my husband to be Cherokee, but just part. Not full-blood, because I'm part, not full-blood. I want to marry someone who is part, so my children's bloodline stays high. It would be good if they were a Cherokee speaker too, but that's not my main criteria." In part, because this young woman was raised in a traditional Cherokee community, she believes she can relate successfully only to a Cherokee man who is similar to her in terms of blood identity—not too much, not too little—though she adds a cultural concern to the mix when she expresses a preference for a Cherokee-language speaker. Her attitudes about race and culture contain a subtle contradiction because at the same time that she rejects a full-blood Cherokee spouse, she wants her own children's bloodlines to "stay high."

This desire to keep Cherokee blood at a certain level is characteristic of traditional Cherokees, who usually prefer some degree of Cherokee blood in their potential spouses, though they have different standards about how much blood is necessary. For instance, we can compare how one traditional Cherokee woman described her one-quarter-blood husband as not looking or acting sufficiently Cherokee to be socially accepted as kin, while another wanted a husband who had a blood quantum similar to her own one-quarter blood degree. For her, a more blooded man would not have been acceptable, presumably because his greater blood quantum would be accompanied by cultural characteristics that would set her apart from him. Traditional Cherokees have different standards about how much blood they want in their potential spouse, because they have different standards about how much blood is necessary for someone to be really Cherokee. Thus, the idea that blood is a quantifiable index of cultural and racial authenticity shapes Cherokee endogamy, though it varies according to these different individual standards. However, degree of blood is not the only consideration for traditional Cherokees looking for a suitable Cherokee spouse.

MOTHER'S BLOOD: MATRILINEAL CLAN EXOGAMY VERSUS TRIBAL ENDOGAMY

For some traditional Cherokees, the lineal source of a person's blood—whether it derives from the father's or the mother's side—can be as meaningful as the amount of that blood, as expressed by blood quantum. For example, Brackette Williams describes the importance of blood origin in the ethnographic case of the Daribi, as studied by Roy Wagner in 1977:

> [N]ot all the shared biogenetic substance of which a human is composed defines . . . the flow of relatedness. From the male substance comes [sic] some elements and from the female other elements of the total biogenetic substance. . . . Consequently, not all of nature is . . . equally significant in the formation of the criteria that allow intensive social relationships to move people to resources and resources to people. (1995: 213)

This passage accurately describes Cherokee kinship relations as well, since some Cherokees make a significant social distinction between a Cherokee mother's blood and a Cherokee father's blood. Traditional Cherokees who make this distinction are often members of the Keetoowah Society, where clan still plays an important ceremonial role.[8] However, all Cherokees who make this distinction do so because at one time Cherokees were primarily a matrilineal society, divided into seven exogamous, matrilineal clans. As I described in chapter 2 and as legal historian John Philip Reid states, "the clan was the exogamous unit of Cherokee society, and marriage within one's own clan or one's father's clan violated exogamy" (1970: 41). Today, many Keetoowahs and other traditional Cherokees maintain that to be a member of a Cherokee clan—some say even to be truly Cherokee—one has to have a Cherokee mother, in other words, to have the blood of a Cherokee mother in one's veins. While their primary concern is simply to marry Cherokee, this often requires finding someone with a clan affiliation different from their own. In this manner, tribal identity is interwoven with clan identity, which causes some traditional Cherokees to search for a spouse with Cherokee mother's blood to form a real Cherokee union that will produce real Cherokee children with a clan identity.[9]

When choosing what they consider to be a socially acceptable Cherokee spouse, some traditional Cherokees may place greater emphasis on the social distinction between matrilineal and patrilineal descent than that between greater and lesser degrees of Cherokee blood. Oftentimes, however, these ideological distinctions regarding blood degree and lineal descent intersect. For example, a middle-aged Cherokee man who was a member of the Keetoowah society told me that before his first marriage

> . . . it wasn't so important to me that my wife be Cherokee. My ex was one-half Cherokee. But now, I wouldn't go below one-half. Mainly, because I

want my children to speak the language, to know their culture and to look Indian. I suppose my ideal mate could be one-half, but her Cherokee blood would have to be from her mother, so our child would know its clan.

Implicitly linking his potential marriage with biological, racial, cultural, and social reproduction, this man wanted his ideal Cherokee mate to have a certain degree of matrilineal Cherokee blood. That way, his wife and his future children would have enough blood—and the right kind of blood—to fulfill his vision of Cherokee racial and cultural identity.

This gender hierarchy regarding lineal descent, in which mother's blood is more important than father's blood, also shapes traditional Cherokee marriage preferences in different ways for Cherokee men and women. Some traditional Cherokee men experience intense social pressure to marry a Cherokee woman with matrilineal blood because their children will have no clan membership without it. Traditional Cherokee women, on the other hand, do not have their field of marriage partners narrowed in the same way. Because a Cherokee woman is the "bearer" of the clan, she has more freedom to seek a marriage partner of either matrilineal or patrilineal Cherokee descent.

Many traditional Cherokees, including Cherokee Baptists, are well aware of this important gender difference and commented upon it frequently. For instance, a Cherokee elder who is a deacon in a local Cherokee Baptist church described how Cherokee boys are socialized differently from Cherokee girls:

> Boys, especially, are taught that it's important to have a Cherokee wife. With girls, it's not so important. Because women carry the clan, the kids will still have a clan if they [women] marry out. But this wouldn't be true for me, if I married white. . . . Personally, for a wife, I never care how much blood, or even if she is traditional. She's just got to be Cherokee, and that means through the mother.

A former Cherokee beauty queen, raised in a traditional Cherokee community as a Cherokee Baptist, also noted this important distinction regarding mother's blood. She said, "Because we are a matrilineal society, the way I look at it, even if I marry a man of another race, our children would still be Cherokee, because I'm Cherokee, and that's all that matters." For this young woman, Cherokee mother's blood is an important guarantor of Cherokee identity. If she marries outside the tribe, or even outside the race, her children will still be socially accepted as Cherokee, as long as they can claim matrilineal Cherokee descent. This strong belief in the power of mother's blood—her own blood—as a carrier of Cherokee identity gives her more latitude in choosing potential marriage partners than her male counterparts.

Already, we might note the subtle contradiction in Cherokee blood/kin ideologies regarding whether or not it is important for Cherokee women to marry Cherokee. Some traditional Cherokees suggest that women have a greater degree of choice than men and can even choose to marry outside the tribe. But these same women are constrained by other social pressures to marry Cherokee. For example, the father mentioned earlier pushed his daughters to marry within the tribe, fearing that if they did not their children would no longer be "genetically separate," would no longer maintain their distinct racial identity as Cherokees. This contradiction results from the fact that traditional Cherokees reckon kinship in different ways, according to competing blood/kin ideologies. On the one hand, most traditional Cherokees define tribal endogamy in terms of a highly racialized, quantifiable blood identity in which there is no distinction between potential marriage partners on the basis of lineal descent; rather, this distinction is based only on blood degree. On the other hand, other traditional Cherokees, particularly Keetoowahs, define tribal endogamy according to a clan system based on matrilineal descent. In such cases, blood quantum may also be an important consideration, but it is secondary to whether or not a potential spouse is of matrilineal descent and a clan member. In other words, it might be preferable for a Cherokee suitor to have one thirty-second mother's blood rather than one-half father's blood. These two competing definitions of endogamy are essentially different definitions of Cherokee identity according to degrees of blood or types of blood.

Not surprisingly, these competing kinship ideologies have different origins, though they share certain elements. Both reflect the originally Euroamerican conflation of blood, race, culture, and nation and the Euroamerican idea that blood is a divisible biological substance, the degree of which can be used to measure different substances of identity. Yet traditional Cherokee kinship ideologies also reflect vestigial traces of the distinctly Cherokee, matrilineal kinship system that I discussed in chapter 2. For instance, traditional Cherokees frequently speak about the importance of matrilineality as an organizing principle in family social organization and in living arrangements. Furthermore, many Cherokee siblings still have especially close relationships with one another, as do maternal uncles with their sister's children. Though these practices also exist in other sectors of the tribal population, ideologies of blood on the basis of matrilineal descent and clan membership are more pronounced among Cherokees living in traditional communities, where they provide a confusing counterpoint to concerns about blood quantum. Having two overlapping standards of determining who is a suitably Cherokee marriage partner has created a complex, two-tiered system in which blood-quantum considerations are weighed against lineal considerations, each according to individual preferences. Increasingly, traditional Cherokees are granting more weight to the ideology of blood quantum, in which the distinction between Cherokees is not at all based on lineal descent but only on blood degree—Cherokee blood, from whatever side, is all that matters. This idea encourages Cherokees to reckon kin on both their mother's and their father's sides. Thus, traditional Cherokees are experiencing the articulation of two different kinship systems, complicating and even obscuring Cherokee definitions of exogamy.

FURTHER COMPLICATIONS OF COUNTING KIN: GENEALOGICAL DISTANCE AND BILATERAL DESCENT

In the beginning he really wanted to find a Cherokee wife, but eventually he just gave up. Wistful, he speaks to the anthropologist who feels sadder and more perplexed as he goes on.

"But why?" she asks him, "Didn't your family want you to marry a Cherokee?"

He looks up at her from across the desk, his hand resting on his chin, then leans forward and says, "I'll tell you a little story, okay?

"When I was young man," he begins, "I dated this beautiful girl, and she was Cherokee. I can still remember her face. It was so young and fresh, and she had the most beautiful eyes. I thought she was great, that the stars just fell from the sky anytime she was near. . . . I remember I first met her at Sunday dinner at church. I was only eighteen years old and I think maybe she was just barely sixteen. We wound up sittin' next to each other, and once we got started, we just couldn't stop talking. We would just sit together and visit all day long. After we had been doing that for a few months, I decided, well, I really like this girl. She's something special, so it's about time I take her home and introduce her to the family. When she first came to our house, I was sort of beside myself, nervous and excited all at the same time. I was like a school kid. Heck, I was a school kid!" he exclaims, "and so was she."

Chuckling a little, he savors the memory, and then continues. "Of course, the first person to meet her when I brought her to the door was my old grandma. She really asked her the questions, boy did she! At dinner, I kept hoping grandma would just pipe down and be quiet, but it didn't happen. It was like my grandma was after something. Well, sure enough, she was. After I finally took the girl home, my grandma pulled me aside and she said, 'you can't date that girl no more. I hate to tell you this, honey, but she's kin to you.' I was so disappointed that evening. Her being kin to me seemed to explain so much, even why we were drawn to one another."

His disappointment is still strong enough for the anthropologist to feel it, and in some small way to share a sense of his loss. Then he tells her something else. "Later, I just got more and more frustrated with dating Cherokee women. I was trying to please my family, and I was also trying to please myself. I really wanted to be with a Cherokee woman, but I just got more and more frustrated, because it seemed that every Cherokee woman I dated was kin to me. I'd take them home and grandma would always have them pegged as some kind of distant relation. She even knew our tenth cousins! How was I going to beat that?"

He doesn't really expect an answer, but he pauses anyway. Then, with what seems like respectful resignation, he says, "The old people were amazing that way, just keeping all that stuff in their heads. . . . I suppose it was out of sheer frustration that I just quit dating girls around here altogether."

As a result of competing blood/kin ideologies, Cherokees have experienced a gradual shift from a matrilineal kinship system to a bilateral one, which has eroded traditional definitions of Cherokee exogamy in more ways than one. As I noted in chapter 2, originally Cherokees reckoned genealogically distant kin within the same matrilineal clan, all of whom were considered unacceptable marriage partners according to the rule of clan exogamy. Now, however, Cherokees have adopted the Euroamerican kinship system of bilateral descent, so that they acknowledge genealogically distant kin on both their mother's and their father's sides. This practice of combining a Euroamerican system of bilateral descent with Cherokee conceptions of genealogical distance makes it increasingly difficult for traditional Cherokees to marry Cherokee without somehow "marrying kin." To understand and untangle this complex conceptual knot, let us first examine how Cherokee kinship diverges from U.S. kinship on the matter of genealogical distance. Then, we can consider how this practice, combined with Euroamerican notions of bilateral descent, affects Cherokee exogamy.

According to Schneider, genealogical distance is "roughly measured by how many intervening categories of relatives there are, or how many generations one must go back before a common relative is found" (1968: 73). He explains that in the dominant U.S. kinship system

> [t]here is . . . a tendency to forget distant collaterals and distant ascendants, but the boundary in either the past or the present is fuzzy and there are interstitial areas which are so faded at any given moment as to be barely visible. The distant ascendants are dead and no relationship obtains with them. Without a relationship, there can be no reason to retain them . . . unless, of course, they are famous, in which case they may be remembered though their descendants along collateral lines, lacking fame, will not be known. The distant collaterals are "too far away." (1968: 72)

Among Cherokees, however, blood ties stretch thinner and farther than among Euroamericans. Distant collateral and ascendant relatives who would be long forgotten in U.S. kinship systems are both acknowledged and remembered in Cherokee kinship reckonings.[10] For instance, I recall my amazement when I asked a Cherokee elder about his family history and he proceeded to sketch a detailed family tree dating back to 1710 on the back of a paper napkin. Euroamericans, on the other hand, typically recognize no more than three or four generations of kin, at least without the aid of genealogical research (Schneider 1968: 67).

Cherokees not only trace their ascendant kin back through multiple generations, but they also know and socially acknowledge their distant collateral kin. On a regular basis, Cherokees whom I interviewed would mention third or fourth cousins on both their mother's and their father's sides with whom they had recently visited.[11] One older Cherokee woman even told me, "The way I was brought up, your fortieth cousin was your close kin." She went on to say that the distinction between close kin and distant kin was not part of the Cherokee kinship system but instead was "a white man's way of thinking." For traditional Cherokees, acknowledging both their distant collateral and ascendant kin as kin is nothing new. The Cherokees have historically relied on these extended kinship networks for economic, social, and political support. In the early nineteenth century, to the utter bafflement of missionaries, Cherokees could tell "without hesitation" the degree of relationship that existed between themselves and any other member of the same clan (Reid 1970: 38). This meant that Cherokees could not marry anyone inside their own clan or their father's clan, "even members whose relationship . . . was by our standard so remote that we would not think them kin" (Reid 1970: 42). While Cherokees were even forbidden to marry distant cousins within their clan, they had no concept of cousinage outside the clan; thus, they could marry a father's brother's offspring without social repercussions (Reid 1970: 42).

Today, what is different is that Cherokees now acknowledge genealogically distant kin on both the mother's side and the father's side, whereas before Cherokee kinship was reckoned solely through the matriline. For instance, one young Cherokee woman when describing her extended family, her third and fourth cousins, said, "I never did see any difference in my mother's side or my father's. They're both equally important." Another Cherokee woman in her thirties, a Keetoowah Society member, said, "My parents taught me the old ways, to marry outside the clan. You could marry a cousin on your dad's side, but in this day and age most people would frown on it because they'd be your kin too."[12] Born of the competing kinship ideologies discussed earlier, this shift from a matrilineal to a bilateral kinship system has important implications for Cherokee marriage preferences and practices. Because traditional Cherokees acknowledge so many genealogically distant kin on both sides, finding a Cherokee spouse has become a troublesome and lengthy task unless one is willing to buck Cherokee society's strictures about "kissing cousins," most broadly defined. Since wanting to marry Cherokee is tied to a pervasive blood hegemony, and since wanting to practice certain types of exogamy is tied to uniquely Cherokee kinship ideologies, many traditional Cherokees find themselves between a rock and a hard place.

I first became aware of the tension between these and other competing ideologies in Cherokee kinship practices when I interviewed the Cherokee elder who told me the above story about his grandmother's intervention in his youthful love affair. His experience was common among traditional Cherokees, who on many occasions told me how they had wanted to marry a Cherokee spouse but had been unable to find someone who was not related to them in some way. The combination of Cherokee and Euroamerican beliefs about genealogical distance and bilateral descent has increased the difficulty of finding a suitable spouse for contemporary Cherokees. While confusing in the abstract, in practice this conflict is the clear source of much frustration. According to the people I interviewed, as dominant ideologies of bilateral descent became entangled with traditional notions of Cherokee kinship about three generations ago, or sometime in the 1940s, most Cherokees began to reckon anyone with any degree of common blood, on either side, as kin. The effect of this shift was that patrilineal relatives, who were once considered eligible marriage partners, were now ineligible, and what was once an easily maintained system of matrilineal clan exogamy had, essentially, broken down.

At one time, Cherokees could marry within the tribe and outside their clan without trouble, but now they define so many people as kin that it is difficult to marry within the tribe without entering a potentially incestuous union.[13] For traditional Cherokees to find a Cherokee marriage partner who is a nonrelative is more difficult than it may sound, because intersecting kin/blood ideologies are constantly restricting the field of potential spouses.[14] As I have attempted to show, traditional Cherokees cannot marry what dominant U.S. society considers to be very distant collateral relatives because they view them as close relatives with whom marriage would be a violation of the incest taboo.[15] At the same time, they are bound by ideologies of blood since they prefer to marry not only someone who has Cherokee blood, but someone who has a certain amount and type of Cherokee blood. The irony is that these competing kin/blood ideologies have the effect of diminishing the very blood that they are intending to preserve. With these overlapping ideologies consistently limiting their choices among potential Cherokee marriage partners, many traditional Cherokees often find themselves falling in love with non-Cherokees and marrying outside the tribe, even though this may not be their first preference.

THE MOVE TO TRIBAL EXOGAMY:
RACIAL HIERARCHIES IN TRADITIONAL
CHEROKEE MARRIAGE PREFERENCES

When traditional Cherokees marry outside the tribe, they face a new set of concerns. In such situations, they find themselves making social distinctions not between different types of kin but between different types of people from many racial and cultural backgrounds. Once again, racial ideologies expressed through the idiom of blood shape the selection of a marriage partner. For Cherokees, marriage is tied to social, racial, cultural, and national "reproduction" through the passage of Cherokee blood from one generation to the next. As a result, if Cherokees want their future offspring to identify themselves and to be identified by others as Cherokee, then they have to consider what type of blood mixture is socially acceptable. If we examine the discourse surrounding Cherokee marriage preferences, it quickly becomes apparent that among traditional Cherokees certain types of blood mixtures are more socially acceptable than others. In fact, traditional Cherokee marriage preferences are based upon a concrete racial hierarchy in which we can see the linkage between the mixing of blood and the mixing of race, class, and culture and, thus, the mixing of national substances.

Concerned that their children be socially identifiable as Cherokee, traditional Cherokees prefer to marry Cherokee, but if an appropriate Cherokee marriage partner cannot be found, then they tend to marry Indian.[16] For example, while we were sitting over lunch, a middle-aged Cherokee man told me, "When I was looking for a wife, I thought to myself, well, if she was Indian, but not Cherokee, that would be second best." Another young Cherokee woman shared this sentiment, saying, "My future husband, he doesn't have to be Cherokee, but he at least needs to be Indian. I want him to share the same interests." An older Cherokee woman lamented her daughter-in-law's identity, complaining that, "If she wasn't going to be Cherokee, I wanted her at least to be Indian, but she's not." Traditional Cherokees seem to recognize the distinct cultural differences between themselves and other Native Americans, but they also believe that other Native Americans are more tolerant of these differences than other racial groups, who would also be less likely to understand the social pulls of family and tribe. Consequently, race is an important consideration for traditional Cherokees looking outside the tribe for a spouse. For them, marrying Indian is the best option next to marrying Cherokee, because other Native Americans not only share common interests and experiences, but they also share a common Indian racial identity that can be passed on to children.[17] Traditional Cherokees prefer marriages with other Native Americans rather than with non-Indians because they consider blood-mixing between Cherokees and other Native Americans to be culture-mixing but not race-mixing. They believe that the offspring of a Cherokee/non-Cherokee Native-American marriage will have a secure racial identity as Indians, even though they will have to make a choice regarding their specific tribal identity and enrollment.[18]

But what if neither Cherokee nor Indian marriage partners are available? Then, traditional Cherokees must consider the option of marrying a non-Indian and having mixed-race children even though this is explicitly and implicitly discouraged in their communities. When traditional Cherokees are faced with this option, usually only after the search for a spouse among available Cherokees and other Indians has been exhausted, then a clear racial hierarchy emerges. For example, I asked an older Cherokee woman if marrying a Cherokee spouse had been an important consideration in the traditional community where she was raised. She told me bluntly, "It was promoted but not enforced that you marry into the tribe, that you marry a Cherokee. Beyond that you marry white. You don't marry black people and you don't marry Mexicans, because Mexicans are in the same class as blacks." Another Cherokee man described this same racial hierarchy in a slightly different way:

> Well, you know my wife . . . and I. My wife's full-blood and we'll be walking down the street and we'll see a white and black couple, and she will be offended by that. She thinks that's bad, and she thinks it's even worse when it's an Indian and black couple. She has this degree of badness. And, you know, I'll tell her what difference does it make if a white and a black come together, because they are not our people. Our people are the Cherokee. And I say, I'm a half-breed, my mother's white, my father Indian. Do you not think that's bad? And she says no, because we [Cherokees] are as good as the white people. We are as good. . . . That's such a bizarre concept to me [laughs]. I just don't understand it, but it's a response I probably couldn't understand, not being a full-blood . . . [to] some isolation or punishment that has been heaped on them [full-bloods] that I just can't conceptualize. Because being half white . . . trying to relate to that experience is real hard for me, so I really couldn't speak to that. But I think there's a lot of prejudice, a lot. But much of it is hard for people to define why they are prejudiced. And I don't think most people can. It's just a learned thing. They heard it in their family.

This quote reveals racial hegemony, the almost unconscious reproduction of the dominant U.S. racial hierarchy, within contemporary Cherokee kinship ideologies. For example, this man's wife associates different "degrees of badness" with different kinds of race-mixing, so that a black/Indian intermarriage is somehow "worse" than a white/Indian intermarriage. For her, a white/Indian marriage is socially acceptable, because Cherokees are equal in status to whites. As she puts it, they are "as good." What is even more interesting is the way this Cherokee man asserts the difference between himself and his wife as one of blood. He believes that he cannot understand his wife's attitudes about race-mixing, because as a "half-breed" he cannot relate to her life experiences as a full-blood.

As suggested by the previous two quotes, because of traditional Cherokees' internalization of a racially hegemonic system that assigns a higher status to white identity, they prefer to marry Euroamericans rather than other non-Indians. Other racialized groups are less preferable or even unacceptable marriage partners.[19] For instance, traditional Cherokees are reluctant to marry Mexican Americans not only because of their assumed racial differences but also because of the lower class status often associated with "Hispanic" identity. For example, when I asked a Cherokee man why traditional Cherokees were reluctant to marry Mexican Americans, he suggested the following:

> I think the prejudice against Mexicans is a prejudice of class, not of color . . . because of the type of work they do when they come over here—mainly nursery work or line work. They work in a lot of the plants. . . . Even though the Cherokees which live in some of these small rural communities are not educated and could work in some of those same kind of jobs, they have the same kind of attitude that most Americans have that, "that's not the kind of job that I want." And the Mexicans, "they can have that job." They [rural Cherokees] consider them to be a lower class, even though color-wise they are similar to us. Probably, genetically, they are related to us by their ancestry. So, I think it is a class distinction, not a color one.

Although he recognizes that Cherokees and Mexican Americans share a common indigenous ancestry, that they are phenotypically similar and perhaps even biologically related, this Cherokee man implies that marriages between the two groups are infrequent because of the local class standing assigned by Cherokees to Mexican Americans. Thus, it seems that for traditional Cherokees blood-mixing with Mexican Americans is not only race-mixing but also class-mixing. Since they believe that mixing of any sort is undesirable because it threatens the continued biological, racial, cultural, and national substance of Cherokee identity, then they try to limit Mexican-American/Cherokee intermarriages. In this case, we can see the articulation of race and class in Cherokee marriage preferences, but this is only one aspect of how racial hegemony, in a more encompassing sense, colors Cherokee marriage preferences.

While traditional Cherokees consider interracial marriages with Mexican Americans to be less preferable than those with Euroamericans, they are even more reluctant to intermarry with African Americans. In fact, because traditional Cherokees have internalized the same racial hegemony shared by many U.S. citizens of different racial and cultural backgrounds, they assign the lowest status to African Americans in general. During my fieldwork, I was often surprised and disheartened to hear traditional Cherokees describe African Americans in a manner similar to what I had heard growing up among southern whites. For instance, an older Cherokee woman who worked at the tribal complex told me, "Blacks and Cherokees, that's a very touchy subject. Most Cherokees feel like there shouldn't be intermingling between Cherokees and blacks. I don't know why that feeling is so strong, but it just seems like that with Cherokees that's a touchy subject." Another traditional Cherokee woman said, "With my daughter, she could marry a non-Indian, as long as they were Christian and could provide for her, but not black." She explained, "It's just the way that society is, the way that society would treat her if she did that. In Stilwell, there are no blacks. But I remember when I was a kid, about twelve or fourteen, that Stilwell would have its annual Strawberry Festival of the World, and my parents wouldn't let me go, because the blacks would be coming to town."[20] This suggests that while they may tolerate some types of race-mixing, many traditional Cherokees consider African Americans to be unacceptable marriage partners. In the case of this traditional Cherokee woman, the racial fears and divisions of her childhood extend to the present, so that she cannot accept the possibility of her daughter's marrying an African American. This racial attitude toward African Americans—that traditional Cherokees stigmatize them more than they do any other racial group—reveals how traditional Cherokees have internalized U.S. racial hierarchy and how this, in turn, has influenced their marriage preferences.

The bottom line is that if traditional Cherokees cannot practice tribal endogamy, then they prefer to marry other Native Americans, Euroamericans, Mexican Americans, and African Americans, in that order. These racial preferences mirror U.S. racial hierarchies, except in one regard: traditional Cherokees would rather practice racial endogamy with Native Americans of other tribes than marry a non-Indian, who might be assigned a higher social status in U.S. society in general. In this instance, maintaining a racial identity as Indian is more important than "marrying up." But if traditional Cherokees cannot marry within the race, then they prefer to marry as near the top of the racial hierarchy as possible. For this reason, when marrying non-Indians, traditional Cherokees are more likely to marry white than to marry black. But traditional Cherokees may also prefer to marry white because, as one middle-aged Cherokee man told me, "Cherokees think white is neutral." Since Cherokees tend to see "whiteness" as a culturally and racially "empty" category, while seeing "blackness" as culturally and racially "full," then they may also prefer to marry whites rather than blacks to avoid the stigma associated with what would be a more socially marked instance of racial and cultural mixing.

CONCLUSION: KINSHIP, RACE,
POWER, AND IDEOLOGY

In this chapter, I have tried to demonstrate how kinship is a site where racial ideologies are negotiated and reproduced in the construction of Cherokee identity. Cherokee kinship is not an innocent cultural system but one where ideologies of race align with power in distinct ways.[21] As we have seen, among traditional Cherokees, marriage preferences and practices are deeply embedded in competing blood/kin ideologies. These ideologies include: (1) a preference for tribal and racial endogamy to preserve national, racial, and cultural substance; (2) a preference, in most cases, to marry individuals with higher degrees of Cherokee blood to maintain high degrees of Cherokee blood in future offspring; and (3) a preference for clan exogamy, for finding a Cherokee spouse of a mat-rilineal clan different from one's own. However, these preferences often come into conflict with the Cherokee practice of reckoning genealogi-cally distant kin and the Cherokee adoption of a bilateral descent sys-tem. These competing, even contradictory, blood and kin ideologies make it increasingly difficult for traditional Cherokees to practice tribal endogamy without marrying kin. Although many traditional Cherokees still manage to negotiate this complex ideological terrain, others find themselves marrying outside the tribe, and as they do so, a clear racial hierarchy has emerged in traditional Cherokee marriage preferences. For a traditional Cherokee, the first preference after a Cherokee spouse is to practice racial endogamy by marrying a Native American from an-other tribe. But if faced with racial exogamy, then traditional Cherokees reproduce the dominant U.S. racial hierarchy.

As these marriage preferences and practices show, traditional Cher-okee kinship systems and dominant racial ideologies are so imbricated in one another that traditional Cherokees evaluate their marriage choices in racial terms without even consciously thinking of race. The fact that traditional Cherokee marriage preferences are racially hierar-chic and racially constituted is an instance in which racial hegemonies have become highly naturalized, almost to the level of Bordieuian "doxa," so that it is rarely subject to any contestation (Bourdieu 1977: 164). At the same time, the interpenetration of kinship and racial ide-ologies in traditional Cherokee marriage preferences demonstrates how ideology, which is expressed at the discursive level, has tangible, mate-rial, and in this case, even genealogical effects.[22] As a result, competing blood/kin ideologies shape the Cherokee national, social, and racial body in concrete ways.

As this chapter has shown, one of the ways in which ideologies constitute the Cherokee social body is in the reproduction of a dominant U.S. racial hierarchy in the marriage preferences of traditional Cherokees faced with racial exogamy. Because traditional Cherokees associate race-, culture-, and class-mixing with the erosion of their national substance, they express what might be called a moral obligation to pick the right kind of kin, to place a priority on maintaining racial, cultural, and national identity by marrying Indian as a first marriage preference. If an Indian spouse is not an option, then Cherokees feel a need to improve the blood, or their national substance, in some other fashion. In the racial hierarchy of the United States, where certain racial groups are assigned more sociopolitical power and status than others, traditional Cherokees tend to choose their non-Indian marriage partners from the top of the hierarchy without even expressing conscious intent, though their parents and grandparents, interestingly enough, seem quite explicit about the racial pecking order.

The interconnection of kinship, race, and power has become a part of Cherokee national culture, just as it is a part of U.S. national culture. But this is more than the simple reproduction of racial hegemony; the particulars of Cherokee national substance and race relations within the tribe have their own specific historical and even ideological trajectory. For instance, because white-Cherokees have historically been imbued with a higher class standing and with greater degrees of political power, contemporary intermarriages between traditional Cherokees and white-Cherokees are far more socially accepted than those between Cherokees and black-Cherokees or freedmen. Nonetheless, Cherokee attitudes against race-mixing with African Americans in general warrant further explanation. I explore them in the next chapter, where I trace the little-known twentieth-century political history of the Cherokee freedmen.

CHAPTER SEVEN

Challenging the Color Line

*The Trials and Tribulations
of the Cherokee Freedmen*

Point. Click. The newly arrived messages roll across her computer screen. In her small room in Tahlequah, Oklahoma, she sits on the edge of her seat, squinting at the rapid-fire procession of names and subjects. She takes a deep breath, feeling anxious and impatient, as she experiments with her research methods, trying to use electronic mail to correspond with Cherokees outside of Oklahoma. As she lets the shades down to get rid of the glare on her monitor, she wonders if anyone will respond to her survey, if they will feel comfortable with the format, if anthropological fieldwork via the internet isn't a bit ridiculous. After all, she moved to the Cherokee Nation to work in this particular community, and now here she is, trying to breach those same confines, sending messages and surveys to Cherokees in every state in the Union. Finally, she sits and begins to pore over the names one by one, exhaling audibly as she realizes that, yes, a few people have responded.

One name she immediately recognizes as that of a Cherokee freedman, one of the many phenotypically black descendants of Cherokee slave-owners and their African slaves.[1] They had spoken on the phone several days ago, and at that time he had suggested that she send him some questions. So she moves the cursor to his name and opens the file, eagerly scanning his responses. Something about question thirteen must have resonated with him, or maybe it was simply the chance to shape her work on this topic. She had asked, "What do you think I should write about?"

His answer was long and impassioned. "I think you should write about the racism that permeates these Indian programs [tribal benefits and who qualifies for them]. And point out that many of the so-called Indians running the Oklahoma tribes are exclusive if the hyphenated Indian is black and inclusive if the hyphenated Indian is white. I think you should go back to the Dawes process and point out how degree of Indian blood was ignored among black people just as degree of European blood did not and does not today affect one's status if one is black. I think you need to argue that these programs need to be made realistic. . . . It is ridiculous to allow white people to take advantage of Indian programs because they have some long lost relative who was classified as an Indian, having some Indian blood on a tribal roll 100 years ago, when a black person who suffers infinitely more discrimination and needs the aid more, is denied it because his Indian ancestry is overshadowed by his African ancestry. Few Blacks are 100 percent African, and to be frank about it, few Europeans whose ancestors come from the South are 100 percent European. . . . Either the descendants of freedmen should be allowed to take advantage of benefits, or the federal government, not these cliquish tribes, should set new standards for who is an Indian—and save itself some money."

While this statement might be considered angry or even inflammatory in Cherokee County, Oklahoma, much of it is also supported by the historical record and my own ethnographic observations. The Cherokee freedmen continue to be one of the most marginalized groups in Native North America, and their story has never received the attention it deserves, in part because many people would prefer that it remain buried. To understand how this came to be, I have sought to unearth contemporary perspectives of freedmen like the one above and to situate them within the local political dynamics of the Cherokee Nation. Only then can we fully comprehend the social and political construction of Cherokee identity.

At the center of the story of Cherokee identity and experience is an absence, an exclusion, a silence where the Cherokee freedmen might have been. The reason for this absence is clear. When Cherokee citizens conflate blood, color, race, and culture to demarcate their sociopolitical community, they often exclude multiracial individuals of Cherokee and African ancestry, who are treated in both discourse and practice in qualitatively different ways than multiracial individuals with Cherokee and white ancestry. As I discussed earlier, this bias against African ancestry has a long history rooted in the practice of plantation slavery among certain sectors of the Cherokee population. African slavery is the most extreme example of the influence of Euroamerican racism on Cherokee attitudes and practices. However, centuries of social, political, and economic relations with Euroamericans also engendered color-prejudice among the Cherokees, a legacy that means, among other things, that Cherokee identity politics has never been simply a question of blood or culture. This prejudice comes into high relief when we consider the situation of multiracial Cherokees with black ancestry. Cherokee freedmen who choose to identify as both Indian and black challenge the prevailing racial ideologies that ask us to choose one racial or ethnic identity, often at the expense of another.

To understand how racial ideologies constrain the multiracial identities of the Cherokee freedmen, it is necessary to examine the historical process of "racial formation" and the ways in which historically situated "racial projects" give rise to local expressions of contradictory consciousness and racial hegemony (Omi and Winant 1994: 55–61). To that end, I have used a variety of sources, including contemporary interviews, field notes, tribal and federal court documents, and other archival records to trace the Cherokee freedmen's legal and political struggles to gain recognition as Cherokee citizens over the past century and a half. Interweaving ethnohistory, legal history, and ethnography, I follow this largely untold story into the present, focusing on how ideologies of race and culture affect the identity formation and the social and legal classification of multiracial Native-and-African-American people.

"A JUDICIAL JUNGLE": THE HISTORICAL AND LEGAL ORIGINS OF THE FREEDMEN CONTROVERSY

Contemporary expressions of contradictory consciousness and racial hegemony among Cherokees reveal the human side of a painful history of racial irresolution originating in the Cherokee adoption of African slavery. Although slavery no longer existed as a legal institution within the Cherokee Nation after the Civil War, its legacy of socioeconomic inequality and political factionalism endured (Perdue 1979: 140). As I described in chapter 3, the Cherokee Nation signed a reconstruction treaty with the United States on July 19, 1866, amid great internal controversy. That treaty extended Cherokee citizenship and "all the rights of Native Cherokees" to the freedmen and their descendents (Wardell 1977: 225). Despite the promises of this treaty, the freedmen were never fully accepted as citizens of the Cherokee Nation, and Cherokees to this day remain divided over the political status of their former slaves.

In an attempt to solidify their own economic and political interests, in 1883 the Cherokee tribal council passed legislation that excluded the freedmen and other tribal citizens without Cherokee blood, such as the Shawnees, Delawares, and intermarried whites, from sharing in tribal assets. In response, the federal government took an increasingly active role in issues related to Cherokee citizenship. As noted in chapter three, Congress responded in 1888 with legislation that required the tribe to share its assets equally with the freedmen and other adopted citizens (25 Stat. at L. 608–609). To determine the number of eligible freedmen and provide for their equitable treatment, Congress sent a federal agent to make a full record of all those who were entitled to share in the dispersal of federal funds within the Cherokee Nation. By 1889, the agent had enrolled 3,524 freedmen in a document that came to be known as the Wallace Roll (Sampson 1972: 126; 25 Stat. at L. 980, 994 [1889]). Although the federal government had created other tribal rolls before and after it, the Wallace roll appeared at time when tribal rolls were linked increasingly to the distribution of economic resources. Quite simply, by the last decade of the nineteenth century, only Cherokee individuals whose names appeared on federal rolls could receive the financial benefits of being Cherokee, at least as far as the federal government was concerned (Hill 1997: 160).

In 1889 with the completion of the Wallace Roll, 3,524 Cherokee freedmen could point to a new federal document to legitimate their claims to Cherokee citizenship, but the Cherokee Nation continued to resist their efforts. Finally, in 1890 the U.S. Congress authorized the federal court of claims to adjudicate the just rights of the Cherokee freedmen (26 Stat. at L. 636). In *Whitmire v. Cherokee Nation and United States*, the court argued that while the tribal council could sell the common property of the tribe, it could not discriminate against a particular class of citizens in deciding who was entitled to share in the proceeds (30 Ct. Clms. 138 [1895]); *R. H. Nero, et al. v. Cherokee Nation of Oklahoma, et al.*). Ruling in favor of the freedmen, the court awarded them $903,365 as their rightful share of $7,240,000 that had been generated from the sale of tribal lands.

The promise of a substantial financial settlement must have raised the spirits of the freedmen fighting for equal treatment from the Cherokee Nation, but disappointment was just around the corner. According to the Cherokee Nation, the entire $7,240,000 had already been distributed to Cherokees by blood, leaving not a dollar for the freedmen (Sampson 1972: 126). As codefendant in the *Whitmire* case, the U.S. government was now responsible for the $903,365 the freedmen had been awarded. Rather than simply compensating the freedmen, the federal government insisted on a new roll to determine eligibility for payment. Some observers might have looked to the recently completed Wallace Roll, but the court chose to ignore it for reasons that have never quite been explained (Sampson 1972: 126). As a result, in 1896 the secretary of the interior generated a brand new list of 5,600 eligible freedmen in what would come to be known as the Kern-Clifton Roll (Littlefield 1978: 148; 10 Ind. Cl. Comm. 117–18 [1961]). These freedmen were now able to receive their portion of tribal funds in accordance with the *Whitmire* ruling, although the dispersal took much of the subsequent decade. With money in their pockets, the freedmen could finally put aside years of legal squabbling and enjoy a brief moment in which their treaty rights seemed secure.

During this same period at the end of the nineteenth century, the groundwork was also being laid for what would amount to a political coup against Native sovereignty throughout the United States. As I described in chapter 3, under the Dawes Act of 1887, Congress adopted a policy of converting tribal lands to individual ownership, hoping this would assimilate Native Americans, diminish their land base, and free the residual land for white settlement. The assumption was that if Indian Territory were to become an American state filled with "civilized" citizens, as many white settlers hoped, then the allotment of tribal land to individual Indians was the logical first step. For six years, the Cherokee Nation and the other Five Civilized Tribes within Indian Territory were not subject to the Dawes Act, but all that changed with the passage of the Indian Appropriations Act on March 3, 1893. In that same year, the Dawes Commission was created to negotiate with the Five Tribes for the purpose of extinguishing tribal title to their lands.

For this purpose the Dawes Commission required yet another roll, and after three years of political resistance on the part of the tribal governments (1893–1896), the commission began taking oral and written testimony from applicants for tribal enrollment. The final rolls of the Five Tribes were to list newborns, minors, and adults in three racial categories—freedmen, intermarried whites, and Indians by blood, with only the latter specifying an Indian blood quantum. Sensing an opportunity to reverse the inroads the freedmen were making in the courts, the Cherokee Nation attempted to frustrate the enrollment of the freedmen, who may have been citizens by law but were not accepted in the minds of the majority of Cherokees (Wardell 1977: 237). Over 53,000 people applied for enrollment in the Cherokee tribe, and when the count was finalized, there were 41,798 enrolled citizens of the Cherokee Nation, 4,924 of them freedmen (Littlefield 1978: 238). Many of these freedmen enrollees had appeared on the Kern-Clifton Roll six years earlier that listed 5,600 freedmen. Of those 5,600 individuals named on the Kern-Clifton roll, however, 1,659 are missing from the Dawes Commission roll of 1902 (Sampson 1972: 128). These excluded individuals, whose absence will be explained below, would later bring their case to court and seek the benefits of Cherokee citizenship (10 Ind. Cl. Comm. 109 [1961]; 161 C. Clms. 787 [1963]; 13 Ind. Cl. Comm. 33 [1964]).

To expedite the process of allotment and to squash tribal resistance, Congress enacted the Curtis Act in 1898, before the Dawes Rolls were even completed. Now the Dawes Commission could proceed with allotment without the consent of the tribal governments, though this was not the Curtis Act's only horrible blow to tribal sovereignty. It also extended the jurisdiction of the federal courts over Indian Territory, abolished the tribal courts, authorized the incorporation of towns and town lots for survey and sale, and allowed the federal government to assume the collection of taxes from white citizens of Indian Nations (Sampson 1972: 128). Soon after the passage of the Curtis Act, the Dawes Commission completed its work, and in 1902 the final rolls of the Cherokee Nation were closed.

The rolls listed many, though far from all, Cherokee freedmen who received allotments on the basis of their inclusion in the document. By 1907, the same year the Cherokee Nation was dissolved and Oklahoma became a state, 4,208 Cherokee freedmen Dawes enrollees had received land allotments, and another 749 freedmen minors were tentatively slated to become property owners as well (Littlefield 1978: 238). The freedmen might have finally been accepted as full citizens, but allotment often brought a new slate of troubles. In an interview in 1996, Idella Ball, a ninety-nine-year-old original-Dawes-Roll freedmen enrollee explained the situation:

IB: When black people started to own property and land then the whites undermined them, too. I had got property in Fort Gibson and a small piece of oil land in Nowata County, about fifteen acres. But the taxes were about to eat it up. So, I was gonna sell five acres to clear up the taxes, and this white man he bought it and beat me out of all fifteen.

CS: You mean you thought you were selling off just five and he took the whole thing?

IB: Yes! He put on the paper fifteen instead of five and I signed.

CS: But you could read. You didn't see it?

IB: That's exactly how they got me, sure I can read, but I didn't know nothing about business and all. I just signed the papers and that was it.

What Ball describes is well documented in the work of Angie Debo, *And Still the Waters Run* (1940). In her classic book Debo demonstrates how those who received allotments were subject to the manipulations of white "grafters," whose greed led them to take advantage of freedmen and Native-American ignorance regarding the rapidly shifting system of land title in Oklahoma. The grafters were so successful that by 1930 the Five-Tribes Indians owned less than 2 million acres of land (Debo 1940: 379), down from a total of 19,525,966 acres in 1890 (Strickland and Strickland 1991: 124).[3]

Violence against African Americans also became more common at the turn of the century, not relenting until the late 1920s, when much of their land was gone (May 1996: 245). In the first decade of the 1900s, several race riots occurred: four in Creek Nation towns and at least one in the Cherokee Nation town of Bartlesville. The most infamous race riot occurred in Tulsa in 1921, when dozens of African Americans were massacred while prominent black communities and business burned to the ground (Ellsworth 1982). Soon thereafter martial law was declared against the Ku Klux Klan's open terrorism in eastern Oklahoma (May 1996: 245). Despite increased violence during the first three decades of the twentieth century, new freedmen citizens on the whole fared better than they had in the antebellum Cherokee Nation. Ever since allotment, they had increased civil rights and were able to get access to the Cherokee courts, sit on juries, serve as elected officials, have some security in their improvements, and enjoy limited school facilities (Littlefield 1978: 249).

But what happened to those 1,659 Cherokee Freedmen who never received allotments, who had been on the Kern-Clifton Roll but were excluded from the Dawes Roll? It appears that the majority of these individuals did not meet the residency requirements set forth by the

Figure 22.   High school built by the Cherokee Nation for the freedmen and their descendents in 1889 for $10,000.00. Located at Double Springs, six miles northwest of Tahlequah, Oklahoma. Burned in 1916. Courtesy of the University Archives, John Vaughn Library, Northeastern State University, Tahlequah, Oklahoma.

Dawes Commission. Either they were no longer citizens because they had not been in Indian Territory during the Civil War, or they were "too lates" who had not returned to the Cherokee Nation within the six-month period set forth by the Treaty of 1866 (Sampson 1972: 128). In 1909 these disgruntled Cherokee freedmen, most of whom lived just outside the boundaries of the Cherokee Nation, filed a supplemental petition in *Whitmire v. United States* (44 Ct. Clms. 453) to test the right of the Dawes Commission to deny them enrollment. The United States was the only defendant because the Cherokee Nation was not held responsible for the actions of the Dawes Commission (Sampson 1972: 129). In the same year the United States Court of Claims ruled in favor of the freedmen, but by 1912 the Cherokee Nation had joined the United States in an appeal to the Supreme Court, which reversed the decision (Sampson 1972: 129, *Cherokee Nation v. Whitmire*, 223 U.S. 108).

The Cherokee Nation continued its quest to restrict the freedmen's property rights and to limit the extent of their citizenship. In 1924, using the Supreme Court's *Whitmire* decision as a precedent, Congress passed a jurisdictional act allowing the Cherokees to file suit against the United States to recover money that had been paid to the Kern-Clifton freedmen. The Cherokee Nation alleged that the United States had diverted to non-Indians and non-tribal members settlement money that actually belonged to the tribe (Sampson 1972: 130). It was not until 1937 that the court of claims reached a decision denying recovery by the Cherokee Nation. The court held that the Kern-Clifton Roll was a one-time-only distribution roll that had served its purpose, and that its validity ceased with the 1894 distribution. Thus, it would not affect future rolls or distributions of the Cherokee Nation in any way (Sampson 1972: 130; *Cherokee Nation v. United States,* 85 Ct. Clms. 76 [1937]).

The Kern-Clifton freedmen applicants who were denied Dawes enrollment were not satisfied with this ruling but had few options left. Nine years later, however, in 1946 the Indian Claims Commission Act was passed, and it stirred activity among people claiming to be descendants of the 1,659 Kern-Clifton freedmen who were denied tribal citizenship. In Kansas and Oklahoma, an organization called the Cherokee Freedmen's Association (CFA) came into being sometime in the late 1940s. The CFA membership included a diverse gathering of about 110 blacks who could show descendency from the Wallace, Kern-Clifton, or Dawes Commission Rolls. Their goals were to secure political and economic rights that they felt the federal and tribal governments had erroneously denied to their members. They collected dues, gathered documentation, and hired a lawyer. On June 13, 1951, they filed their first petition with the Indian Claims Commission in Tulsa, Oklahoma (Docket 123), though the commission did not actually begin to hear the case until early November 1960. Even then, the commissioners had to make numerous inquiries regarding past litigation to grasp the "judicial jungle," as one writer described it in the *Tulsa Tribune* on November 12, 1960. While the case was still in litigation in 1961, the Cherokee Nation received a $14.7 million settlement from the United States as payment for the Cherokee Outlet nonreservation lands in north-central Oklahoma. The members of the CFA took notice of their prospective share of the money, but their hopes were dashed when the Indian Claims Commission denied their collective claim to tribal citizenship on December 28, 1961 (Sampson 1972: 131). The commission decided that the freedmen's claims were individual in nature and that it had no jurisdiction over them.

The CFA appealed the decision in the United States Court of Claims, contending that they were entitled to share in the funds paid to the Cherokee Nation because of their 1866 Treaty-based citizenship rights. They asserted that their treaty rights superseded the Dawes Commission rolls, which were created for the sole purpose of allotment and not other tribal matters. Nonetheless, the court of claims affirmed the findings of the Indian Claims Commission on two grounds. First, the freedmen's claims were individual and would require a case-by-case examination. However, this was made impossible by the court's second ground that the claims were no longer subject to consideration since they had already been adjudicated when the Supreme Court had denied their claim to citizenship in the 1912 *Whitmire* case (Sampson 1972: 132). However, the court of claims realized that some new considerations had been raised and suggested that the freedmen intervene in the remaining portion of the Cherokee Outlet case before the Indian Claims Commission (Sampson 1972: 131–32).

On November 12, 1964, the Indian Claims Commission granted the CFA's request, allowing them to intervene in Docket No. 173-A, but the outcome was the same as it had been in 1961. The Indian Claims Commission determined that it did not have jurisdiction over the freedmen matter at hand, although this time for different reasons. First, the distribution of an award was a political question that needed to be settled by Congress and not by the commission. Second, membership in a tribe was a political controversy to be resolved by the tribe as a fundamental attribute of sovereignty. Finally, the commission had no jurisdiction over intratribal disputes, whether they were between two separate tribes or between two factions within a single tribe (Sampson 1972: 133; 22 Ind. Cl. Comm. 417–20 [1971]). The freedmen made a last-ditch appeal to the court of claims in 1971, but the court quickly affirmed the Indian Claims Commission's 1964 decision. After twenty years of legal struggle and few victories, the Cherokee Freedmen's Association finally laid their case to rest with nothing to show for their efforts.

Even in denying the freedmen's claims, the courts had treated them in a way that suggested the potential validity of their quest for citizenship in the Cherokee Nation. From the beginning, the CFA's claims to citizenship were challenged on the grounds that most of them were not on the Dawes Rolls, which was considered the final authority on who was and who was not a Cherokee citizen, regardless of race. Yet the Indian Claims Commission ruled in part that it had no jurisdiction over the freedmen case because the conflict was an internal tribal matter. This assertion seems to assume that the freedmen had some legitimate claim or were seen in the eyes of the court as possibly falling within the margins of Cherokee citizenship. In fact, thirteen years later a group of elderly freedmen, most original Dawes enrollees, would bring the question of their citizenship rights to trial again. But this time, the legal arguments would change dramatically, sometimes in complete opposition to statements made in earlier cases, and charges of racial discrimination would become a central focus of the litigation. These people were undeniably legitimate Cherokee freedmen listed on the Dawes Rolls, but the question was whether they and their descendants continued to have "all the rights of native Cherokees" as they had been promised in the treaty of 1866.

BREACHING THE DAWES ROLLS:
THE STRANGE CASE OF THE REVEREND ROGER NERO

On June 18, 1983, the Reverend Roger H. Nero and four other Cherokee freedmen went to the Muskogee courthouse to cast their votes in the Cherokee Nation's elections for principal chief. These Dawes enrollees had received allotments and shares in at least two cash land settlements over the past twenty years. When Congress finally had given the tribe back the right to elect its own officials in 1970, these descendants of black-Cherokee slaves had voted in the first tribal elections (*Baltimore Sun,* July 29, 1984). Cherokee freedmen occasionally received certain educational and housing benefits but had not been allowed health care and most federal benefits granted to other tribal members. Their treatment by the tribe had always been inconsistent, yet Nero and his companions were shocked when Cherokee election officials turned them away from the polls in 1983, saying freedmen no longer had the right to vote.

The justification for this denial was based on blood. In an unpublished interview, Ross Swimmer, chief of the Cherokee Nation (1975–85), stated that five years earlier in 1977–78 both the voter registration committee and the tribal membership registration committee had established new rules. These rules declared that according to the new Cherokee Constitution of 1976, an individual must have a certificate degree of Indian blood (CDIB) to be registered as a tribal citizen or voter (interview by D. Goodwin, 1984).[4] However, the 1976 Cherokee Constitution specifies in Section 1 of Article 3, "All members of the Cherokee Nation must be citizens as proven by reference to the Dawes Commission Rolls." As mentioned earlier, the Dawes Rolls were divided into separate categories for Cherokees by blood, freedmen, and intermarried whites. Presumably, a descendent of any of these three groups would be eligible for tribal citizenship, since the 1976 Cherokee Constitution refers only to the Dawes Rolls and does not limit tribal membership to Cherokees by blood.

This inclusive reading of the rolls would seem to open the door to the Cherokee freedmen, but in practice the Cherokee Nation grants citizenship only to lineal descendants of Cherokees by blood listed on the Dawes Rolls. When applying for tribal membership, individuals must simultaneously apply for a CDIB.[5] If individuals are able to document through state and federal records that they are direct descendents of a Cherokee by blood on the Dawes Rolls, then Cherokee blood quantum is assigned and tribal membership is automatic. To most contemporary Cherokees, blood has become a potent hegemonic construct, a symbolic medium uniting all Cherokees to one another. Cherokee blood, in part, defines "Cherokeeness" and anyone without Cherokee blood would automatically fall outside the boundaries of the Cherokee community. For this reason, Cherokee tribal leaders deny freedmen's claims to Cherokee citizenship. For example, in 1984 Wilma Mankiller, then deputy chief to Ross Swimmer, said that the freedmen, "should not be given membership in the Cherokee tribe. That is for people with Cherokee blood." And tribal member Jimmy Phillips said, "Whether they are white, black or red, if they've got the blood then they are tribal members. Without it . . . no" (*Baltimore Sun*, July 29, 1984).

When the Cherokee Nation reorganized its government between 1970 and 1976, the resulting changes in blood legislation had important implications for the freedmen and for race relations within the tribe. During that period, the freedmen were quietly disenfranchised and denied their rights to citizenship. Paradoxically, at the same time these rights were extended to tribal members with minimal Cherokee blood. In December 1977, the tribe successfully challenged the one-quarter blood quantum limitation for Indian health services. A variety of new economic incentives, including free health care, lured many long-assimilated white-Cherokees to return to the tribal fold. As a result, in the decade between 1970 and 1980 the Cherokee Nation became progressively whiter at the same time that it rid itself of most of its black citizens.

These changes occurred without the knowledge or input of the Cherokee freedmen. When the Reverend Roger Nero and his companions went to vote in the Cherokee elections in 1983, they found that the definition of a Cherokee citizen had been changed to exclude them, which came as a surprise since Nero had voted in the last tribal election in 1979. What had happened between 1979 and 1983? According to Chief Ross Swimmer, the tribal election committee attempted to use the CDIB to determine eligibility to vote as early as 1975. But the committee had soon realized that the CDIBs were unreliable since the whole process of application had been mishandled under the BIA. Many people had simply purchased membership within the Cherokee Nation or had provided a Dawes Roll number that was not verified through any other documentation. In 1975 the tribe began to purge its rolls and to take control over the certification process. Still struggling to straighten out the mess, the tribe decided the election of 1979 would be the last in which people with old registration cards could vote. Ostensibly, this is why Nero could vote in 1979 but was turned away in 1983.

This heightened sense of blood as the primary basis of Cherokee national identity began to take hold as early as 1975. Yet only one year before, on October 8, 1974, Chief Swimmer wrote in a letter regarding freedmen eligibility for public health service benefits to Jack Ellison, area director of the BIA in Muskogee:

> I have been advised by the local Health Service unit that the BIA does not recognize enrolled Freedmen for benefits and that this is carried over to IHS [Indian Health Services]. . . . The IHS says they cannot participate . . . because the people are Freedmen instead of Indians. It would appear that since the government had us include Freedmen on our rolls they should be entitled to similar benefits of other enrolled Indians. I can understand the blood-quantum problem, but again it would appear that the Freedmen would be taken as a class and would have the same status as 1/4 blood.

Surprisingly, this letter demonstrates that in 1974 the principal chief of the Cherokee Nation viewed the freedmen as citizens and argued that they were eligible for the same benefits given other enrolled Cherokees. But federal benefits come with strings attached to federally imposed, racially discriminatory policies. Between 1975 and 1983, the Cherokee Nation increasingly began to administer to its own members. When the Cherokee Nation began processing applications for CDIBs and tribal membership, it had to conform to federal standards. As a result, in its own blood-based policies of administration, the Cherokee Nation reproduced many of the racial ideologies that lay at the base of federal Indian policy.

These administrative changes did not come into being without struggle. The Cherokee Nation shifted its stance back and forth, contradicting its own newly derived policies. In 1983 the Cherokee election committee decided to waive the CDIB requirement for any original enrollee, including freedmen and intermarried whites (Ross Swimmer, interview by David Goodwin, 1984). In a similar vein, federal administrators also debated whether the freedmen were eligible to participate in Cherokee elections. On April 21, 1983, the Muskogee area director of the BIA wrote a memorandum to the deputy assistant secretary of Indian affairs. He stated that according to his interpretation of the Cherokee Constitution, "the Freedmen, who have rights of Cherokee citizenship, but who do not possess any degree of Cherokee blood, would not be eligible to participate as candidates, but would be eligible to vote." Therefore, according to the Cherokee election committee's new policy regarding original enrollees and federal interpretations of the Cherokee Constitution, Nero and any other Cherokee freedmen listed on the Dawes Commission rolls should have been permitted to vote in the 1983 elections.

Yet the fact remains that Nero and other freedmen were turned away at the polls because of the race-based assumption that they had no Cherokee blood and thus did not have rights to tribal citizenship. This set the stage for freedmen resistance, as the freedmen could not believe that blood had become the main criteria for Cherokee citizenship. As Nero put it, "We weren't allowed to vote because we were freedmen. They said that we didn't have Cherokee blood, but when I was born my birth certificate said that I was declared a citizen of the Cherokee Nation" (*Tahlequah Daily Press*, June 21, 1984). He also said, "We had a guarantee we'd have the same rights as the Indian as long as the water flowed and the grass growed. Well, it's still flowing and growing" (*Baltimore Sun*, July 29, 1984). Angered by the delegitimization of his lifelong identification as a black-Cherokee citizen, Nero began to stir up resistance among freedmen original enrollees and their descendants living in the Fort Gibson area near Muskogee, Oklahoma. His cause was aided by his calling: he was a prominent Baptist preacher who spent much of his time traveling from congregation to congregation.

On July 7, 1983, Nero and five other original enrollees filed a letter of complaint with the Civil Rights Division of the Department of Justice. It stated that, because they had been denied the right to vote, their civil rights had been violated and that it was "humiliating, embarrassing and degrading of Freedmen, such as ourselves, to be treated as second class tribal citizens." And then, one year from the date they were denied the

Figure 23.   Rare photograph of the Reverend Roger H. Nero. Fort Gibson,
Oklahoma, 1984. Courtesy of *The Baltimore Sun.*

right to vote, on June 18, 1984, Nero and sixteen other freedmen plaintiffs filed a class-action suit against Chief Swimmer, the tribal registrar,
a tribal council member, the tribal election committee, the United States,
the Office of the President, the Department of the Interior, the Office of
the Secretary of State, the Bureau of Indian Affairs, and three BIA em-
ployees. They complained that they had been denied the right to vote
and tribal benefits from federal funds because their lack of verifiable

Cherokee blood prevented them from obtaining registration cards. Because the Cherokee Constitution also restricts office holding to members of the tribe with Cherokee blood, the freedmen alleged that the tribe had systematically discriminated against them on the basis of race.

These legal actions were the culmination of the long-term frustration of the freedmen, who with only minor exceptions had been treated as an invisible faction within the Cherokee Nation for decades. At one point, Nero said, "We are not using any hatred or trying to put the Council in misery by our actions. All we are trying to do is fight for our rights. We want them to see us" (*The Oklahoma Eagle,* July 5, 1984). The freedmen sought almost $750 million in compensatory and punitive damages and wanted the Cherokee election to be declared null and void. This last request seems to suggest, in part, that the freedmen may have been, consciously or not, political pawns in an ongoing conflict between Ross Swimmer and Perry Wheeler, another candidate for chief. In the 1983 election for principal chief and deputy chief, Ross Swimmer and Wilma Mankiller ran on a ticket against Perry Wheeler and Agnes Cowen. At the polls, Wheeler received 3,300 votes to Swimmer's 2,437. But on the strength of a large absentee vote, Swimmer came back to win the election by fewer than 500 votes (*The Washington Post,* December 2, 1983). The race was so close that Wheeler and Cowen demanded a recount, stoking the fires of controversy. The subsequent recount prompted Cowen to say, "I have never seen such a farce. They had ballots strewn all over the world. They had them open. They didn't know which came from which county. It looked like a bunch of kids playing mudpies" (*The Washington Post,* December 2, 1983). Wheeler, Cowen, and their attorney, L. V. Watkins, brought their case before the Cherokee judicial appeals tribunal and the U.S. district court. They alleged that the election proceedings were corrupt on several counts and that the freedmen were disenfranchised from voting because they were Wheeler party allies. Although their case was defeated in both tribal and federal venues, the freedmen continued to fight, and L. V. Watkins brought the situation to the attention of Tulsa attorney Jim Goodwin, a prominent African-American leader in the city. Goodwin became the attorney for the freedmen and used their case as an opportunity to raise the charges of election fraud again.

When the Nero case came under public scrutiny, Ross Swimmer was particularly sensitive to the allegation that he and the tribe had discriminated against the freedmen on the basis of race. In self-defense, he stated that, according to the Cherokee Constitution,

To run for office you must be a Cherokee by blood. I can't argue with that. I think it means what it says. The President of the US must be a natural born citizen. Even a German immigrant or Spanish immigrant . . . who goes before the judge and is naturalized as an American citizen and has all the rights of an American citizen can never be the President of the US, because the Constitution specifically requires that the President of the US must be an American by blood. . . . The Cherokee Nation, good, bad or otherwise, specifically says that to be an elected official you must be a Cherokee by blood. . . . The best evidence . . . has been a Certificate of Degree of Indian Blood. . . . We provide services from the federal government using the federal government's guidelines. . . . Every program we get comes from the federal government and it comes with strings attached. (Interview by David Goodwin, 1984)

This statement is a good example of contradictory consciousness at work in the Cherokee Nation, even at the highest level of political power. Chief Swimmer conflates place of birth and nationality with blood, a hegemonic construction, but he uses this hegemonic argument to buttress his political stance and manipulate racial hegemony until it becomes political ideology.

In the same interview Chief Swimmer also stated that the freedmen should have first tried to seek a tribal remedy by bringing their case to the Cherokee judicial appeals tribunal. "This class of freedmen have said we're not going to give the tribunal an opportunity to address it. We're just going to go to federal court and the heck with you all. Which I think is a little unfair. . . . They [the tribunal] could have very easily made a decision. The Constitution of 1975 did include descendants of freedmen." That the freedmen had failed to exhaust their tribal remedies before taking their case to federal court would become the first line of defense in the legal arguments of the Cherokee Nation against Nero.

On July 10, 1984, the Cherokee Nation filed a motion to dismiss the suit, and various federal defendants quickly followed suit with their own motion to dismiss on August 28, 1984. The Cherokee Nation argued that the court had no jurisdiction over the matter at hand without congressional authorization, and that they were immune from suit according to the Indian Civil Rights Act, premised in part on sovereign immunity, a keystone of American-Indian law. They asserted that their right to determine tribal membership was a fundamental attribute of sovereignty, even if the basis of exclusion or inclusion was deemed unconstitutionally discriminatory. The Cherokee Nation maintained that the only hope was for the freedmen to bring their case before the Cherokee judicial appeals tribunal in Tahlequah, Oklahoma. Furthermore they argued that the case at hand was an intratribal political dispute and not a question for the courts. Congress might deem at some future date that the freedmen had legal rights to some tribal assets because of the Treaty of 1866, but the Cherokee Nation continued to assert that the freedmen had no political rights as tribal members (892 F. 2d. 1457–60, 1463 [10th Cir. 1989]; *Nero v. Cherokee Nation*, Defendant's Reply Brief 1986b: 8–12).

The freedmen countered these claims by arguing that to bring their case before the Cherokee tribunal would be an exercise in futility. In the earlier Wheeler controversy, L. V. Watkins had brought the freedmen issue before the tribal court, and the charges had been summarily dismissed. Furthermore, the freedmen believed that the entire machinery of the Cherokee elections had been compromised and that under the influence of the current Cherokee administration they could not get a fair hearing. Because their civil rights had been violated, the freedmen argued that their case belonged in the federal courts. They also alleged that the Cherokee Nation was subject to federal law because of a clause in its 1976 constitution that arguably waived the tribe's rights to sovereign immunity. The clause read, "The Cherokee Nation is an inseparable part of the State of Oklahoma and the Federal Union, therefore the Constitution of the United States is the supreme law of the land" (Article 1, Section 1). The next section of the document states, "The Cherokee Nation shall never enact any law which is in conflict with any State or Federal law" (Article 1, Section 2). Finally, the freedmen asserted that because federal treaties are the supreme law of the land, their 1866 treaty rights superseded the Cherokee Nation's claims to sovereign immunity.

After hearing the arguments from both sides, the district court in Oklahoma decided that the plaintiffs had failed to establish a claim against the tribe and granted a motion to dismiss. The Cherokee freedmen quickly filed an appeal before the Tenth Circuit Court of Appeals. The final decision on the Nero case came down on December 12, 1989, with the court of appeals affirming the decision of the district court. The court of appeals held that the dispute between the freedmen and the Cherokee Nation was an intratribal affair over which it had no jurisdiction. The decision followed the arguments of the Cherokee Nation closely but added that the Cherokee Nation had a right to remain a culturally and politically distinct entity (892 F. 2d. 1463 [10th Cir. 1989]).

In doing so, the court ignored the freedmen's long history of cultural and political association with the tribe by conflating race with culture and politics. The more accurate summary of their position would have been that the Cherokees had a sovereign right to remain a *racially* distinct community, but the court skirted this controversial issue.[6] However, from the eighteenth century on, the tapestry of Cherokee culture had been woven with efforts of "white, black, and red" Cherokee citizens. While racial self-definition may be a sovereign right upheld by the federal courts, in practice the Cherokees have long been a multicultural and multiracial people. These characteristics, often misunderstood as in the case of the freedmen, have had dramatic effects on the political trajectory of the Cherokee Nation and are reflected by the ongoing litigation between the Cherokee freedmen and the Cherokee Nation from 1889 to 1989.

RACIAL POLITICS IN THE CHEROKEE NATION: A QUESTION OF BLOOD

Through a century of legal wrangling with its black citizens, the Cherokee Nation resisted the incorporation of the freedmen by progressively narrowing its definition of Cherokee identity. In the 1890s, the Cherokee Nation argued that the only legitimate class of Cherokee freedmen was listed on the Dawes Rolls. By the time of the Nero case in the 1980s, the Cherokee Nation had shifted its position, claiming that Dawes enrollment was no longer sufficient. In March 1988, the tribal council passed a statute approving the rules and regulations of the tribal registration committee that had been in practice since 1978 (11 CNCA, Section 12). Now by tribal law, a Cherokee citizen had to be a Cherokee by blood, which excluded the freedmen, who generally lacked the requisite documentation to prove blood descent. I say generally because there is good evidence that many of the freedmen listed on the Dawes Rolls did in fact have Cherokee ancestry. At the turn of the century, the Dawes Commission rolls enumerated 4,208 adult Cherokee freedmen. Of that number, approximately 300 had some degree of Indian heritage, as the census cards indicate in various ways. Some cards say they are "colored" or "Cherokee-Black." Others state that the person is "Cherokee by blood," "part Indian," or "mixed." At least 7 percent of the Cherokee freedmen original enrollees had Cherokee blood but were classified as freedmen solely on the basis of their black phenotype.

Further evidence for racial "misclassification" is found in the testimony of members of the Cherokee Freedmen's Association before the Indian Claims Commission on November 14, 1960. On that day, Gladys

Lannagan, a descendent of freedmen parents, took the stand. "I was born in 1896 and my father died August 5, 1897," she testified before the court. "But he didn't get my name on the roll. I have two brothers on the roll by blood—one on the roll by blood and one other by Cherokee Freedmen children's allottees." Not only was Lannagan not listed on the Dawes Roll, even though her siblings were included, but her brothers were enrolled separately in different racial categories—one as a Cherokee by blood and the other as a Cherokee freedmen minor. She also stated that one of her grandparents was Cherokee and the other was black and that she was seeking whatever rights to which she was entitled. Lannagan was not alone among the freedmen in her claim to Cherokee ancestry. During a century of litigation, many of the freedmen asserted that they were of Cherokee descent, implying that if blood were to be the primary criterion, then they would have enough biological collateral to be legitimate citizens of the Cherokee Nation.

In recent years, the Nero case offered numerous examples of this sentiment. Almost all the plaintiffs in the case claimed they had some Indian ancestry. Curtis Vann said that his grandfather was a Cherokee by blood, and Cornelius Nave stated that his father was three-quarters Indian. Although I was unable to verify their statements in the Dawes records, I was able to locate Berry Niven's birth affidavit of October 16, 1903, which provided further clues to a confused system of racial classification. The affidavit showed that Niven's father and mother were both citizens of the Cherokee Nation. The mother was a citizen by marriage and the father by blood, but the father was enrolled as a freedman. As in the case of the Reverend Mr. Nero's birth affidavit, normally if a Cherokee citizen were listed on the freedmen roll, then they would be a citizen by adoption and not by blood.

People with mixed ancestry fell between the cracks of the tri-racial system of classification that existed in Indian Territory at the turn of the century. This system pushed individuals into categories that did not reflect their personal experiences or their familial connections. The rules of hypodescent played out in such a way that people with any degree of African-American blood were usually classified exclusively as black.[7] For example, three out of four possible multiracial ancestries would result in an individual with a black social classification (see the accompanying list of the most common racial classifications of individuals with multiracial ancestry). Based on this generalized chart, multiracial individuals with black ancestry were always considered black, and those with white ancestry were never considered white. As one Cherokee freedmen descendent put it, "This is America where being to any degree black is the same thing as being to any degree pregnant" (Sam Ford, e-mail interview, March 14, 1996). In a similar vein, those with Native-American and white ancestry were often classified as Indian, in part because "whiteness" was seen as an empty cultural and racial category (Frankenberg 1993, Ware 1992). Whiteness was a hegemonic identity that was taken for granted and was no longer marked in any particular way. Using the analogy of mixing paint, a little red paint in a can of white will turn the whole thing pink, implying that one's whiteness is no longer culturally "blank" or racially "pure."

Black/White	Black
Black/Indian	Black
Black/Indian/White	Black
Indian/White	Indian

At the same time, pink is not red, and to some extent a fourth racial category developed in Oklahoma. People of mixed European and Indian ancestries who were phenotypically and culturally ambiguous were usually classified as mixed-bloods. But this was the exception rather than the rule, and the majority of individuals with multiracial identities were pushed into a single-ancestry classification, usually the one with lower status. The critical point here is that the social and often political reaction to racial hybridity varied according to the components of each individual's identity. Multiracial individuals with African-American ancestry were treated in qualitatively different ways from those without it.

This different treatment was the result of a number of factors. Some were economic, as seen in the 1960 testimony of freedwoman Tessie Claggett Payne before the Indian Claims Commission:

> My grandfather and grandmother are on the full blood Cherokee roll, the 1880 roll. . . . All of the children, there was six of them, got allotments, and my mother, and it happened to be in the Nowata oil pool, and they changed us to Freedmen's, from the blood roll to the Freedmen roll, and that give them access to handle or change the land or dispose of it, or we could dispose of it, but none of us ever sold it. It wasn't supposed to be taxable but they sold it for taxes.

In this instance, the racial classification of a multiracial family changed between the 1880 rolls and the Dawes Commission rolls, to open up their allotted land for grafter manipulations.

The motivations for "misclassifying" black-Cherokees went beyond economic greed. For instance, in a recent interview with me, a Cherokee man described a one-time Cherokee citizen named Mary Walker, a woman of multiracial heritage who was supposedly one-eighth black, three-eighths Cherokee, and four-eighths white:

> When she went to the Cherokee citizenship commission [Dawes] to enroll, they looked at her face and they saw a Cherokee woman and said, "through whom do you claim," you know, what are your parents' names and what is your degree of Indian blood. They put it all down, and then someone comes in and says, "She ain't no Cherokee. She's a nigger. That woman is a nigger and you are going to put her down as a nigger." . . . So the Dawes Commission had to go back and research her family and get all the documentation and tell this poor woman that not only are you going to be on the freedmen rolls but so are your children.

The vocal denial of Walker's Cherokee and white ancestry and the concerted effort to push her into a solely black racial category reflect the level of emotion in controversies over racial classification. After all, multiracial offspring were the undeniable result of a broken taboo, interracial sex. The mere existence of multiracial individuals like Mary Walker demonstrated the widespread practice of illegal sexual unions despite community norms and the Cherokee Nation's own antimiscegenation laws.

Consider the background of Mary Walker: she had black, Cherokee, and white ancestry as a result of three generations of illicit sexual relations between prominent mixed-blood Cherokee masters and their black slaves. At the time of the Dawes enrollment, Mary Walker was having a love affair with a wealthy Cherokee man named James French, with whom she had several children. Their offspring might have been considered a threat to the French family fortune if French's paternity could be established. But because Mary Walker was socially categorized as a freedwoman, the kinship connections between her, her children, and other Cherokees and whites were probably severed. Emotions ran high when Mary Walker came before the Dawes Commission and claimed a Cherokee identity because this one individual brought to mind all the issues of illicit sex, matrimonial betrayal, denied love, fatherless children, and economic greed.

Despite such hostile responses to multiracial individuals with African-American ancestry, in general the Cherokee community more readily accepted Native and white unions. One reason for this differential treatment may have been a long-held Cherokee bias against dark skin. In an interview, a Cherokee consultant explained this in the following manner:

> My wife's grandmother was born in 1897, and she talked about her childhood, which was a long time after slavery, but she talked about black people in terms of them being culturally similar to us, that they were community type people. You know she didn't have any prejudice against them as far as their behavior. Her prejudice all came from the fact that they were black. Skin color, it was just skin color. And this was a full-blood Cherokee woman who didn't speak any English. She was a very traditional type person.

In spite of cultural commonalties, a Cherokee bias against black skin usually maintained the social distance between Cherokees and their ex-slaves. Another more recent story concerned a pregnant Cherokee woman who used Indian medicine (a tea of sycamore bark) to lighten the child she was carrying. When I asked the same informant whether this color bias existed among Cherokees today, he said that in his opinion, "Cherokees have always prided themselves in being a light-skinned people." A Cherokee bias against dark skin, the result of their adaptation of a system of African racial slavery in the eighteenth and nineteenth centuries, provides the simplest and most direct explanation for their social treatment and racial classification of multiracial individuals with black ancestry even today.

As this bias demonstrates, Cherokee identity politics has never been simply a question of blood. Multiracial individuals who identify as both Indian and black challenge the prevailing racial ideologies that ask them to "choose one" among several ethnic options. Freedmen with Cherokee ancestry are confronted with questions of racial belonging influenced by ideas associated with blood, color, money, and sex. These symbolically laden objects of repulsion and desire weigh heavily upon most systems of racial classification. To negotiate them at the cost of being named a "race traitor" or facing other social pressures can become a heavy burden that few are willing to share. Thus, it is not surprising that today of the over 4,000 multiracial individuals of Cherokee and black ancestry, relatively few seek recognition as Cherokee citizens.[8]

THE CHEROKEE FREEDMEN TODAY

For most Cherokee freedmen, tribal citizenship was not a question of blood but a question of law: regardless of their blood ancestry, most Cherokee freedmen identified as Cherokee citizens on the principle that the tribe had formally adopted them in the Treaty of 1866. Tribal citizenship meant social and political continuity and economic security for the Cherokee freedmen, and when this citizenship was challenged, they were willing to fight in the federal courts for full recognition of their treaty rights. Although these battles were mostly unsuccessful, the Cherokee freedmen continued to resist because they knew the stakes involved: the older generation of original enrollees feared that if they were not successful, the younger generation would grow up not knowing their rights, and their real history would be lost. As Nero said with uncanny prescience in 1984, "Over the years they [the Cherokees] have been eliminating us gradually. When the older ones die out, and the young ones come on, they won't know their rights. If we can't get this suit, they will not be able to get anything" (*The Oklahoma Eagle,* July 5, 1984). With the death of Nero in 1994 and the passing of the older generation of freedmen, this is exactly what happened. Today, the younger descendants of Cherokee freedmen rarely identify as Cherokee in any fashion. They may have a dim awareness that Cherokee masters enslaved their ancestors, but the details of this relationship are often confused. For example, one descendent said, "Honestly, I don't know much other than we had a link to the Cherokees because both my parents and my maternal grandmother in the mid-1960s received what they called their Indian money. I sort of assumed we were part Indian." Other than vague memories of this sort, recent generations of Cherokee freedmen have retained little knowledge of their specific, historical rights to Cherokee citizenship.

During the course of my fieldwork in the Cherokee Nation, I struggled to find freedmen descendants who were willing to talk with me about their Cherokee heritage. In Tahlequah, where I was based, I asked around to see if anyone knew of freedmen families living in the area. Usually my questions were met with suspicion as to why I would be interested in such a thing, but many people chalked it up to the unaccountable eccentricities of the outsider. Again and again, I was told that there were no freedmen in Tahlequah and that those families had long since moved the twenty miles or so to Muskogee and Fort Gibson, both of which contain a large percentage of African Americans. Eventually, I got a helpful response and was directed toward a section of town locally known as "nigger hill." Although the name made me bristle, it would prove to be the only neighborhood in Tahlequah where I could locate men and women who on the surface appeared to be African American.

She parks her car on the "hill," steps onto the cracked pavement and notices a rusty mailbox with "Vann" glued across the side in shiny gold letters. The contrast between the textures amuses her, and she smiles at the irony of another prominent mixed-blood Cherokee surname marking the unique history and identity of this freedmen community. As she takes in the scene, she notices other contrasts, like run-down, dingy white clapboard houses with neat yards and colorful geraniums. She is reminded of the state advertising campaign, "Oklahoma: Native America," with its superficial images of Indian powwows and white pioneers masking the black reality behind many parts of the state's history. How many times had she heard local people say, "Yeah, we got rid of all our blacks, pushed them down south to Muskogee," or "We don't have any of them around here. I've seen 'em before but they stick to themselves, and we don't have much to do with 'em." She had read about some redneck hate crimes, and even a drive-by shooting a few hours south of town in "Little Dixie", where a couple of crackers with shotguns had done something straight out of the days of reconstruction. The shotguns were unloaded on some young black men from out of state who stopped in the wrong bar at the wrong time. No one died, but it wasn't for a lack of trying.

Not too surprising, she supposes, given that the worst race riot in U.S. history happened just sixty-five miles northwest of here in Tulsa in 1921. Thirty city blocks were destroyed, and the homes of 15,000 blacks reduced to ashes, but it never made the national newspapers, or even the history books, until the early 1970s. Even today the state is deeply divided over how to deal with the event—or how to keep denying its importance.

Yet despite this racist history stands this quiet and solitary neighborhood, a single block of people who refuse to move. Several old ladies work in their gardens, while others sit on their porches fanning themselves in the shaded canopies of ancient blackjack oaks. The people seem as old as the trees, and she notices only one youngster as he runs across his yard to greet his next-door neighbor. As she walks down the street greeting those few folks who catch her eye, it comes home to her that this is the first time she has seen a group of black people in the months since moving to town.

Residential communities are de facto segregated along racial lines in northeastern Oklahoma, and it was difficult for me as a phenotypically white woman to cross those boundaries.[9] I tried to overcome this social geography with the telephone, hoping that a telephone call would feel less intrusive than a knock on the door and that I would be given the opportunity to explain my intentions. But the phone presented new obstacles. With each call, I awkwardly explained who I was and why I was interested in an interview. Too often, however, I was nervous about the racially sensitive nature of my questions and tried to hide this fact behind academic jargon. Most of my contacts found this confusing, but one thing was clear: as soon as I hid behind the mantle of academia, my class status shifted, creating more social distance between me and whomever I was trying to interview. Because of perceived race and class barriers and my early bumbles on the phone, most freedmen declined an interview, saying that they were too old to get involved in any controversy with the Cherokees.

Although the issues of race and class never faded, sometimes I was able to get around them with a stroke of good luck. When one freedman descendent finally consented to an interview, a whole network of freedmen families and communities opened up to me. From then on when I called people, I was able to build trust by saying, "Morris, your cousin in Tahlequah gave me your number and said that I should talk to you." Then, when I met people face-to-face, I was more comfortable and so were they. My gender and youth worked to my advantage, because I was perceived as less threatening than an older, white male might have been. My own rural, southeast Texas background also weighed heavily in my favor, since my accent and bearing were familiar and reminded people that we had a rural, southern culture in common. As I shared pictures of my family's small farm with its own outhouse and cypress siding, and as we exchanged stories about milk cows, roosters, winter gardens, buttermilk cornbread, and poke salad greens, the social barriers between us began to crumble, at least in part.

Once I got to know several freedmen families, I was surprised to find that very few cared whether or not they were recognized by the Cherokee Nation. Adults between the ages of thirty and fifty recalled freedmen elders who spoke Cherokee as children and later sat around talking about the "glory days" of the Cherokee Nation. As one freedmen descendent put it, "My older relatives liked the Indians and they seemed to feel some kinship towards them, but it was vague and not personal at all. . . . However, I did note that all of them had an affinity for the land called Indian Territory, and my dad, although he did not want to be buried in Fort Gibson with the other relatives, insisted on being buried in the Cherokee Nation." Many adult freedmen remembered the court battles against the Cherokee Nation and the important role that the Reverend Roger Nero played in their community. Although the current generation was frustrated with Nero's lack of success and did not see the point in continuing the fight, some freedmen sought the occasional concession from the tribal government. One of their most recent efforts had been to take their children, nieces, and nephews to the Cherokee Nation's registration department, hoping to get them enrolled so they would be eligible for educational scholarships. Not only were they denied enrollment, but they claimed they were "snubbed" and "snickered at" when they applied for tribal membership.

Wary of such slights, younger freedmen descendants were often unwilling to seek tribal membership, even if they were eligible by treaty or by virtue of their documented blood descent. Another factor was a sense of disconnection from their Cherokee past. As one freedmen descendent said:

> I live in this American society and my view of myself is as an African American. The Cherokee history is interesting, but since I have no familial or social links to the Cherokee Indians, I look at them as a people who are admirable but they're not me. I view them and Oklahoma Indians in general as people who share many of the prejudices of Europeans about black people. However, that's my view. . . . Several years ago, I asked Seminole tribal council member, the late Lawrence Cudjoe, why as a black man he wanted to be a Seminole. He replied that it wasn't a question of wanting or not wanting, it was just who he was. Were I like him . . . I'd probably feel as he did.[10]

Like the main body of enrolled Cherokees, the freedmen have adopted dominant Euroamerican racial ideologies that negate multiracial identities. Although my consultant's identity is constituted in multiple ways, it is difficult for him to see himself as anything but African American, thereby negating his potential racial, legal, and political identity as a Cherokee citizen.

Some Cherokees are working to change this situation, with the belief that the freedmen's claims are historically valid and politically potent in the present. One current tribal council member stated, "If we don't have to keep our treaty, then why should the U.S. government keep theirs? A promise is a promise." One Cherokee who sees the contemporary political impact of honoring such promises is David Cornsilk, managing editor of the *Cherokee Observer*, a local independent newspaper. Cornsilk is also one of the founders of the Cherokee National Party, a new grassroots political organization that uses the *Cherokee Observer* to reach a large audience of Cherokee voters. Cornsilk believes that in or-

der for the Cherokee Nation to be a successful leader, it needs to honor
its 1866 treaty by recognizing the freedmen as tribal citizens. When I
asked Cornsilk why he was interested in raising the issue he said:

> I don't really have a very deep moral drive to give citizenship to the freedmen.
> I believe that we have a moral obligation to them, but that's not the driving
> force. My driving force is that the Cherokee Nation has to realize that it has
> jurisdiction there, and that in order to protect that jurisdiction, it must exert
> that jurisdiction over as many of the people who reside here as possible,
> including the freedmen. Whether they are black or not, whether they have
> Cherokee blood or not, if we can control their destiny basically by being their
> government, then they are not going to agitate against us. They are not going
> to be our enemy.

Cornsilk's motivation is primarily political: if the freedmen were recognized as tribal citizens, then the Cherokee Nation would extend its
power base and placate, if not silence, some of its most persistent critics.

Cornsilk's realpolitik vision also takes into account the issue of race.
Given the current political climate of this country, Cornsilk believes that
the Cherokee Nation cannot continue to identify its citizenry on a
strictly racial basis. He fears that tribal citizens who are more white than
Indian are in danger of being reclassified as non-Indian, thereby diminishing the size and power of the Cherokee Nation:

> That's why I think the freedmen are so important to bring them [the freed-
> men] in, because then it's a nonracial issue. We are a nation and we have
> become a nation that is big enough and moral enough to realize its respon-
> sibilities to the people that it held as slaves. It's like what [a tribal official]
> said, "Great nations like great men keep their word." . . . It's to our advan-
> tage to separate ourselves as far as possible from the fact that we are an
> ethnic and racial group and just stand behind our identity as a political entity.
> Then we have strength and power beyond any other ethnic group. . . . We
> can't be sifted out. . . . We have to be dealt with on that level.

Cornsilk understands how racial identities can be manipulated for political purposes, and he believes the Cherokee Nation must beat the federal government to the punch. The potential exists for the Cherokee
Nation to lose over half its citizens if the federal government imposes a
more conservative definition of Indianness according to blood quantum.
For this reason, he sees freedmen recognition as critical to the Cherokee
Nation's self-preservation.

But Cornsilk has encountered a great deal of resistance among Cherokees, in part because nationalism of any sort is always tied to ideologies
about race and culture. Cherokee national identity is based on a unique

sense of peoplehood, one that is intertwined with primordial notions about blood and cultural belonging that seem to exclude the freedmen in the minds of most Cherokees. This is a misperception, since the freedmen in many cases possess as much if not more Cherokee culture—and even blood—than many white-Cherokees enrolled in the tribe.[11] Even if a move away from race to a strictly legal and political self-definition would not necessarily undermine the cultural identity of the Cherokee Nation, it is precisely because the tribe has a reputation for cultural and racial dilution that most Cherokees find the possibility of freedmen citizenship so threatening.

Individuals like David Cornsilk are exceptional among Cherokees in their desire to put political self-preservation before race or culture. Cornsilk spent the past several years trying to find a freedmen descendent who would pursue with him the following scenario to seek tribal recognition. First, a freedmen descendent of a Dawes enrollee would apply for tribal membership, which would be denied because the applicant did not have any Cherokee blood. Then, Cornsilk and the applicant would take the case before the Cherokee judicial appeals tribunal, where Cornsilk believes they could use the Cherokee Constitution of 1976 to win their case.

Like me, Cornsilk had little luck in finding a contemporary freedman descendent who thought tribal recognition was worth the trouble. One responded to his request saying, "Why would I want to switch races?" Another man agreed to work with Cornsilk but soon backed out after he received threatening telephone calls and began to fear for his life. Finally in 1997, after several years of searching, Cornsilk found the ideal candidate, a seventy-eight-year-old widow by the name of Lela Boggs [pseudonym]. A long-time resident of Tahlequah, Boggs is the offspring of parents and grandparents who were all original Dawes enrollees. In fact, her father spoke some Cherokee, and her grandfather served in the Indian home guard of the Union Army under Principal Chief John Ross. Boggs herself has a Cherokee Nation voter registration card that dates to 1975, and she voted in the 1975 elections to ratify the current Cherokee constitution. Given these significant social and political ties, Boggs was shocked when she attempted to register as a Cherokee tribal citizen in 1988 and was turned down. Still smarting from the rejection almost ten years later when Cornsilk approached her, she was open to his proposal to take this issue to the Cherokee courts.

In the summer of 1998, I sat with Lela Boggs on her front porch while she fed the numerous wild rabbits, pigeons, and wrens that frequent her yard, and I asked why she had agreed to participate in the case. She told me that she "just want[s] to have the same rights," that all her life she has identified as a black-Indian, and that although it has been tough, she wants to have some acknowledgement of "who she is." She identifies as a black-Indian not only because of her freedmen lineage but also because of her own Cherokee ancestry. Her paternal grandfather, Joseph Rogers, was both the offspring and slave of a full-blood Cherokee by the name of Will Rogers (not the famous humorist). Although this fact was noted on her grandfather's application for tribal enrollment under the Dawes Commission, he was still enrolled as a freedman and not as a Cherokee by blood. As for Will Rogers, he was never listed on the Dawes Rolls because he died shortly before they started taking applications. As a consequence, Lela Boggs is one-eighth Cherokee by blood but cannot be enrolled as a tribal citizen because she can trace her lineage only to freedmen and not to her Cherokee Indian ancestors.

In the fall of 1996, Boggs, with the help of Cornsilk, filed her case in the Cherokee district court (*DC Case No. CIV 96–09*). However, the judge dismissed the case, saying that the Cherokee judicial appeals tribunal was the proper venue for it. Cornsilk then enlisted the aid of attorney Kathy Carter-White, who as a member of the Cherokee Bar Association was familiar with the nuances of Cherokee law. They petitioned the judicial appeal tribunal to review their case on February 24, 1997, but it would be more than a year before the case would go to trial. The main delay was the eruption in tribal politics that occurred a day after their petition, on February 25, 1997, when Cherokee marshals served a search warrant on Principal Chief Joe Byrd. This action precipitated a serious crisis that would interrupt the functioning of all aspects of the Cherokee government, including the judicial branch, where the chief justices of the court had been impeached for upholding the actions of the Cherokee marshals in carrying out their duties.[12]

Only in the fall of 1997 did the Cherokee court system become fully functional once again. At that point, the Massad Commission—a special commission authorized by the Cherokee Nation tribal council—issued a report upholding the existing Cherokee courts and denouncing the impeachment of the Cherokee justices as an illegal action. However, over a century's worth of Cherokee court records were in complete disarray following a raid on the Cherokee courthouse by Chief Byrd's forces in the summer of 1997. Only with several months of backbreaking work on the part of a handful of people were the records reassembled

into a usable form. While the court records were being put back together, the docket for the case expanded as the Cherokee Nation lawyers
filed several motions to dismiss, and members of the tribal council tried
to intervene. As these efforts to dismiss Boggs's case proved unsuccessful,
both sides filed for more time so they could gather their evidence, find
appropriate witnesses, and hone their arguments before going to trial.
Finally, on June 12, 1998, the freedmen's case was heard in the Cherokee
Nation's own court system (*JAT 97–03-K*).

In her opening statements, Carter-White asked that the court uphold
Lela Boggs's rights to Cherokee citizenship, that it disregard any statutes
or regulations that might have eliminated her eligibility, and that it base
her rights on the Treaty of 1866 and the 1976 Cherokee Constitution.
The Cherokee Nation lawyers contended that Boggs's application had
never been denied, but that the registration department had only asked
for further information. In the defense's opinion, Boggs had filed an
appeal before exhausting her administrative remedies. However, the specific information that the registrar requested was that Boggs provide the
roll numbers of ancestors who were listed on the Dawes Rolls with a
degree of Cherokee blood. Carter-White argued that because the Dawes
Roll listed no blood quanta for freedmen, fulfilling their request was
impossible, and all freedmen descendents eventually would be denied
their rights to Cherokee citizenship on a categorical basis. She later argued that for the tribal registrar to require a CDIB as a measure of
citizenship would have the same effect as "requiring a degree of Native
American genetic stock ancestry," an act that essentially eliminates the
freedmen from tribal participation. As Cornsilk testified before the
court, "I think what we're talking about, and this is strictly my opinion,
is an apartheid situation." He stated that the freedmen were people who
"one day were citizens of the Nation with the rights of suffrage, and the
very next day they found themselves disenfranchised and no longer citizens of the Nation in which they had resided and participated for several
generations."

The defense then countered, arguing that both the Curtis Act and the
Dawes Act had abrogated the Treaty of 1866 because both treated the
freedmen as a special class apart from Cherokees by blood. Furthermore,
because the Cherokee Nation had a sovereign right to determine its own
membership, the registration committee had the authority to limit tribal
membership in any way it saw fit. However, Carter-White countered
that the practice of limiting citizenship to Cherokees by blood was a
decision that was made by the rules and regulations of the registration

committee, not the Cherokee people themselves. Because Cherokee citizens were never given the opportunity to vote on whether or not the
freedmen should be categorically excluded from citizenship, the rights
of the freedmen had to be based on the 1976 Cherokee Constitution,
which had been ratified by the people and did not specifically exclude
the freedmen. The upshot of the arguments before the judicial appeal
tribunal seemed to rest on whether or not the Cherokee Nation, as a
sovereign entity, had included or excluded the freedmen in its own legislation. On the one hand, the Treaty of 1866 and the current Cherokee
constitution seem to support the freedmen's claim, whereas other legislation, such as the Curtis Act and the Cherokee Nation's own internal
statutes, do not.

As of June 2000, the Boggs case had been heard, and the Cherokee
justices still had the difficult job of interpreting the convolutions of Cherokee national law. Almost two years had passed since the case was
brought to trial, and still no decision had been made. During those two
years, a new principal chief had been elected, ushering in a new era of
tribal administration, and two of the three Cherokee justices who heard
the case had stepped down from the bench. In May 2000, I asked people
in the judicial branch of the Cherokee government whether a decision
would be made anytime soon. They assured me that the case had come
up on several occasions but said the judges were wary of making such
a controversial decision, especially because two of them had not heard
the case firsthand and had to base their decision on the trial transcript
and other supporting documents. Furthermore, the Cherokee Nation
had endured so much political controversy over the past several years
that many people wanted the tribal government to stabilize for a while
before a final decision was made.

David Cornsilk is not one of those people—he feels a great deal of
pressure to get the issue settled quickly, before other political events
muddy the waters. One complication was the Cherokee Nation's
constitutional convention in February 1999, which fulfilled a promise
to the Cherokee people that their constitution would be subject to revision twenty-five years after its initial passage in 1976.[13] Cornsilk contends that powerful people in the Cherokee Nation wanted to add a
clause to the constitution that would specifically restrict tribal membership to Cherokees by blood. With the simple addition of those two
words—*by blood*—the issue would have been settled, and the vast majority of freedmen (approximately 93 percent) would have been
eliminated forever from Cherokee citizenship. However, the delegates

to the Cherokee constitutional convention in February 1999 decided the freedmen should be eligible for citizenship as descendents of Dawes enrollees but should be precluded from voting or holding office because they do not have Cherokee blood. The new constitution was adopted by the delegates in March 1999 and was sent to the BIA for approval. According to current Cherokee law, any amendment to the Cherokee constitution is subject to the approval of the president of the United States or his agent, in this case the BIA. The BIA reviewed the new Cherokee constitution but refused to endorse it on several grounds, one of which was its inconsistency regarding the freedmen. The BIA felt that the freedmen could not be citizens and yet be denied the rights of suffrage or holding office. Though the question of the freedmen was only one of several issues, Cherokee officials responded to the BIA's rejection by invoking their sovereign right to self-government and self-definition. In a motion before the tribal council, they moved to strike the amendment in the 1976 constitution requiring presidential approval of their new constitution. Now, the freedmen's fate is up to the Cherokee people, who will have to vote on whether or not to accept a substantially revised constitution.

Of course, Lela Boggs will not participate in the vote. Instead, Cherokees with verifiable blood ancestry will make the decision, including the justices who interpret the new Cherokee constitution when deciding the outcome of her case. It is unclear where the future of the Cherokee freedmen will lead. Whether Boggs and Cornsilk are successful or the Cherokee Nation denies the freedmen their claims to citizenship once and for all, the decision will be made with little input from the freedmen themselves, whose views are rarely offered and never solicited. Their collective silence can be interpreted either as a refusal to struggle any longer against barriers of racial discrimination or as a dignified acceptance that where they find themselves located is perfectly comfortable, even happy. Although it might cost the freedmen in an economic sense, they will no longer be buffeted by the political whimsy and prejudice of others; no longer will they have to fight for a place at a table that does not welcome them. Yet the group with the most at stake in this contest is not the freedmen but the citizens of the Cherokee Nation, who shape their own fate as they decide the freedmen's. If they formally choose to exclude the freedmen, then their own blood policies might be turned against them at some future date, giving the Cherokee Nation a painful lesson in racial politics—the same one they have been teaching the freedmen for over a century.

CHAPTER EIGHT

Closing

Five minutes before grand entry at the Tahlequah powwow: a Cherokee man in his mid-thirties fluffs the neon pink feathers of his bustle. Tired of the vibrant Disney colors popular among fancy dancers a few years ago, he now wishes he had the money for new regalia. At least with a home crowd, they won't care if he's a little behind the times. As he gently shakes himself loose, warming up muscles and tendons, he takes in all the family and friends, the people from his home community and church, who have come to watch tonight's events.

Carla, a pretty Cherokee woman he used to date in high school, greets him as she squeezes past, making her way to the concession stand. "Hey, Jim, long time no see. How's it going?" she says, before introducing him to the tiny, four-year-old boy she has in tow. "Jim, this is my son, David. Last time you saw him was about three years ago. I think it was at that wild onion dinner in Marble City."

"Hi there, little man. You having a good time?" Jim asks the boy, who takes one look at Jim's feathers and says, "Look, Momma, a real Indian!"

With a wry smile, Carla shakes her head in disbelief that a full-blood Cherokee child who knows his family and community could say such a thing. "Oh, David," she says with quiet amusement.

Jim reaches down and pats the little boy on the head. "You know what? You're an Indian, too," he says.

"No, I'm a Cherokee," the boy is quick to respond.

Laughing, Jim asks, "Well, what do you think Cherokees are?"
With eyes wide, the boy looks at him intently for a moment, then turns
to his mother and buries his head in the folds of her skirt.

Heavy rains are falling for the third straight day in a row. Forced
indoors, a ten-year-old Cherokee boy named Matt is playing with
a set of Hot Wheels at the feet of his great-aunt Betty Sixkiller. He has
lived with Betty in her small three-room house for the past four
months, ever since his mom got a job at the new factory outside of
town. He loves his "auntie" but gets bored easily because there aren't
many children in the neighborhood. Mostly he occupies himself by
building forts or visiting other kids at church when Betty is attending
services or teaching Cherokee language classes. Today, his routine
has been interrupted not only by the rain but also by a visitor, a young
anthropologist who has come to ask his auntie a bunch of questions
about Cherokees. He pushes his cars around the carpet and half-
listens to their conversation, paying closer attention when he hears
them mention his name.
   The anthropologist asks, "If Matt here is going to grow up to
identify as Cherokee, then what do you think is the most important
thing for these future generations to maintain their sense of Cherokee
identity?"
   "I think the blood," Betty replies without hesitation, but before she
can finish her thought, Matt interrupts with an innocent question:
"How do you know if you're a Cherokee?"
   "Cherokee? How do you know?" Betty says, taken aback by what
she is hearing. As Betty chuckles about the question, the anthropologist
asks the boy, "How do you think you know?" After a shy moment
of racing his cars up and down his own pants leg, Matt looks to
his auntie, who answers for him. "Well, my parents were Cherokees,"
she says, as if that was all that mattered.
   But Matt is not satisfied so easily. "How do you *know* you're
Cherokee?" he insists, still pushing his cars in small circles on his thigh.
   Betty sits up in her chair a little. "How do I know I'm Cherokee?
Well, because my parents were Cherokee!" she says more emphatically.
Turning to the anthropologist, Betty continues, shaking her head in
exasperation, "I tell you what, we get into some of the craziest things.
Like yesterday he asked the oddest question about what happens to
people's stuff when they die. . . . Can you believe questions like that?
And coming from a child, no less!"

Like the generations that came before them, these two little Cherokee boys ask questions of deceptive simplicity—who is Cherokee, who is Indian, how do we know, and who gets to decide? These questions are on everybody's minds, but many adults prefer not to discuss them directly, so awkward and confusing can they be. Even when they are not articulated as bluntly as they were by these two boys, these questions of identity have long been unavoidable for Cherokee children, Cherokee adults, and other Native Americans who encounter competing definitions of racial and cultural identity in the multicultural and multiracial society around them. These questions are rarely fully resolved for individuals in the Cherokee Nation. No matter how cut and dried the laws of blood descent may seem to make Cherokee identity, the reality of lived experience is infinitely more complex, especially when personal experience conflicts with a world of discourse that labels those experiences and assigns them meaning.

For Cherokees and other Native Americans who fall under direct federal oversight, one of the most significant and confusing idioms of identity is that of blood, as I have tried to show in the course of this book. Although Cherokee identity is not strictly about blood in any literal or even metaphoric sense, the vast majority of Cherokees use blood as a measure of racial, cultural, social, and national belonging. Federal Indian policy and Cherokee national policy both have fetishized and objectified Native-American blood, and as a result, racially hegemonic notions have been reinforced and then reproduced by individual Cherokee citizens at the local level. Multiracial Cherokees often question their own identity and the identity of others in racially hegemonic terms, such as blood, race, color, and culture. Although these terms are analytically distinct, they are conflated in both discourse and practice and serve as the building blocks of both Cherokee "nationhood" and "peoplehood." These categories of identity are important criteria in most systems of racial classification, but "blood is what you make of it," as Otis Payne says in John Sayles's film *Lone Star*. With this in mind, I have tried to show how Cherokee blood has been made into a particularly potent substance for Cherokee identity, one that aligns with power in unique ways.

One of the most telling examples is in regard to black-Cherokees and white-Cherokees. Because of a double standard, multiracial white-Cherokees have experienced a qualitatively different process of racial formation than multiracial black-Cherokees. For white-Cherokees, having a little Indian blood has proven to be a valuable commodity, ensuring them a political identity and access to economic resources in the Cherokee Nation. The Cherokee freedmen have not fared so well, oppressed as they are by the logic of hypodescent that denies their Cherokee blood while it emphasizes their social and political blackness. White-Cherokees have actively used ideologies of blood to wrest power from other segments of the Cherokee population, while the Cherokee freedmen have been progressively stripped of their basic rights of citizenship and political representation in the Cherokee Nation. The result has been that as white-Cherokees have become increasingly central to Cherokee national identity, freedmen have become increasingly marginal.

These differences of power and experience among multiracial Cherokees point to the fact that racial formation is not a monolithic process but is deeply and historically contingent. We need to recognize these differences of experience, and the tensions and antagonisms that they create, as a fundamental aspect of Cherokee history. To a large extent, Cherokee history is about the continual formation of Cherokee culture and identity "through the assertions, rejections, and necessarily incomplete acceptance of the forms of knowledge and ways of being that power creates" (Sider and Smith 1997: 13). In a significant way, Cherokee people's experience of Euroamerican contact and colonialism is about how the meanings they attached to Cherokee blood and identity shifted from being solely about town residence, matrilineal kinship, clan, and culture to include powerful Euroamerican ideas about patrilineal kinship, race, and nationalism. Today, questions of identity, of who is Cherokee and who is not, and how these questions are articulated, arise in part from the workings of power as they occurred in the very real historical experiences of colonialism, nation-building, and incorporation into U.S. society.

That these different historical experiences helped foster race-thinking among Cherokees raises some important questions about the nature of power and its effects on political discourse. For instance, does the Cherokee Nation's continued discrimination against the Cherokee freedmen imply that Cherokee nationalism is somehow a "derivative discourse," one that simply reproduces the racism inherent in the U.S. federal model? (Chatterjee 1993). The answer is both yes and no. Cherokee political leaders have created a state apparatus, modeled on the federal government, that operates as a bureaucratic center of control. In fact, the Cherokee bureaucracy does what the federal Bureau of Indian Affairs used to do by providing certificate degrees of Indian blood and policing Cherokee identity on the basis of genealogy and race. Yet more than mere replication is at work. Cherokees have also remade racial hegemony in their own image so that dominant ideas linked to race have been filtered through their own unique historical and national experiences. As a result, anti-black sentiments among some segments of the Cherokee population reflect not only the dominant U.S. racial hierarchy but also their own unique legacy of African slavery. The larger point is that Cherokees have neither completely internalized nor resisted the powerful racial ideologies to which they are subject and to which they subject others. Instead, they simultaneously reproduce, reinterpret, and resist dominant race-thinking, as race is mediated through their own local and national categories of meaning.

We see this mediation in practice when Cherokee political leaders in the nineteenth and twentieth centuries borrowed Euroamerican ideologies of race and nationalism to create a myth of Cherokee national homogeneity and unity through the symbolism of blood. Because the Cherokee Nation is neither homogeneous nor unitary, its leaders have tried to use Cherokee blood to symbolically cohere what has become an increasingly diverse population. Although blood as a racial metaphor has become central to Cherokee national identity over the last two centuries, it has also remained in dialogue with other aspects of identity, such as phenotype, social behavior, language, religious participation, and community residence, all of which are significant at the local level. As a result, individual Cherokee people interpret blood in multiple ways, factoring in these different aspects of identity in a complex fashion.

In Cherokee practices of social classification, these different aspects of identity are conflated with one another and with race, so that race and culture have come to stand for one another as they move back and forth along what I have described as a race-culture continuum. Although race neither determines Cherokee identity nor is distinct from Cherokee culture, there is a circular logic behind Cherokee practices of social classification. For instance, a full-blood is usually seen as a culture bearer in the eyes of the local Cherokee community, so that his or her presumed fullness of culture denotes a fullness of blood, which is itself a metaphor for culture. While, on the one hand, a full-blood might be a Cherokee-speaking midwife who actually has considerable Euroamerican racial ancestry, he or she might also be someone with solely Indian ancestry who can document that fact through the Dawes Rolls. As a result, the cultural production of blood and race varies significantly among Cherokees, revealing how the individual interpretations and meanings of

Cherokee identity are shaped by the ongoing tensions between local, community standards of Cherokee identity and those of the Cherokee national government.

The potentially relevant ideologies surrounding Cherokee practices of social and racial classification are so complex and variable that Cherokees express a highly diverse racial consciousness. The heterogeneity of Cherokee racial consciousness finds expression in the racial ideology, hegemony, and counterhegemony that we have seen in the course of this book. It accounts for why some individual Cherokees are able to resist explicit racial ideologies, such as blood quantum, and even implicit racial hegemonies, such as the idea that Cherokees have to be Indian. Yet even in this heterogeneous field of discourse, I have not seen evidence of resistance to race-thinking in any large-scale, socially transformative way. Instead, as a result of local blood politics, what most Cherokees experience on a day to day basis seems to me to be best described by the Gramscian idea of contradictory consciousness, which combines uncritically absorbed dominant ideas and implicitly critical ideas that arise from lived experience.[1] Cherokees express contradictory consciousness when they say that being Cherokee is a question of blood but not degree of blood, or when they claim that being Cherokee is a political identity open to multiracial whites but not multiracial blacks. If we pay attention to this slippage between hegemony and counterhegemony inherent in the experience of contradictory consciousness, then we can better understand the complex, "messy," and partial forms of domination and resistance expressed in Cherokee discourses and practices regarding blood, race, and nation.

I also point to this slippage because in it lies the hopeful possibility that Cherokees might resist racial hegemony in a socially transformative way that has so far been absent. For instance, some Cherokees reject hegemonic understandings of Cherokee racial identity by drawing on the implicitly critical ideas that arise from their cultural knowledge and lived experiences. These insights are akin to what Nietzsche describes when he says that each of us carries inside ourselves "an enormous heap of indigestible knowledge stones that occasionally rattle together inside [the] body. . . . And the rattle reveals the most striking characteristic of these modern men [and women]—the opposition of something inside them to which nothing external corresponds, and the reverse" (1949: 23). Transposed to a Cherokee context, this passage describes how some contemporary Cherokees are able to draw upon their own unique ways of knowing, their internal "good sense," to build collective fronts that both recognize and celebrate their differences (Gramsci 1971: 322, 333).

We see this process at work when individual Cherokees suggest that their collective identity as a people centers not on race but on their shared historical experiences and their political status as a sovereign nation. For example, a seventy-six-year-old Cherokee man whom I interviewed, a fluent Cherokee speaker, suggested that "For someone to be registered [as a tribal member] who's 1/2000 Cherokee, that's really splitting hairs. But you must remember that their ancestors came over on the Trail of Tears just the same as mine did or an equivalent. They suffered the same consequences and the same hardships and probably lost many of their relatives that way." In this man's opinion, because the federal government did not discriminate on the basis of race when it forced all the Cherokees—white, black, and red—to leave their homeland, then the descendents of those various individuals should all have rights to Cherokee citizenship.

Another Cherokee man in his late thirties echoed these sentiments when he said:

> Does the federal government have the right to define a racial category for the responsibility that it has to a nation? I would say no. I think they have a responsibility to all the citizens of that nation. . . . It is not a federal relationship where it is saying we were discriminating against you on a racial basis and that is why we are making these reparations. We didn't steal your land because you are Indians. You just had land we wanted and you could have been Martians for all we cared. . . . If the federal government was to say because your complexion is now whiter or blacker, we are not going to have anything to do with you, there is [a] huge Supreme Court case in there somewhere. After all, what is their responsibility to the tribe? Is it to the individuals because of their race, or is it to the tribe because of an historic relationship?

Cherokees who define their identities in political and historical terms, as these speakers do, are trying to distance themselves from dominant race-thinking, including federal definitions of Indianness that are measured on the basis of blood or color.

A few politically minded Cherokees with whom I spoke took these arguments a step further, suggesting that to protect their tribal sovereignty and rights to self-determination, they needed to deracialize their own national identity. These individuals believe the Cherokee Nation might be able to do this if it redefines tribal citizenship in terms of territorial residence or allows fluent Cherokee speakers without documentation of Cherokee blood to become tribal citizens. Some even want the Cherokee Nation to naturalize non-Indians who are willing to make an oath of allegiance, as an act of sovereignty. The challenge to enacting these sweeping changes lies with convincing other tribal members of the logic of their position—that if Cherokees deracialize their national identity, at least at a political level, then intermarriage between Cherokees and non-Indians would no longer pose a threat to tribal continuity because Cherokee national substance would no longer be defined in terms of Cherokee blood.

Although this move away from race toward a more historical, political, and geographic definition of Cherokee national identity may seem to be a simple solution, it has complex ramifications. Using nationalism as a self-determining framework is as much a cultural borrowing as race and can be just as contradictory. As I have argued throughout, all nations are created using normative racial and cultural ideologies that shape discourses of social belonging. The question of what is a nation if not a race is one that is still hotly debated around the globe, often with violent repercussions.[2] Furthermore, the suggestion that Cherokees abandon race-based definitions of national identity seems impractical, particularly given that federal definitions of Indianness are so intimately tied to racial essentialism. Even now, the federal government might at any time decide to set a new standard of racial identity and suddenly reclassify most Cherokee citizens as non-Indians in order to save itself some money. Such a response would not be surprising, considering that federal economic needs have often taken priority over Native-American rights of sovereignty and self-determination. The Cherokee Nation is well aware of the power of the U.S. federal government. If the Cherokee Nation went so far as to recognize non-Indians as citizens, then it might draw attention to its racial diversity and run the risk of losing federal funding, even federal recognition, which could result in economic and political chaos for the tribe.

The suggestion that Cherokees abandon race-based definitions of national identity raises other challenges. In a careful analysis, we may recognize Cherokee identity as a social construct, one that is intimately tied to the workings of history and power, whether it is defined in racial, cultural, and/or national terms. However, the fact remains that most Cherokee people still live and imagine their identity as something rooted in essence, inextricably linked to their race, biology, genetics, phenotype, blood, and culture. As a result, social constructivist arguments about Cherokee identity, whether made by Cherokee politicians trying to expand their electoral support or anthropologists looking for the analytical high ground, run the risk of undermining or ignoring something that has become fundamental to many indigenous peoples' claims about nationhood and identity.

In this book, I have tried to walk a fine line between constructivist and essentialist understandings of Cherokee identity, to show how race is a productive category that both enables and limits certain political arguments. Although I have maintained that Cherokee identity is a deeply historical construct, the product of the shifting relations of power and struggle over time, I also want to acknowledge the power that racial, cultural, and national essentialism holds in many Cherokee people's lives (as is true for most people). Discourses of racial essentialism, which are themselves social, cultural, and historical products, shape Cherokee identities and consciousness not just at some superficial or ephemeral level. They also have very real material, political, economic, and even genealogical effects. Ideas about racial essentialism, which are often expressed in terms of blood, have profound effects on who gets recognized as a Cherokee citizen, who gets access to financial scholarships, who gets to represent the Cherokee Nation as Ms. Cherokee, and who gets to run for tribal office. They also shape the contours of different Cherokee lives in less overtly political ways, as Cherokees make important decisions about who they want to marry, and who they consider to be kin—decisions that will shape the racial, cultural, and national identities of future generations.

In Cherokee blood politics, part of the controversy over what constitutes Cherokee identity results from the fundamental contradiction between Cherokee national policy, which defines Cherokee identity in terms of blood, and the very different experiences of those who live as members of different Cherokee communities and societies. As a political entity, the Cherokee Nation imagines itself as a confederation of lived communities, united by a common racial and cultural bond. But because of recent demographic shifts in the Cherokee Nation, most Cherokee citizens do not participate in this same cultural and racial community that they imagine as the basis of their nationhood. Most Cherokee citizens do not fit their own racial and cultural definitions of Indianness. For example, if most Cherokee citizens believe that speaking the Cherokee language is a cornerstone of national cultural difference, then what happens when only 10,000 of the 200,000 enrolled tribal citizens speak the language? Because the majority of tribal citizens are nonspeakers, Cherokee culture as a shared national possession continues to be imagined around linguistic exceptionalism but has become something else in practice.[3]

The tension in the Cherokee national polity between the lived and the imagined results from the fact that Cherokee culture is not a monolithic experience, as some of the Cherokee Nation's policies might imply. Today, a meeting of the Cherokee genealogical society is as much a part of the Cherokee Nation as a Cherokee Baptist sing, a Keetoowah stomp dance, or a certificate degree of Indian blood, for that matter. As a result, the Cherokee Nation is a highly diverse polity that has been ideologically realized through the various symbols of blood, race, culture, and nation. These powerful ideologies have been imposed upon, internalized, and resisted by different Cherokee residential communities, cultures, and social networks. These ideologies do the work of reifying these various Cherokee cultures and societies as a singular political entity, but to what extent are they unified? The cultural experiences of a Cherokee genealogist in Sacramento, California, and a Keetoowah stomp dancer in Vian, Oklahoma, do converge in important ways. Most Cherokee citizens share less obvious cultural and social bonds, such as a shared political and tribal identity; a common experience of being interpellated, or named as Cherokee; and a shared subjection to bureaucratic racism (Althusser 1971: 173). Even though its citizens share these common bonds, as we have seen in the course of this book, the Cherokee Nation is yet another hegemonic force that both includes and excludes different Cherokee cultures, societies, and lives.

Today, the Cherokee Nation is a diverse body of multiply constituted individuals who coalesce in socially significant ways around different aspects of their identities. Blood, race, culture, language, religion, national politics: any or all of these aspects of personal subjectivity can both unite and divide Cherokee citizens along different lines. However, many Cherokees perceive these differences not as a source of social and political factionalism but as one of strength. I remember early in my fieldwork, a Cherokee woman in her mid-thirties made this point by telling me what she described as "an old story about Rabbit and Bear." At the time, I recognized the story as being similar to something that I had read in James Mooney's *Myths of the Cherokees* (1900: 273–74), so I was careful to record it. I am glad I did, because it proved to be significant. Here is the story, taken from my field diary, as it was told to me in early fall 1995.

Rabbit and Bear are sitting in the woods and are good friends. The bear says, "Rabbit, why are we so different from one another? Why are you so small and I'm so big?" The rabbit replies, "I'm not sure, Bear." The rabbit notices that Bear is kind of depressed and down in the mouth. So, Rabbit decides to help Bear and cheer him up. Rabbit says, "Bear, why don't you come over to my house for dinner?" Bear accepts his invitation, so Rabbit runs home and cleans up his house and begins to cook supper. Rabbit puts on a big pot of water and boils carrots, onions, and other vegetables. Usually, Rabbit just eats his vegetables raw, but because Bear is such a good friend and is Rabbit's guest, Rabbit cooks for Bear, knowing that he prefers his food cooked. However, it suddenly dawns on Rabbit, "Oh no! Bear likes to eat meat and he's coming over soon! Where can I find some meat for my friend, Bear?" Because Rabbit doesn't eat meat and Bear does, he is concerned about his friend.

After a little while, Bear arrives at Rabbit's house. Bear smells this wonderful, fragrant aroma of dinner and says, "Oh, Rabbit, what a marvelous smell. What have you made for dinner?" But then Bear notices that Rabbit isn't as peppy as he was earlier. In fact, Rabbit looks pale and weak. Bear rushes to frail little Rabbit and sees that Rabbit is growing faint. Why? Because Rabbit has cut a piece of himself from his own leg and put it in the soup so his friend, Bear, could eat.

When Bear realizes what Rabbit has done, he scoops up Rabbit gently in his arms and carries him to the woods. Because Bear is good with medicine, he finds roots and herbs, bundles up Rabbit's leg, and carries him back to bed so he can heal and rest. Bear takes care of his friend, Rabbit, until he is all better. Then, Bear tells him, "Rabbit, now I understand why we are so different. Each of us can take care of the other. This is why we are such good friends."

Like all culture, this story has changed with the passage of time to reflect a new context, one in which a highly diverse group of Cherokee people brings their own unique gifts and abilities to the table. Cherokee national identity is and always has been about how multiple forms of difference come together in socially and politically meaningful ways to constitute complex subjects. These differences of identity among Cherokees—whether they are defined in terms of blood, race, culture, or some other national substance—are not innate possessions, nor are they

passing illusions. Instead, they reflect the meaningful interactions between groups of people struggling with themselves and others over access to power, including the rights of self-determination and self-
definition that have long been promised to them. As we enter a new
millennium, Cherokee identities will continue to be forged in the everyday practices of Cherokee cultures and lives and in the overt political
discourses of Cherokee citizens. Although these tribal citizens will continue to differ from one another in significant ways, in the coming years,
the ones with the power to heal and create will find a way to utilize
those differences as a source of ongoing vitality and strength. They will
find a way to devise a stable polity that does not reduce Cherokee cultures to culture and societies to society. If we look back over the long
trajectory of Cherokee history, the Cherokee Nation has risen and fallen
time and time again, and it may well do so again. But we need not fear
this possibility, for what will endure is what has always endured—not
the Cherokee Nation as a unified or singular political entity, but these
highly diverse Cherokee cultural and social worlds.

Notes

CHAPTER ONE

1. I view race as a Western social and political construct around various biological fictions that is nonetheless "real" because of its impact on lived experience. It is created to explain social difference and justify inequality, and its meaning varies over time according to shifting relations of power and struggle. I deal with the concept of race in greater detail later in this chapter.

2. In general, I use the term *multiracial* to avoid the negative connotations and biological fictions associated with the more familiar expression *mixed blood,* which is found both in the literature on Native North America and in Native American communities. The term *multiracial* highlights the fluid and multiple nature of identity while describing people whose cultural and biological ancestry encompasses more than one racial category. I also use the noun *racial hybridity,* which should be read as synonymous with the adjective *multiracial.* Occasionally, I employ the term *mixed blood* because its familiarity might make the meaning I am trying to convey clearer. But with all of these labels, I point to race specifically, because it is those same hegemonic or "taken for granted" racial categories that I wish to disentangle from other aspects shaping identities.

3. The biological standard of "one-quarter Indian blood" was challenged by the 1985 *Zarr v. Barlow, et al.* case in California. The case set an important legal precedent, namely, that the federal government can not legally discriminate against Native Americans on the basis of blood quantum. Unfortunately, the implications of this case have not had much effect on the political relationship between federal and tribal governments.

4. For more information on Native American demography, see Russell Thornton's two excellent books, *American Indian Holocaust and Survival: A Population History since 1492,* Norman: University of Oklahoma Press (1987),

214 Notes to Pages 4–18

and *The Cherokees: A Population History,* Lincoln and London: University of Nebraska Press (1990).

5. Throughout the book, I alternate between the terms *Indian* and *Native American.* I believe that, of the two, *Native American* is more accurate, whereas *Indian* is Columbus's misnomer. However, during my fieldwork in Tahlequah, if I used the term *Native American* I was immediately marked as an outsider. Only then did I realize how completely Cherokee people have adopted the term *Indian* as their own.

6. A Mongolian spot refers to a dark, bluish, bruise-like spot that appears at the base of the spine of newborn infants of Native American or Asian heritage. Commonly, members of other racial groups who are born with this spot have mixed indigenous heritage, such as African Americans and Latinos. The spot fades with maturity.

7. Other fieldworkers, when conducting research outside of their home cultures, have experienced these points of convergence. For example, in *Mama Lola,* Karen McCarthy Brown related well to her primary informant, a Haitian-American voodoo priestess, on the basis of their shared gender and marital status (1991). In *Learning Capitalist Culture,* Doug Foley identified with white male, high-school athletes in south Texas because of his own personal experiences growing up as a "jock" in Nebraska (1990).

8. I would argue that Native American culture is ignored in part because it is falsely seen as "dying" or "something from the past" instead of as a living and dynamic force in the lives of contemporary Native Americans.

9. Adair County is one of five counties within the Cherokee Nation with the highest population of Native Americans. Adair County is 43.78 percent Indian; Cherokee County is 33.42 percent, Delaware County 26.6 percent, Sequoyah County 26.9 percent, and Mayes County 18.24 percent (Office of Research and Analysis, May 1993 (1): 2. These five counties are frequently referred to as the five-county area and are considered by most people in northeastern Oklahoma to be the heart of the Cherokee Nation. These demographic statistics have been taken from "Cherokee People . . . Cherokee Tribe . . . ," a periodic in-house publication of the Office of Research and Analysis, an executive support unit of the Cherokee Nation, Tahlequah, Oklahoma, with Steve Woodall as acting director.

10. Examples of this new wave include Alonso 1994, Gregory and Sanjek 1994, Smith 1995, 1997, 1998, and Williams 1989, 1991, 1993.

11. For a discussion of this issue, see Baird 1990: 4.

12. The southeastern tribal complex refers to the southeastern region of the United States that was originally inhabited by the Cherokees, Choctaws, Chickasaws, Seminoles, and Creeks, among others. Interestingly, these five large tribes are otherwise known as the Five Civilized Tribes.

13. Anthropologist Albert L. Wahrhaftig in four separate field-stays conducted the last ethnographic research among the Oklahoma Cherokees in the period between 1963 and 1972.

CHAPTER TWO

1. Red Bird Smith is an important spiritual leader in Cherokee history, a man who provided religious guidance to the Nighthawk Keetoowahs in the wake of tribal dissolution and Oklahoma statehood in 1907 (Littlefield 1971: 412). In general, the Keetoowah society is a non-Christian segment of Cherokee society dating to 1859. For more on this topic, see this chapter and the section on Cherokee religious identity in chapter 5.

2. The historical and ethnohistorical literature on the Cherokees is quite extensive. A good, though somewhat dated, introduction to the literature can be found in Raymond Fogelson's *The Cherokees: A Critical Bibliography* (1978), Bloomington: Indiana University Press. Other favorites of mine include works by Thomas Hatley (1993), William McLoughlin (1986, 1993), Theda Perdue (1979, 1998), Sarah Hill (1997), and Wilma Mankiller (1993). See bibliography for full citations.

3. From the oral histories of the Cherokees themselves and from the written records of Europeans, we know that Cherokees first encountered European explorers sometime in the sixteenth century. Most scholars of Cherokee history agree that in 1540 Hernando de Soto and members of his expedition were likely the first Europeans to set foot in Cherokee territory, but the evidence is not as strong as it is for the arrival of another Spanish explorer twenty-seven years later. In 1567, Juan Pardo and other members of the Spanish militia appear to have crossed through at least five different Cherokee towns, for the historical records mention these towns by name (Hill 1997: 66).

4. Because Cherokees are speakers of an Iroquoian language, some scholars have argued, based on historical linguistic reconstructions, that the Cherokees migrated from the Northeast and arrived relatively late in the Southeast, somewhere between several hundred and 1,000 years ago (Hill 1997: 64). However, according to the Cherokees' own oral histories, they believe they either originated further to the South, in what would now be Latin America, or that they had been in the Southeast for millennia (Mankiller and Wallis 1993: 18).

5. The Cherokees followed what is typically referred to in the anthropological literature as a "Crow" kinship pattern, which is common among people with a strong matrilineal descent organization. The Crow kinship system is somewhat unusual in that it does not distinguish between certain kin of different generations. For example, among Cherokees, all members of their matrilineal clan, regardless of generation, were known as brothers and sisters, except for the mother, her sisters, her brothers, and grandparents (Gilbert 1943: 208). However, women of the same generation as one's biological mother, such as maternal aunts, were also referred to as mothers.

6. Anthropologist Raymond Fogelson argues that based on Cherokee theories of procreation, which I discuss later in the chapter, Cherokee kinship was literally understood as a relationship of blood (1990: 173). While I agree with this reading in general, it is important to note that at that time Cherokee kinship ideologies did not correspond with Euroamerican ones. Thus, we have to be careful not to impose European notions of consanguineality onto the Cherokees

when interpreting the historical record. While this is a subtle distinction between kinship ideologies that requires further research and analysis, it seems to me that the Cherokee incest taboo against marrying within the mother's clan *and the father's clan* provides some evidence that fathers may have been understood as kin, but kin of a different sort. If, as Fogelson suggests, Cherokees believed that fathers provided bone to the developing child in the form of semen, then maybe this was also another "substance" of Cherokee kinship besides blood (Fogelson 1990: 174).

7. In a footnote, Gearing quotes a Buttrick informant (from the Payne-Buttrick manuscripts) as stating, "one cannot marry with individuals having blood connexions" (Gearing 1962: 114). This statement suggests a linkage between the Cherokees' incest taboo and their beliefs about blood as the basis of kinship.

8. According to James Mooney, who was writing in 1900, Cherokees had "strains of Creek, Catawba, Yuchi, Natchez, Iroquois, Osage and Shawano blood, and such admixture implie[d] contact more or less intimate and continued" (234). However, to what extent Cherokees had intermarried with other Native Americans in the first half of the eighteenth century is unclear. But even if intermarriage with other Native Americans had been extensive and prolonged, as Mooney suggests, it probably would not have disrupted Cherokee social classification to the same extent as later intermarriages with Europeans.

9. Although the historical record is vague, we can reasonably assume that Cherokee women who practiced tribal exogamy chose to marry European men over African or other Native American men in order to create and cement alliances that reflected an already established race/power hierarchy. In addition, there is good evidence that by the late 1700s, Cherokees were beginning to internalize European racial ideologies. See my arguments later in this chapter.

10. For more on the history of Cherokee women, see Fogelson 1990, Hill 1997, and Perdue 1998.

11. Although I use the terms *myth* and *mythology* to refer to certain Cherokee origin stories, I do not mean to imply that these stories are untrue, only that they refer to a unique and sacred "place-time," when foundational events in the Cherokee cosmos occurred.

12. My understanding of Cherokee blood ideologies is greatly indebted to the work of Ray Fogelson. His 1990 article, "On the 'Petticoat Government' of the Eighteenth-Century Cherokee," in *Personality and the Cultural Construction of Society* , edited by David K. Jordan and Marc J. Swartz, is my primary source in the following discussion.

13. *Wodí* also means "paint," as in Painttown (Margaret Bender, personal note, Apr. 11, 2000).

14. In 1735, James Adair, a Scots-Irish trader who lived among the southeastern tribes, estimated that the number of Cherokee "villages" was sixty-four, although in 1789, William Bartram, a naturalist from Philadelphia who left detailed records of his observations, estimated that the number of Cherokee "villages" was closer to forty-three. It may be that a number of Cherokee towns consolidated during this period or that Adair was referring to the number of Cherokee residential communities instead of "town" political units. Gearing,

who usually is taken to be an authority on such matters, argues that the Cherokee towns were even fewer, somewhere between thirty and forty, because a larger population was needed to supply sufficient numbers of old men to fill important political offices (1962: 3).

15. Because town membership was related to matrilineal kinship ties, Cherokee men who married women from other towns and then went to live in their wife's community, as was the standard practice, were likely to have maintained political allegiances to their own town despite no longer being residents.

16. *Beloved* was used as a term of honor and respect for Cherokee elders. Cherokee men who had gray hair were known as beloved, as were Cherokee women who had reached menopause. In the scholarly literature, *beloved man* also is used as a synonym for a Cherokee priest-chief, but most elder Cherokee men had the ceremonial and religious knowledge that was necessary to fulfill this role.

17. The social roles and identities of Cherokee men, as with Cherokee women, shifted according to political context. Age, warrior status, clan, and town were different aspects of male identity comprising a strategic repertoire that could be called upon as needed. For instance, when older Cherokee men assumed authority in the White position, younger men often continued to organize themselves much as they would in the Red position. They may have deferred to their elders within the context of town politics, but they also formed militaristic age-grades on the side. With their own chiefs, rules, professional codes, and secrets, these highly cohesive bands of youth, known as pony clubs, spent much of their time involved in horse raiding (McLoughlin 1986: 55). Their ongoing activities often brought them into conflict with other tribal political interests, which is one of the reasons why the tribe as a whole organized itself along Red lines—so that older warriors could check the behavior of the young men.

18. In 1730, there were seven "mother towns" among the Cherokees that commanded a great deal of respect from their affiliated "daughter towns." According to Duane Champagne, however, these mother towns in no way undermined the autonomy of the daughter towns (1992: 25). Still, the mother towns did provide a precedent for leadership when coordination among Cherokee towns was necessary.

19. The Hicks quote can be found in the *Panopolist and Missionary Herald* 14 (1818): 415–416 and is cited in Champagne (1992), 268–69 n. 67. For more on the differentiation of clan roles and politics in Cherokee society, I recommend this particular note as well as chapter 2 of Champagne's book. In his note, Champagne responds to the observations made by Hicks in view of the overall literature. Although Champagne and I reach somewhat different conclusions, these differences are more of degree than kind.

20. Fred Gearing posits that by the late 1760s Cherokees had actually created an indigenous state (1962: 7). However, I agree with Duane Champagne that the term *state* does not accurately describe Cherokee political organization during this period, since the Cherokee polity went through a series of structural changes, none of which were stable or permanent enough to consolidate control over the practice of blood revenge (1992: 275). A more accurate description of

the Cherokee polity is as a confederacy, a term that is fairly standard in the scholarly literature on southeastern Indians. For specific treatments of the Creek confederacy see Knight's chapter in Hudson and Tesser (1994); for the Choctaw, see Galloway's excellent book, *Choctaw Genesis, 1500–1700* (1995).

21. For a comparative analysis of state formation among southeastern tribes, see Duane Champagne's *Social Order and Political Change: Constitutional Governments among the Cherokee, the Choctaw, the Chickasaw, and the Creek* (1992), Stanford: Stanford University Press. Though other southeastern tribes were under pressures similar to the ones that produced Cherokee centralization, Champagne argues that the Cherokees were the first to create a national state because they had greater social and political solidarity via their kinship system. All seven clans had representatives in all Cherokee towns, which enabled the Cherokees more readily to become politically centralized. At the same time, he argues that the Cherokee kinship system was differentiated from their political system, more so than in other southeastern tribes during the same period. However, this is a point to which I take exception above.

22. Ethnohistorians have been the most prolific in their treatment of this topic. Some key scholarly references on perceptions of the Indian in the white imagination include Berkhofer (1978), Bieder (1986), Dickason (1984), Sauer (1971), Stedman (1982), and Vaughan (1982).

23. *American State Papers*, Class 2: *Indian Affairs*, 2 Vols. Washington, D.C. (1832) 1: 41; also quoted in Shoemaker 1997: 642.

24. According to Durbin Feeling, the Cherokee Nation's tribal linguist, the term *atsi nahsa'i* is currently used to mean "employee" in everyday conversation.

25. The historical account in this section of this chapter is greatly influenced by the work of Theda Perdue (1979). Her excellent book provides, among other things, a rare perspective on precontact slavery practices among the Cherokees. For a broader perspective on the Cherokee freedmen, other recommended authors include Halliburton (1977) and Littlefield (1978). The historiographic material post-1866 is very limited with the important exceptions of Littlefield (1978), Wardell (1977), and Wilson (1971). However, their work extends only through the first decades of the twentieth century.

26. *American State Papers*, Class 2: *Indian Affairs*, 2 Vols. Washington, D.C. (1832) 1: 461.

CHAPTER THREE

1. One of the most important examples of cultural syncretism during this era of Cherokee nation building was the creation of a unique Cherokee writing system—the Cherokee syllabary. The Cherokee syllabary was the brainchild of Sequoyah, a Cherokee man also known as George Guess. Sequoyah had seen the power of writing in the hands of white men and women and wanted to harness that power for Cherokee use, to find a way to capture his own native language on paper. In 1821–22, Sequoyah created a syllabary, a writing system that differs substantially from an alphabetic one. Instead of each letter standing for a sound, in a syllabary each character stands for a syllable. This more efficient system was an important social leveler within the Cherokee nation because

it provided even monolingual Cherokee speakers with a new means of self-expression and a new sense of power (McLoughlin 1986: 350). It also helped to buttress a separate Cherokee national identity, as seen through the Cherokees' creative use of various forms of print media (Bender 1996: 36). For more on this topic, see Margaret Bender's 1996 dissertation, Department of Anthropology, University of Chicago.

2. Some scholars have suggested that a change-oriented planter class seeking to protect its economic interests was the driving force behind the emergence of a Cherokee state (Perdue 1979: 56–57, McLoughlin 1986: 289). That Cherokees codified 115 laws in the first quarter of the nineteenth century, 48 of which were specifically concerned with economic issues, provides some evidence for this assertion (Hill 1997: 95, McLoughlin 1986: 289). But given that similar conditions and class interests existed among other tribes in the Southeast, why were the Cherokees the only ones to create a constitutional government during this period? According to Duane Champagne, the difference lies in the role of the social conservatives, the mass of the Cherokee people (1992: 286–87). Because they believed that a state would protect them from further loss of land and guarantee their political autonomy, everyday Cherokee citizens—including the numerous town and clan chiefs—consented to the process of consolidation and agreed to share their political authority (Champagne 1992: 107). Without this consent, elite Cherokees had little power. Only by speaking to the interests of the broader Cherokee community were they eventually able to help bring about these significant changes in the political structure of the tribe.

3. Some evidence suggests that Cherokees organized themselves for removal along town lines (Fogelson and Kutsche 1961: 100). Thus, communities in Oklahoma may correspond on some level with original Cherokee towns in the East, though this topic has yet to be examined on a systematic basis.

4. For more general information on the development of scientific racism in the late nineteenth century, see the work of Nancy Stepan (1982) and Elazar Barkan (1992). For a more specific treatment of how this scientific discourse was applied to Native Americans, particularly by physical anthropologists, refer to David Beaulieu's excellent article in *American Indian Quarterly* (1984).

5. The federal government used this second racial ideology, as a by-product of the racial logic of the nineteenth century, both intentionally and unintentionally, to undermine Native-American economic autonomy, as I will discuss in greater detail below. To define Native Americans using notions of blood as race was an almost unquestioned, hegemonic practice, which also happened to conveniently serve the federal government's purposes when it came to vying for Native-American land.

6. Besides race, there were other measures of national belonging that arose during this period. For instance, in 1810, Cherokee citizenship was defined, in part, by residence within a certain set of geographical boundaries and by loyalty to the representative national council (McLoughlin 1986: 110).

7. For more on this topic, see Nash 1974 and Perdue 1979.

8. This racial hierarchy partially accounts for why many Cherokees were more willing to accept Europeans into their communities while at the same time rejecting African Americans in the same manner as their southern neighbors.

9. Racist ideologies fade slowly, if at all. Forty years later, the notorious pseudoscientist and craniologist Josiah C. Nott expressed the same ideas when he said that the civilization of the Cherokees meant nothing, because "whatever improvement exists in their condition is attributable to a mixture of races" (Nott 1844: 36–38).

10. The following account of Shoe Boots is based on McLoughlin 1983: 343–45 and May 1996: 63.

11. Return J. Meigs interview with Shoe Boots, October 19, 1803, M-208, quoted in McLoughlin 1983: 344.

12. Payne Papers, 2: 32–37 in McLoughlin 1983: 344–45.

13. The Treaty of New Echota was signed by only 500 Cherokees against the wishes of the remaining 15,665, who protested the treaty by formal petition to the U.S. government.

14. In several memorials before Congress, Cherokees argued for their own rights to national sovereignty and independence, using language that reflected the influence of Euroamerican models of nationhood (Walker 1997: 222, Krupat 1992: 156–63).

15. The use of the term *traditional* in reference to Native Americans is problematic and has drawn a great deal of criticism from scholars and activists alike. Please see my discussion in chapter 6 under the heading "Traditional Cherokee Communities."

16. There is much scholarly debate regarding population losses resulting from Cherokee removal. The most commonly cited figure is about 4,000, which accounts for my estimate. Some scholars have suggested a more conservative figure of 2,000, whereas Cherokee demographer Russell Thornton has used population projections that suggest well over 10,000 deaths (Thornton 1990: 74–76).

17. Linguistic exchange provided one point of divergence from the slaveholding practices of Euroamericans because many monolingual Cherokee masters depended on their bilingual slaves to act as interpreters.

18. The growth of the particular population is clear, though it is difficult to know if this figure is accurate because most of the censuses after 1835 classified a Cherokee with any degree of African ancestry as exclusively black.

19. After McLoughlin 1974: 381. Copyright by the American Studies Association. Reprinted by permission of the Johns Hopkins University Press.

20. There is some evidence that Cherokees saw blood as a nonindividual but quantifiable substance, which may help explain why it would lend itself so readily to the codification of Cherokee racial identity. In his early studies of Cherokee beliefs concerning death, anthropologist John Witthoft writes, "The third soul, that of circulation, is located in the heart, and blood its secretion. This soul is non-individual and quantitative; it takes a month to die, its substance gradually diffusing back into nature as a life force" (1983: 70). In my reading of this material, because the blood soul is nonindividual, it connects all Cherokees who share in its substance. At the same time, this blood soul can be lost because it is a quantifiable, measurable life substance. Seemingly, an analogy could be made between this blood soul and the use of blood as a measure of Cherokee identity.

21. "Full-blood" Cherokee Stand Watie, as it is noted prominently on a historical marker in downtown Tahlequah, was a brigadier general in the Confederate Army and the last Confederate general to surrender. The U.S. Post Office recently issued a stamp that depicts him riding horseback with his arm upraised.

22. Eventually, the Keetoowah society broke into two somewhat antagonistic organizations. In 1890, Red Bird Smith revived the old nucleus of the ultra-conservative Nighthawk Keetoowahs, which broke ranks with the larger society (Champagne 1992: 217). Even within the Nighthawks, there was a subgroup known as the pins, or pin Indians (Champagne 1992: 179–80).

23. The Cherokee Outlet was a long, narrow strip of land running east to west from the eastern edge of the Oklahoma panhandle to the northwest corner of the Cherokee Nation.

24. I was able to locate a complete legal record of *Cherokee Freedmen and Cherokee Freedmen's Association, et al. v. United States,* 10 Ind. Cl. Comm. 109 (1961), Dockets No. 173-a and 123, in the Earl Boyd Pierce Collection, Archival Box 75, at the Cherokee National Historical Society (CNHS), Park Hill, Oklahoma. Earl Boyd Pierce was the Cherokee tribal attorney during that period, and the CNHS has his complete papers, which are well indexed and underutilized.

25. This fact seems to imply that the Cherokee officials on the Dawes Commission had transcended race-thinking. To some extent this is true, since inter-married whites were granted citizenship on the basis of marriage and on the assumption that they would have Cherokee "blooded" children. However, the freedmen were a different issue. Cherokees had been forced by the federal government to recognize their former African-American slaves as tribal citizens in an 1866 reconstruction treaty. That they then received allotments was a source of political controversy for decades, as I demonstrate in chapter 5.

26. The idea here was that the state and federal governments believed that Native Americans of one-half or more Indian blood were incapable of understanding the newly imposed land allotment system. Therefore, their land allotments were held in federal trust. Fuller bloods were often declared incompetent to handle their own legal affairs and frequently assigned a court appointed legal guardian. On the other hand, those Native Americans with less than one-half Native American blood were not so encumbered. For more on this topic, see Debo (1940) and the historically based but fictionalized account of Hogan (1990).

CHAPTER FOUR

1. "Blood" is a cultural construction that has shifted its meaning over time. Blood predates biology as a symbolic bearer of cultural identity. However, once the Mendelian notion of genetics was accepted at the turn of the nineteenth and twentieth centuries, blood became more entangled with biology as a powerful symbol of racial identity. Thus, today, blood signifies both race and culture, and I use the term in this sense. For more on this topic see Stepan 1982, particularly chapter 4.

2. For a discussion of the various definitions of Indianness employed by federal agencies at different points in time, see Nagel 1996: 243–44.

3. For more information on the Dawes Rolls, see chapter 3, pp. 78–81.

4. The second largest Native American tribe in the United States is the Navajo Nation, located in parts of Arizona, Utah, and New Mexico on approximately 15 million acres of reservation land. In 1991, the Navajo Nation had approximately 143,000 enrolled tribal members, while the Cherokee Nation only had 120,000. Today, the Navajo Nation continues to have a more "blooded" enrollment than the Cherokee Nation. Unlike the Cherokee Nation, the Navajo Nation sets a one-quarter blood quantum for tribal enrollment. It also differs from the Cherokee Nation in its social and geographic isolation. Therefore, Navajos tend to marry other Navajos, and there are far more Navajo full-bloods than Cherokee full-bloods (Utter 1993: 20, 37–38, 111, 281).

5. These figures from January 1996 are based on information provided by the Cherokee Nation's database in its department of registration.

6. For instance, if a Cherokee citizen resides within the tribal jurisdictional service area (TJSA), then the Indian Health Service requires no minimum blood quantum for free medical services. But Cherokee citizens who live outside of Oklahoma must meet a one-quarter blood quantum to be eligible for exactly the same services in another state. The TJSA corresponds with the historical boundaries of the Cherokee Nation in the northeastern corner of Oklahoma.

7. This section chronicling the rise of the Cherokee state in the 1970s is greatly indebted to the work of anthropologist Albert Wahrhaftig. His unpublished dissertation is one of the only sources providing accurate and detailed historical and political information on the Cherokees during the early twentieth century. See Albert L. Wahrhaftig, 1975, "In the Aftermath of Civilization: The Persistence of Cherokee Indians in Oklahoma," Ph.D. diss., Department of Anthropology, University of Chicago.

8. The terms *white-Cherokee* and *white-Indian* are commonly used among Cherokees in northeastern Oklahoma. These terms refer to an elite class of Cherokees who are descended from prominent mixed-blood families and who actively strove to maintain the class status of their ancestors. For them, like their grandchildren today, being Cherokee was a source of great pride, an integral part of their identity. However, this pride partially stemmed from the fact that they, as mixed-blood Cherokees, had a unique history not to be confused with that of Cherokee traditionalists, whom they often saw as backwards. White-Cherokees manipulated these race, class, and cultural connotations and used them to justify their right to political power.

9. As Wahrhaftig describes, these forces from outside the region include TV networks looking for material regarding the "war on poverty" and the Senate hearings in 1968, directed by Robert Kennedy, on the education of Indian children (1975: 66). This national media attention embarrassed the Cherokee Nation because it drew attention to the fact that there was a white-Cherokee political elite running tribal affairs, who disempowered the poor, fuller-blood Cherokees in rural communities (Wahrhaftig 1975: 66).

10. I do not have recent demographic data regarding the Cherokee birth rate. However, according to Thornton, in the decade between 1970 and 1980, Cherokees "increased their representation in the total American Indian population at the rate of about .08 percent per annum" (1990: 199). If we assume that the Cherokee birth rate has remained fairly constant in the following decade, then the phenomenal Cherokee population growth since 1982, charted in Figure 14, cannot be accounted for simply by an increase in Cherokee births versus deaths.

11. Most of the people whom I interviewed tended to be toward the higher end of the blood-quantum spectrum. The social geography of the Cherokee Nation is such that Cherokees who reside within the historic boundaries of the Cherokee Nation tend to have a higher blood quantum than those who live outside the fourteen-county area. However, I also interviewed Cherokee citizens with blood degrees in triple-digit fractions, some of whom resided in Oklahoma but many of whom resided in California, where I was living the year before and the year after my fieldwork.

12. For more on race and nationalism, see chapter 1.

13. Actually, the literature put out by the Cherokee Nation's public affairs office at the time referred to Chief Byrd as a full-blood and to Deputy Chief Eagle as seven-eighths Cherokee. However, most Cherokee people also referred to the deputy chief as a full-blood.

CHAPTER FIVE

1. I address this issue at length in chapter 7, where I show how the social classification of multiracial Cherokees differs significantly, depending on whether or not they have African ancestry.

2. My decision to explore these various indexes of identity is patterned after anthropologist Virginia Domínguez's work on social classification in Creole Louisiana (1994: 205), although I have developed different categories.

3. These words translate as "hello," "okay," and "thank you," respectively.

4. One of the most telling exceptions to this tendency to privilege language above race occurs in the case of multiracial black-Cherokees. Although a few of these individuals who speak Cherokee are socially accepted as members of Cherokee communities, they most often are seen as racially distinct. This is not the case for multiracial white-Cherokees, who are usually accepted as Cherokee and even as full-bloods if they speak the Cherokee language. I discuss this qualitative difference in the social classification of white-Cherokees and black-Cherokees in chapter 7.

5. Cherokees from all walks of life describe their encounters with the "little people," who seem to be a small version of themselves with certain magical properties. According to local legend, little people live in undeveloped areas away from whites. If Cherokees live a good life, then the little people will appear to them more frequently and will help them in various ways. For example, chores will get done mysteriously or money will appear in the road. An interesting side note is that many Cherokees feel a bond with the Irish because the Irish have their own version of little people in leprechauns. One Cherokee man went so

far as to tell me that the Irish were a "lost tribe" of Cherokees. In fact, Cherokees have extensively intermarried with Euroamericans of Irish descent, but whether or not this is the work of the little people, I cannot say.

6. It is difficult to estimate the number of Cherokees who are active members of the Keetoowah Society because it has long been a secret organization. Also, the number of participants varies from night to night. Still, Keetoowahs are a significant minority in the tribal population. Keetoowahs may be associated with one of two ceremonial grounds in Northeastern Oklahoma—either the Red Bird Smith/Nighthawk Keetoowah grounds or the Stokes-Smith ceremonial grounds. My observations and interviews centered on the Stokes-Smith ceremonial grounds, the older and more continuous of the two. Outsiders often confuse the Keetoowahs with the United Keetoowah Band of Cherokee Indians (UKB), a small, federally recognized tribe that also has its headquarters in Tahlequah, Oklahoma. However, the first is a religious society and the second is a formal tribal government. There are Cherokees who are members of both, but there is no necessary connection between the two entities. The history of the UKB and its often tense relations with the Cherokee Nation of Oklahoma is a complex and fascinating topic, but not one that I have time and space to develop here. For more information on the recent history of the UKB, see Leeds 1996.

7. Both the Keetoowah and Cherokee Baptist religions are expressions of religious syncretism. For more on this topic, see Donaldson 1995 and McLoughlin 1994.

8. There is another subcategory to the term *full-blood*. Often, when Cherokees want to refer to someone with all Cherokee ancestry, instead of all Indian ancestry, then they will use the term *pureblood*. Supposedly, this biological distinction between purebloods and full-bloods has phenotypic consequences. As one Cherokee man explained to me, "A pureblood will be short and have rounded features and will usually be fat or husky. A full-blood will have the same basic features but can be any height." Despite this slight phenotypic differentiation, which may be anomalous, Cherokees tend to conflate the two groups as racially Indian and as culture bearers.

9. Because of the diffuse nature of cultural borrowing, Cherokees who use this term are probably unaware that Uncle Tom was a strong and noble character in Stowe's novel and that his name was reinterpreted to stand for any submissive behavior in the African-American community.

10. *Freedmen*, of course, is a term used across the American South for over a century to refer to African-American former slaves.

CHAPTER SIX

1. Marriage connotes a variety of rights, some of which may include legal fatherhood, legal motherhood, a monopoly of sexual access, rights to domestic services and labor, and rights over property and inheritance (Barnard 1994: 798). Many of these rights tend to assume eventual biological reproduction, and this has had important social repercussions along the lines of race, class, and gender. For instance, Martinez-Alier (1989) shows how in nineteenth-century Cuba marriage and mating patterns were linked to race and class, so that the

sexuality of upper-class white women was circumscribed in order to maintain race and class distinctions, while lower-class women of color were encouraged to make liaisons of concubinage with lighter-skinned men. However, there are other expressions of "marriage" that are not based on assumptions about pro-creation. For instance, the Nayar case in South India is a now classic example (Fuller 1976), as well as "woman marriage" and "ghost marriage" among the Nuer of Africa (Evans-Pritchard 1951). More recent kinship studies, like those of Kath Weston, have also examined domestic partnership and "marriages" among gays and lesbians in the United States (1992).

2. Many traditional Cherokees view race-mixing as a threat to their unique sense of peoplehood—their sense of nationality—as it is based on their ideas about cultural and racial essence. White-Cherokees, on the other hand, have often taken quite a different stance and, in the past, have manipulated the legal definition of Cherokee identity to be more inclusive of race-mixing in order to build a larger and more powerful Cherokee Nation.

3. In the mid-1960s, anthropologist Albert Wahrhaftig made extensive de-mographic surveys of traditional Cherokee settlements in Northeastern Oklahoma. His may be the only demographic survey of Oklahoma Cherokees to make distinctions between different types of Cherokee communities. My ex-perience in the late 1990s suggests that little has changed in terms of the size of these communities; thus, I continue to reference his work. Unfortunately, more current demographic work on the part of the tribe itself and other scholars is based either on U.S. census data or on the tribal citizenry as whole; therefore, it does not take intratribal racial and cultural diversity into consideration. Clearly, more accurate demographic fieldwork in these communities is needed.

4. Information on Cherokee housing is taken from *Cherokee People . . . Cherokee Tribe . . .* , an internal publication of the Cherokee Nation Office of Research and Analysis, No. 5, Winter 1993–94.

5. The following information on economic conditions by race is taken from *Cherokee People . . . Cherokee Tribe . . .* , Cherokee Nation Office of Research and Analysis, No. 4, December 1993.

6. Wahrhaftig estimates that the traditional Cherokee population was 9,500 in 1964 (Wahrhaftig 1975: 25), while Thornton estimates that between 1970 and 1980 the growth of the Cherokee population nationwide was 43 percent (Thornton 1990: 199). Thornton's figure is based on U.S. census data and makes no distinction between Cherokees living in Oklahoma and the rest of the United States. However, I believe that if we apply this growth percentage to Wahrhaf-tig's population count, we can get a rough estimate of the traditional Cherokee population today. Thus, between 1970 and 1980, the traditional Cherokee pop-ulation would have grown to 13,585. If this trend continued, then between 1980 and 1990 the traditional Cherokee population would have further increased to 19,427 individuals.

7. In this instance, when I use the term *blacks,* I am referring to Cherokee and non-Cherokee blacks, both of whom would be considered unacceptable marriage partners for maintaining Cherokee racial distinctiveness. The white category, on the other hand, is somewhat more fluid, and many Cherokee trad-itionals would classify certain light-skinned Cherokee citizens as whites. These

white-Cherokees might also make unacceptable marriage partners for traditional Cherokees as I have defined them here.

8. Based on fieldwork he conducted in the late 1930s, anthropologist Alexander Spoehr states that the ceremonial function of the matrilineal clan system
had all but disappeared among Oklahoma Cherokees (1947: 201). However,
almost sixty years later, I found that clan identity still carried significant meaning
within the context of Keetoowah Society ceremonialism, where people usually
sat around the sacred fire in their specific clan arbors and often danced as representatives of their clans. For more on Cherokee kinship practices in the early
decades of the twentieth century, see Spoehr 1947: 108–202. For comparative
data on Eastern Cherokee kinship, particularly the matrilineal clan system, collected during the same period, see Bloom 1939: 266–68.

9. The continued significance among traditional Cherokees of maintaining
clan identity and clan exogamy is evident in a small survey that I conducted
among traditional Cherokees who had chosen to marry within the tribe. Of
these twenty-five individuals who were raised in Cherokee-identified communities and were members of Cherokee religious institutions, fifteen, or well over
50 percent, knew their clan identity. Seven did not know their matrilineal clan,
and three had no clan because they had white mothers and thus were Cherokee
on only their father's side. The sample was almost evenly divided between Cherokee Baptists and Keetoowah Society members. What is most striking is that
for each population, almost half maintained the rule of clan exogamy, marrying
into a clan different from their own. The others who married Cherokees were
more concerned with tribal endogamy than clan exogamy.

10. That Cherokees reckon distant kin and are so conversant with the va-
garies of bloodlines may partially explain why some of them tolerate Cherokee
national policy, which sets no minimum blood-quantum standard for tribal enrollment.

11. Several older Cherokees whom I interviewed claimed that their grandparents or great-aunts and great-uncles knew and acknowledged their cousins
to anywhere between the sixth and tenth degree. In the course of my fieldwork,
I never saw this claim verified, but many traditional Cherokees did mention and
socialize with their third and fourth cousins.

12. This woman's husband, who was also a member of the Keetoowah Society, was one-half Cherokee through his father. Because he had no matrilineal
clan, he often chose to sit with his father's or his wife's clan on ceremonial
occasions.

13. Traditional Cherokees who do marry Cherokee tend to find marriage
partners in other, geographically distant, traditional Cherokee communities.

14. In my sample survey of twenty-five traditional Cherokee marriages, five,
or 20 percent, had violated the incest taboo either by marrying distant cousins
(to the sixth degree or greater) or by marrying within their own clan. All traditional Cherokees who violated this taboo said that they were socially stigmatized to some degree for doing so.

15. Because Cherokees socially classify one another on the basis of blood
degree, I believe that this incest taboo does not necessarily extend to distant,
mixed-blood collateral relatives. In other words, Cherokees are less likely to

identify a highly mixed-blood individual as a relative. In this instance, however, intermarriage with a distant, less-blooded collateral relative—defined as both non-Cherokee and, thus, non-kin—would violate the rule of endogamy but not the prohibition against incest.

16. Because Cherokees prefer to make marriage alliances with other Native Americans rather than whites, this practice directly contradicts the dominant U.S. racial hierarchy.

17. This secondary preference for an Indian spouse is one manifestation of racial hegemony. In the past, endogamy and exogamy among Cherokees concerned maintaining their cultural distinctiveness apart from other tribes. Now, however, Cherokees also want to maintain their racial distinctiveness as Indians apart from other races. Thus, intermarriage with another tribe is a more socially acceptable option.

18. The hegemonic notion that multiracial or multicultural individuals have to choose one among several identity options also applies to Native Americans of multitribal descent. The Bureau of Indian Affairs and the vast majority of tribes require that multitribal Native Americans choose among their ancestries, formally enrolling as a member of only one tribe. Thus, an Oklahoma Cherokee with Kiowa, Cherokee, and Choctaw ancestry, even if he or she had enough blood to qualify for membership in each, must enroll in only one tribe. It would be an interesting study to find out if there was any patterning to this choice, possibly based on blood degree or on a tendency to identify more with the father's or mother's side.

19. Very few Asian Americans reside in northeastern Oklahoma relative to the population as a whole. Therefore, the races that tend to be mentioned in Cherokee discourses about intermarriage are limited to Native American, Mexican American, and African American.

20. Stilwell is a well-known, more commercially developed Cherokee town— what I describe as a large checkerboard Cherokee community.

21. I would argue that ideology as a cultural construct is always aligned with power, because culture itself is aligned with power. Historically, anthropologists have tended to assume that kinship systems were somehow innocent of these power connotations. Here, I have tried to directly link kinship ideologies to the "power-full" social construct of race and racial reproduction.

22. This is particularly interesting considering that as an anthropologist, trying to understand and uncover racial ideology and its impact on the Cherokee community, I had to rely on discourse, on what Cherokee people said to me, as "data." Yet even these discursively based data revealed how ideology also had material and social repercussions.

CHAPTER SEVEN

1. Although the term *freedmen* is gender biased, I have chosen to use it to maintain historical continuity and to avoid the awkwardness of phrases such as "freedmen and freedwomen," or "freedpeople," which might jeopardize meaning. However, when referring specifically to the female sex, I use the term *freedwomen*.

2. I was able to locate a complete legal record of *Cherokee Freedmen and Cherokee Freedmen's Association, et al. v. United States,* 10 Ind. Cl. Comm. 109 (1961), Dockets No. 173-a and 123, in the Earl Boyd Pierce Collection, Archival Box 75, at the Cherokee National Historical Society (CNHS), Park Hill, Oklahoma. Earl Boyd Pierce was the Cherokee tribal attorney during that period, and the CNHS has his complete papers, which are well indexed and underutilized.

3. For a fictional treatment of this phenomenon in Oklahoma, see Linda Hogan's 1990 novel, *Mean Spirit* (New York: Ivy Books).

4. Virtually all of my information on the Nero cases comes from the files of Jim Goodwin, attorney at law, of Goodwin and Goodwin, Tulsa, Oklahoma. Mr. Goodwin was the attorney for the freedmen in the Nero cases, and he and his staff were very helpful to me during the course of my fieldwork. Mr. Goodwin has two sons, Jerry Goodwin, who runs the *Oklahoma Eagle,* the only newspaper written for the African-American community in Tulsa; and David Goodwin, who was a contributor to the paper. David and his father conducted a series of important taped interviews with Ross Swimmer, R. H. Nero, and Agnes Cowen in 1984. The tapes and transcripts are located in Jim Goodwin's files.

5. The process by which someone obtains Cherokee tribal citizenship is explained in greater detail in chapter 4.

6. My analysis of the freedmen controversy crosses the same theoretical bridge linking critical race theory to the progressive critical legal studies (CLS) movement of the early 1980s. Today, CLS challenges ahistoricism and insists on a contextual/historical analysis of the law. Critical race theory, on the other hand, focuses on race as a social and political construction, arguing that inattention to race flaws critiques of human rights legislation.

7. In the numerous interviews that I conducted, I found only one exception to this general tendency. A Cherokee woman in her late sixties recounted that her mother's brother's wife, her aunt, had been a black woman without Cherokee ancestry. Because she had been orphaned at a young age in the early 1900s and raised by a full-blood Cherokee family in Hulbert, she understood Cherokee culture and Cherokee was her first language. As a result, this woman was accepted into the community as a Cherokee. She married a full-blood Cherokee-language speaker and had children who were fluent speakers and who also married within the tribe.

8. The number of 4,000 black-Cherokee individuals is from Thornton 1990: 169.

9. Cemeteries are also segregated in practice. Not only do Cherokees tend to bury their dead in their own community graveyards, but the freedmen do so as well. The freedmen descendents whom I interviewed did not bury their dead in the main Tahlequah cemetery but in what is known as the Ross cemetery. This cemetery belonged to the Ross family, who used it as a place to bury their deceased slaves. Today, you can find it next door to the W. W. Hastings Indian Hospital in downtown Tahlequah.

10. This quote is interesting for two reasons. It links the Cherokee freedmen case with this book's introductory vignette about black-Seminoles taken from

John Sayles's 1996 film *Lone Star*. The quote also points to the fact that multi-racial identity is not a homogeneous experience. Different groups of Native/African-American people, here black-Seminoles and Cherokee freedmen, have very different historical experiences of racial formation and social incorporation.

11. Many Cherokees admit that contemporary freedmen descendants share Cherokee foodways as well as economic and religious practices. A case in point is that the freedmen community churches are usually Baptist and hold socio-religious observances on the same days as Cherokee traditional holidays. In fact, there is a history of interaction and exchange between freedmen and Cherokee Baptist churches, as explained by the Reverend Roger Nero in a taped interview with David Goodwin, and by Daniel Downing in the Duke Oral History Collection 1969: 4–25, Western History Collections, University of Oklahoma. Several Cherokees I interviewed said they could relate more easily to the freedmen than to whites because the freedmen were also a community-focused people.

12. For more on this recent political crisis, refer to chapter 4 of this volume.

13. The Cherokee Constitutional Convention was first convened in 1996. However, its progress was seriously impeded by the political controversy involving Principal Chief Joe Byrd and the judicial branch of the Cherokee government. Under the new chief, Chad Smith, the tribal council passed an act creating a formal constitutional commission with over seventy delegates.

CHAPTER EIGHT

1. All people experience contradictory consciousness, particularly as they are influenced by powerful ideas about racial and cultural essentialism, nationalism, class, gender, and sexuality. However, because Cherokees and other Native Americans have been subjected to federal policies that police their identities in terms of blood and race, this experience may be even more intensified, at least in regard to these particular aspects of identity.

2. This insight is indebted to anthropologist Karen Blu, who read this manuscript on more than one occasion with great care. I am fortunate to have such a perceptive and challenging reader.

3. While this is a common problem among Native-American communities, where American Indian languages are on the wane, other tribes with few or even no remaining language speakers have responded by defining their national culture on some other basis.

Bibliography

Abu-Lughod, Lila.
 1986.   *Veiled Sentiments: Honor and Poetry in Bedouin Society*. Berkeley and Los Angeles: University of California Press.
 1990.   "The Romance of Resistance: Tracing Transformations of Power through Bedouin Women." *American Ethnologist* 17 (1): 41–55.

Adair, James.
 1775.   *The History of the American Indians*. London: Edward and Charles Dilly.

Alonso, Ana Maria.
 1994.   "The Politics of Space, Time, and Substance: State Formation, Nationalism, and Ethnicity." *Annual Review of Anthropology* 23: 379–405.

Althusser, Louis
 1971.   *Lenin and Philosophy*. New York: Monthly Review Press.

Anderson, Benedict.
 1983.   *Imagined Communities*. London: Verso.

Anderson, William L. (ed.).
 1991.   *Cherokee Removal: Before and After*. Athens and London: University of Georgia Press.

Ankersmit, F. R.
 1989.   "Historiography and Postmodernism." *History and Theory* 28 (2): 137–53.

Anzaldúa, Gloria.
 1987.   *Borderlands/La Frontera: The New Mestiza*. San Francisco: Spinsters/Aunt Lute.

Baird, W. David.
    1990.   "Are There Real Indians in Oklahoma? Historical Perceptions
                    of the Five Civilized Tribes." *Chronicles of Oklahoma* 68 (1):
                    4–23.
Barkan, Elazar.
    1992.   *The Retreat of Scientific Racism: Changing Concepts of Race
                    in Britain and the United States between the World Wars.* Cam-
                    bridge: Cambridge University Press.
Barnard, Alan.
    1994.   "Rules and Prohibitions: The Form and Content of Human
                    Kinship." In *The Companion Encyclopedia of Anthropology:
                    Humanity, Culture, and Social Life.* T. Engold (ed.). London:
                    Routledge.
Bartram, William.
    1853.   "Observations on the Creek and Cherokee Indians, 1789, with
                    Prefatory and Supplementary Notes by E. O. Squier." Reprint.
                    Transactions of the American Ethnological Society 3 (1). New
                    York: G. P. Putnam.
Beaulieu, David L.
    1984.   "Curly Hair and Big Feet: Physical Anthropology and the
                    Implementation of Land Allotment on the White Earth Chip-
                    pewa Reservation." *American Indian Quarterly* 8 (4): 281–
                    314.
Behar, Ruth.
    1993.   *Translated Woman: Crossing the Border with Esperanza's
                    Story.* Boston: Beacon Press.
Bender, Margaret C.
    1996.   "Reading Culture: The Cherokee Syllabary and the Eastern
                    Cherokees, 1993–1995." Ph.D. diss., Department of Anthro-
                    pology, University of Chicago, Chicago, Illinois.
Berkhofer, Robert F., Jr.
    1978.   *The White Man's Indian: Images of the American Indian from
                    Columbus to the Present.* New York: Knopf.
Bickham-Mendez, Jennifer.
    1996.   "Ideologies of Race/Ethnicity, Culture, and Nationalism: The
                    Uprising of 1932 in El Salvador." Department of Sociology.
                    University of California, Davis. Unpublished ms.
Bieder, Robert E.
    1986.   *Science Encounters the Indian, 1820–1880: The Early Years
                    of American Ethnology.* Norman: University of Oklahoma
                    Press.
Bird, S. Elizabeth. (ed.).
    1996.   *Dressing in Feathers: The Construction of the Indian in Amer-
                    ican Popular Culture.* Boulder, Colorado: Westview Press.
Bloom, Leonard.
    1939.   "The Cherokee Clan: A Study in Acculturation." *American An-
                    thropologist* 41 (2): 266–68.

Blu, Karen.
  1980.   *The Lumbee Problem: The Making of an American Indian People*. New York: Cambridge University Press.
Bordewich, Fergus M.
  1996.   "Revolution in Indian Country." In *American Heritage* 47 (4): 34–46.
Bourdieu, Pierre.
  1977.   *Outline of a Theory of Practice*. Cambridge: Cambridge University Press.
Brewton, Barry.
  1963.   *Almost White: A Study of Certain Racial Hybrids in the Eastern United States*. New York: McMillan.
Calloway, Colin G.
  1986.   "Neither White nor Red: White Renegades on the American Indian Frontier." *Western Historical Quarterly* 17 (1): 43–66.
Campisi, Jack.
  1991.   *The Mashpee Indians: Tribe on Trial*. New York: Syracuse University Press.
Champagne, Duane.
  1992.   *Social Order and Political Change: Constitutional Governments among the Cherokee, the Choctaw, the Chickasaw, and the Creek*. Stanford: Stanford University Press.
Chatterjee, Partha.
  1993.   *Nationalist Thought and the Colonial World: A Derivative Discourse*. Minneapolis: University of Minnesota Press.
Cherokee Freedmen and Cherokee Freedmen's Association, et al. v. The United States and The Cherokee Nation.
  1971.   Appeal No. 5–70, U.S. Court of Federal Claims, Washington, D.C.
Cherokee Nation of Oklahoma, Office of Research and Analysis.
  1993.   "Population and Geography." In *Cherokee People . . . Cherokee Tribe . . .* No. 1, May.
  1993.   "Sex and Age," In *Cherokee People . . . Cherokee Tribe . . .* No. 2, June/July.
  1993.   "Age Structure Analysis," In *Cherokee People . . . Cherokee Tribe . . .* No. 3, August/September.
  1993.   "Economic Conditions," In *Cherokee People . . . Cherokee Tribe . . .* No. 4, December.
  1993–1994.   "Housing," In *Cherokee People . . . Cherokee Tribe . . .* No. 5, Winter.
Cherokee Nation of Oklahoma, Registration Department.
  1996.   Monthly Report for February.
Cherokee Nation v. Georgia.
  1831.   Peters 5: 1.
Clifford, James, and George E. Marcus (eds.).
  1986.   *Writing Culture: The Poetics and Politics of Ethnography*. Berkeley and Los Angeles: University of California Press.

Clifton, James A.

1989.   *Being and Becoming Indian: Biographical Studies of North American Frontiers.* Chicago: Dorsey Press.

1990.   *The Invented Indian: Cultural Fictions and Government Policies.* New Brunswick: Transaction.

Cohen, Felix S.

1971 (1942).   *Felix S. Cohen's Handbook of Federal Indian Law.* Albuquerque: University of New Mexico Press.

Collier, John.

1934.   *Memorandum.* Hearings on HR 7902 before the House Committee on Indian Affairs, 73rd Congress, 2nd. Session. U.S. Department of the Interior, Washington, D.C.

Comaroff, Jean, and John Comaroff.

1991.   *Of Revelation and Revolution: Christianity, Colonialism, and Consciousness in South Africa.* Vol. 1. Chicago: University of Chicago Press.

Corkran, David H.

1962.   *The Cherokee Frontier: Conflict and Survival, 1740–1762.* Norman: University of Oklahoma Press.

Cornell, Stephen.

1988.   *The Return of the Native: American Indian Political Resurgence.* New York: Oxford University Press.

Crowe, Cameron.

1975.   "Indians and Blacks in White America." In *Four Centuries of Southern Indians.* Charles M. Hudson (ed.). Athens: University of Georgia Press.

de Certeau, Michel.

1986.   *Heterologies: Discourses on the Other.* Minneapolis: University of Minnesota Press.

Debo, Angie.

1940.   *And Still the Waters Run: The Betrayal of the Five Civilized Tribes.* Princeton: Princeton University Press.

Deloria, Vine, Jr.

1969.   *Custer Died for Your Sins: An Indian Manifesto.* New York: Avon.

Derrida, Jacques.

1978.   *Writing and Difference.* London: Routledge.

di Leonardo, Michaela.

1984.   *The Varieties of Ethnic Experience: Kinship, Class, and Gender among California Italian-Americans.* Ithaca: Cornell University Press.

Dickason, Olive Patricia.

1984.   *The Myth of the Savage and the Beginnings of French Colonialism in the Americas.* Edmonton: University of Alberta Press.

Domínguez, Virginia R.

1994.   *White by Definition: Social Classification in Creole Louisiana.* New Brunswick: Rutgers University Press.

Donaldson, John K.
  1995.   "The Themes of Reciprocity and Renewal in Traditional Cher-
                 okee Culture." Ph.D. diss., Department of American Civiliza-
                 tion, George Washington University.
Dowd, Gregory E.
  1992.   *A Spirited Resistance: The North American Indian Struggle
                 for Unity, 1745–1815.* Baltimore: Johns Hopkins University
                 Press.
Eagleton, Terry.
  1991.   *Ideology: An Introduction.* London: Verso.
Ellsworth, Scott.
  1982.   *Death in a Promised Land: The Tulsa Race Riot of 1921.* Baton
                 Rouge: Louisiana State University Press.
Evans-Pritchard, E. E.
  1951.   *Kinship and Marriage among the Nuer.* Oxford: Clarendon
                 Press.
Feraca, Stephen E.
  1990.   *Why Don't They Give Them Guns? The Great American
                 Indian Myth.* Lanham, Maryland.: University Press of Amer-
                 ica.
Fogelson, Raymond D.
  1977.   "Cherokee Notions of Power." In *The Anthropology of Power.*
                 Raymond D. Fogelson and Richard N. Adams (eds.). New
                 York: Academic Press.
  1978.   *The Cherokees: A Critical Bibliography.* Bloomington, Uni-
                 versity of Indiana Press.
  1990.   "On the 'Petticoat Government' of the Eighteenth-Century
                 Cherokee." In *Personality and the Cultural Construction of So-
                 ciety: Papers in Honor of Melford E. Spiro.* David K. Jordan
                 and Marc J. Swartz (eds.). Tuscaloosa: The University of Ala-
                 bama Press.
Fogelson, Raymond D., and Paul Kutsche.
  1961.   "Cherokee Economic Cooperatives: The Gadugi." In *Sympo-
                 sium on Cherokee and Iroquois Culture.* William N. Fenton
                 and John Gulick (eds.). Bureau of American Ethnology Bulletin
                 180: 87–123.
Forbes, Jack.
  1993 (1988).   *Africans and Native Americans: The Language of Race and the
                 Evolution of Red-Black Peoples.* Urbana: University of Illinois
                 Press.
Foucault, Michel.
  1979.   *Discipline and Punish: The Birth of the Prison.* New York: Vin-
                 tage Books.
Frankenberg, Ruth.
  1993.   *White Women, Race Matters: The Social Construction of
                 Whiteness.* Minneapolis: University of Minnesota Press.

Fuller, C. J.
   1976.   *The Nayars Today*. Cambridge: Cambridge University Press.
Funke, Karl A.
   1976.   "Educational Assistance and Employment Preference: Who Is
                  an Indian?" *American Indian Law Review* 4 (1): 1–45.
Galloway, Patricia K.
   1995.   *Choctaw Genesis, 1500–1700*. Lincoln: University of Ne-
                  braska Press.
Gearing, Fred O.
   1962.   "Priests and Warriors: Social Structures for Cherokee Politics
                  in the Eighteenth Century." *American Anthropologist*. Mem-
                  oir 93, 64 (5): Part 2.
Giddens, Anthony.
   1987.   *The Nation-State and Violence*. Vol. 2 of *A Contemporary Cri-
                  tique of Historical Materialism*. Berkeley and Los Angeles: Uni-
                  versity of California Press.
Gilbert, William H.
   1943.   "The Eastern Cherokees." Smithsonian, Bureau of American
                  Ethnology Bulletin, 133 (23): 169–413.
Gilroy, Paul.
   1987.   *There Ain't No Black in the Union Jack: The Cultural Politics
                  of Race and Nation*. Chicago: University of Chicago Press.
Gist, Noel P. and Anthony G. Dworkin.
   1972.   *The Blending of Races: Marginality and Identity in World Per-
                  spective*. New York: Wiley-Interscience.
Goldberg, David T. (ed.)
   1990.   *Anatomy of Racism*. Minneapolis: University of Minnesota
                  Press.
Gramsci, Antonio.
   1971.   *Prison Notebooks*. New York: International Publishers.
Green, Rayna.
   1988.   "The Tribe Called Wannabee: Playing Indian in America and
                  Europe." *Folklore* 99 (1): 30–50.
Gregory, Steven, and Roger Sanjek. (eds.).
   1994.   *Race*. New Brunswick: Rutgers University Press.
Gulick, John.
   1958.   "Language and Passive Resistance among the Eastern Chero-
                  kees." *Ethnohistory* 5 (1): 60–81.
   1973.   *Cherokees at the Crossroads*. Chapel Hill: University of North
                  Carolina Press.
Hagan, William T.
   1985.   "Full-Blood, Mixed-Blood, Generic, and Ersatz: The Problem
                  of Indian Identity." *Arizona and the West* 27 (4): 309–26.
Hall, Stuart.
   1986.   "Gramsci's Relevance for the Study of Race and Ethnicity."
                  Journal of Communication Inquiry. 10 (2): 5–27.

1988.   "New Ethnicities." *ICA Documents* 7 (1): 27–31.

1991.   "Old and New Identities, Old and New Ethnicities." In *Culture, Globalization, and the World System: Contemporary Conditions for the Representation of Identity*. A. King (ed.). Binghamton: SUNY Press.

Halliburton, Rudia, Jr.

1977.   *Red over Black: Black Slavery among the Cherokee Indians.* Westport, Connecticut: Greenwood Press.

Hatley, M. Thomas.

1993.   *The Dividing Paths: Cherokees and South Carolinians through the Era of Revolution.* New York: Oxford University Press.

Hendrix, Janey E.

1983.   "Redbird Smith and the Nighthawk Keetoowahs." *Journal of Cherokee Studies* 8 (1): 22–39.

Hertzberg, Hazel.

1971.   *The Search for an American Indian Identity.* New York: Syracuse University Press.

Hill, Sarah H.

1997.   *Weaving New Worlds: Southeastern Cherokee Women and Their Basketry.* Chapel Hill: The University of North Carolina Press.

Hogan, Linda.

1990.   *Mean Spirit.* New York: Ivy Books.

Horsman, Reginald.

1981.   *Race and Manifest Destiny: The Origins of American Racial Anglo-Saxonism.* Cambridge: Harvard University Press.

Hudson, Charles.

1976.   *The Southeastern Indians.* Knoxville: The University of Tennessee Press.

Indian Claims Commission.

1961.   10: 109, 117–18.

Isaacs, Harold R.

1975.   *Idols of the Tribe: Group Identity and Political Change.* New York: Harper.

Jaimes, M. Annette.

1990.   "Federal Indian Identification Policy." Ph.D. diss., Department of American Indian Studies. Arizona State University.

1992a.   "Federal Indian Identification Policy: A Usurpation of Indigenous Sovereignty in North America." In *Native Americans and Public Policy*. Fremont J. Lyden and Lyman H. Letgers (eds.). Pittsburgh: University of Pittsburgh Press.

1992b.   (ed.) *The State of Native America: Genocide, Colonization, and Resistance.* Boston: South End Press.

1994.   "American Racism: The Impact on American-Indian Identity and Survival." In *Race*. S. Gregory and R. Sanjek (eds.), New Brunswick: Rutgers University Press.

Jennings, Francis.

1975.   *The Invasion of America: Indians, Colonialism, and the Cant of Conquest.* Chapel Hill: University of North Carolina Press.

Knight, Vernon James, Jr.

1994.   "The Formation of the Creeks." In *The Forgotten Centuries: Indians and Europeans in the American South, 1521–1704.* Charles Hudson and Carmen Chaves Tesser (eds.). Athens: University of Georgia Press.

Kolchin, Peter.

1993.   *American Slavery, 1619–1877.* New York: Hill and Wang.

Krupat, Arnold.

1992.   *Ethnocriticism: Ethnography, History, Literature.* Berkeley and Los Angeles: University of California Press.

Leeds, Georgia R.

1996.   *The United Keetoowah Band of Cherokee Indians in Oklahoma.* New York: Peter Lang.

Limerick, Patricia N.

1987.   *The Legacy of Conquest: The Unbroken Past of the America West.* New York: W. W. Norton & Co.

Littlefield, Daniel F., Jr.

1971.   "Utopian Dreams of the Cherokee Fullbloods, 1890–1934." *Journal of the West* 10 (3): 404–27.

1978.   *The Cherokee Freedmen: From Emancipation to American Citizenship.* Westport, Connecticut: Greenwood Press.

Lowe, Lisa.

1991.   "Heterogeneity, Hybridity, Multiplicity: Marking Asian American Differences." *Diaspora* 1 (1): 24–43.

Malkki, Liisa.

1992.   "National Geographic: The Rooting of Peoples and the Territorialization of National Identity among Scholars and Refugees." *Cultural Anthropology* 7(1): 24–44.

Mankiller, Wilma, and Michael Wallis.

1993.   *Mankiller: A Chief and Her People.* New York: St. Martin's Press.

Marcus, George E., and Michael M. J. Fischer.

1986.   *Anthropology as Cultural Critique: An Experimental Moment in the Human Sciences.* Chicago: University of Chicago Press.

Martin, Joel W.

1990.   "'My Grandmother Was a Cherokee Princess': Representations of Indians in Southern History." In *Dressing in Feathers.* S. Elizabeth Bird (ed.). Boulder, Colorado, and Oxford: Westview Press.

Martinez-Alier, Verena.

1989 (1974). *Marriage, Class, and Colour in Nineteenth-Century Cuba.* Ann Arbor: University of Michigan Press.

Martz, Ron.
  1986.   "Indians Maintain U.S. Trying to Erode Tribal Sovereignty: Cultural Significance Said to Be Goal." Cox New Service, Pierre, South Dakota, October 26, 1986.

May, Katja.
  1996.   *African Americans and Native Americans in the Creek and Cherokee Nations, 1830s to 1920s: Collision and Collusion.* New York: Garland Publishing.

McLoughlin, William G.
  1974.   "Red Indians, Black Slavery, and White Racism: America's Slaveholding Indians." *American Quarterly,* 26 (4): 367–85.

  1986.   *Cherokee Renascence in the New Republic.* Princeton: Princeton University Press.

  1993.   *After the Trail of Tears: The Cherokees' Struggle for Sovereignty, 1839–1880.* Chapel Hill: University of North Carolina Press.

  1994.   "The Cherokees and Christianity, 1794–1870." In *Essays on Acculturation and Cultural Persistence.* Walter H. Conser, Jr. (ed.). Athens: University of Georgia Press.

McLoughlin, William, and Walter H. Conser, Jr.
  1989.   " 'The First Man Was Red'—Cherokee Responses to the Debate Over Indian Origins, 1760–1860." *American Quarterly* 41(2): 243–64.

Mooney, James.
  1900.   *Nineteenth Annual Report of the Bureau of American Ethnology to the Smithsonian Institution, 1897–98.*Part 1. 1900. Government Printing Office, Washington, D.C. Rpt. 1995 as *Myths of the Cherokee.* New York: Dover Publications, Inc.

Moulton, Gary E. (ed.)
  1985.   *The Papers of Chief John Ross.* Norman: University of Oklahoma Press.

Mulroy, Kevin.
  1993.   *Freedom on the Border: The Seminole Maroons in Florida, Indian Territory, Coahuilla, and Texas.* Lubbock: Texas Tech University Press.

Nagel, Joane.
  1996.   *American Indian Ethnic Renewal: Red Power and the Resurgence of Identity and Culture.* Oxford: Oxford University Press.

Nash, Gary B.
  1974.   *Red, White, and Black: The Peoples of Early America.* Englewood Cliffs, New Jersey: Prentice Hall.

Nero, R. H., et al. v. Cherokee Nation of Oklahoma, et al.
  1986a.   Case files of Jim Goodwin, attorney at law, Goodwin and Goodwin, Tulsa, Oklahoma, regarding No. 84-C-557-C, U.S. District Court for the Northern District of Oklahoma.

1986b.   Appeal No. 86–1271, U.S. Court of Appeals for the Tenth Circuit, Denver, Colorado.

Nietzsche, Friedrich.

1949.   *The Use and Abuse of History*. Indianapolis: Bobbs-Merrill.

Nott, Josiah C.

1844.   *Two Lectures on the Natural History of the Caucasian and Negro Races*. Mobile: Dade and Thompson.

Omi, Michael, and Howard Winant.

1994.   *Racial Formation in the United States: From the 1960s to the 1990s*. New York: Routledge Press.

Peletz, Michael G.

1995.   "Kinship Studies in Late Twentieth-Century Anthropology." *Annual Review of Anthropology* 24: 343–72.

Perdue, Theda.

1979.   *Slavery and the Evolution of Cherokee Society, 1540–1866*. Knoxville: University of Tennessee Press.

1998.   *Cherokee Women: Gender and Culture Change, 1700–1835*. Lincoln: University of Nebraska Press.

Peterson, Jacqueline, and Jennifer S. H. Brown.

1985.   *New People: Being and Becoming Métis in North America*. Lincoln: University of Nebraska Press.

Quinn, William W.

1990.   "The Southeast Syndrome: Notes on Indian Descent Recruitment Organizations and Their Perceptions of Native American Culture." *American Indian Quarterly* 14 (2): 147–54.

Reid, John P.

1970.   *A Law of Blood: Primitive Law of the Cherokee Nation*. New York: New York University Press.

Root, Maria P. P.

1992.   *Racially Mixed People in America*. Newbury Park, California: Sage Publications.

Sampson, Bill.

1972.   "Justice for the Cherokees: The Outlet Awards of 1961 and 1972." Master's thesis, Department of History, University of Tulsa.

San Juan, E., Jr.

1992.   *Racial Formations, Critical Transformations: Articulations of Power in Ethnic and Racial Studies in the United States*. Atlantic Highlands, New Jersey: Humanities Press.

Sauer, Carl Otwin.

1971.   *Sixteenth Century North America: The Land and the People as Seen by the Europeans*. Berkeley and Los Angeles: University of California Press.

Schneider, David M.

1969.   "Kinship, Nationality, and Religion in American Culture: Toward a Definition of Kinship." In *Forms of Symbolic Action*.

R. F. Spencer (ed.). Proceedings of the American Ethnological Society. Seattle: University of Washington Press.

1980.   *American Kinship: A Cultural Account*. 2nd ed. Chicago: University of Chicago Press.

Shoemaker, Nancy.

1997.   "How Indians Got to Be Red." *American Historical Review* 102 (3): 625–43.

Sider, Gerald M.

1994.   *Lumbee Indian Histories: Race, Ethnicity, and Indian Identity in the Southern United States*. Cambridge: Cambridge University Press.

Sider, Gerald M., and Gavin Smith (eds.).

1997.   *Between History and Histories: The Making of Silences and Commemorations*. Toronto: University of Toronto Press.

Smith, Carol A.

1995.   "Race/Class/Gender Ideologies in Guatemala: Modern and Anti-Modern Forms." *Comparative Studies in Society and History* 37 (4): 723–49.

1997.   "The Symbolics of Blood: Mestizaje in the Americas." *Identities: Global Studies in Culture and Power* 3(4): 495–522.

1998.   "North American Treatments of Race and Racism in Guatemala: A Critical Genealogy." Forthcoming in *Identidades y Racismo en Guatemala*. G. Palma and C. Arenas (eds.) FLACSO, Guatemala.

Snipp, Matthew C.

1986.   "Who Are American Indians? Some Observations about the Perils and Pitfalls of Data for Race and Ethnicity." *Population Research and Policy Review* 5 (3): 237–52.

Spickard, Paul R.

1989.   *Mixed-Blood: Intermarriage and Ethnic Identity in Twentieth-Century America*. Madison: University of Wisconsin Press.

Spoehr, Alexander.

1947.   *Changing Kinship Systems: A Study in the Acculturation of the Creeks, Cherokee, and Choctaw*. Pub. 583. Anthropological Series, Field Museum of Natural History, 33 (4): 202.

Stack, Carol.

1974.   *All Our Kin: Strategies for Survival in a Black Community*. New York: Harper & Row.

Stedman, Raymond W.

1982.   *Shadows of the Indian: Stereotypes in American Culture*. Norman: University of Oklahoma Press.

Stepan, Nancy.

1982.   *The Idea of Race in Science: Great Britain, 1800–1960*. Oxford: McMillan Press.

Stolcke, Verena.

1991.   "Conquering Women." *NACLA Report on the Americas* 24 (5): 23–28.

Strickland, Rennard, and William M. Strickland.
1991.   Beyond the Trail of Tears: One Hundred Fifty Years of Cher-
               okee Survival. In Cherokee Removal: Before and After. W. L.
               Anderson (ed.). Athens and London: University of Georgia
               Press.
Strong, Pauline, and Barrik Van Winkle.
1993.   "Tribe and Nation: American Indians and American Nation-
               alism." Social Analysis 33 (1): 9–26.
1996.   "'Indian Blood': Reflections on the Reckoning and Refiguring
               of Native North American Identity." Cultural Anthropology
               11 (4): 547–76.
Swanton, John R.
1946.   "The Indians of the Southeastern United States." Bulletin of
               the Bureau of American Ethnology 137: 664.
Tanner, Adrian.
1983.   The Politics of Indianness: Case Studies of Native Ethnopoli-
               tics in Canada. Saint John's, Newfoundland: Institute of Social
               and Economic Research, Memorial University of Newfound-
               land.
Thomas, Robert K., and Albert L. Wahrhaftig.
1971.   "Indians, Hillbillies, and the 'Education Problem.'" In Anthro-
               pological Perspectives on Education. Murray L. Wax, Stanley
               Diamond, and Fred O. Gearing (eds.). New York: Basic Books.
Thompson, Gary L.
1993.   "Green on Red: Oklahoma Landscapes." In The Culture of
               Oklahoma. H. F. Stein and R. F. Hill (eds.). Norman: Univer-
               sity of Oklahoma Press.
Thornton, Russell.
1987.   American Indian Holocaust and Survival: A Population His-
               tory since 1492. Norman: University of Oklahoma Press.
1990.   The Cherokees: A Population History. Lincoln and London:
               University of Nebraska Press.
United States Federal Court of Claims.
1895.   30: 138.
United States Statutes at Large.
1890.   26: 636.
1889.   25: 608–9, 980, 994.
Unrau, William E.
1989.   Mixed-Bloods and Tribal Dissolution: Charles Curtis and the
               Quest for Indian Identity. Lawrence: University of Kansas
               Press.
Urban, Greg.
1994.   "The Social Organizations of the Southeast." In North Amer-
               ican Indian Anthropology: Essays on Society and Culture. Ray-
               mond J. DeMallie and Alfonso Ortiz (eds.). Norman: Univer-
               sity of Oklahoma Press.

Utter, Jack.
  1993.   *American Indians: Answers to Today's Questions.* Lake Ann,
                 Michigan: National Woodlands Publishing Company.
Vaughan, Alden T.
  1982.   "From Whiteman to Redskin: Changing Anglo-American Per-
                 ceptions of the American Indian." *American Historical Review*
                 87 (4): 917–53.
Vizenor, Gerald.
  1990.   *Crossbloods: Bone Courts, Bingo, and Other Reports.* Min-
                 neapolis: University of Minnesota Press.
Vogt, Anita.
  1974.   "Eligibility for Indian Employment Preference." *Indian Law
                 Reporter* 6(1): 32–37.
Wagner, Roy.
  1977.   "Analogic Kinship: A Daribi Example." *American Ethnologist*
                 4 (4): 643–62.
Wahrhaftig, Albert L.
  1968.   "The Tribal Cherokee Population of Eastern Oklahoma." *Cur-
                 rent Anthropology* 9 (5): 510–18.
  1975.   "In the Aftermath of Civilization: The Persistence of the Cher-
                 okee Indians in Oklahoma." Ph.D. diss., Department of An-
                 thropology, University of Chicago.
Walker, Cheryl.
  1997.   *Indian Nation: Native American Literature and Nineteenth-
                 Century Nationalisms.* Durham, North Carolina: Duke Uni-
                 versity Press.
Wardell, Morris L.
  1977 (1938).   *A Political History of the Cherokee Nation, 1838–1907.* Nor-
                 man: University of Oklahoma Press.
Ware, Vron.
  1992.   *Beyond the Pale: White Women, Racism, and History.* Lon-
                 don: Verso.
Wax, Murray L.
  1971.   *Indian Americans: Unity and Diversity.* Englewood Cliffs,
                 New Jersey: Prentice-Hall.
West, Cornel.
  1993a.   *Race Matters.* Boston: Beacon Press.
  1993b.   *Keeping Faith: Race and Philosophy in America.* New York:
                 Routledge.
Weston, Kath.
  1992.   *Families We Choose: Lesbians, Gays, Kinship.* New York: Co-
                 lumbia University Press.
White, Hayden.
  1978.   *Tropics of Discourse: Essays in Cultural Criticism.* Baltimore:
                 Johns Hopkins University Press.

Williams, Brackette F.
    1989.   "A Class Act: Anthropology and the Race to Nation Across the
                    Ethnic Terrain." *Annual Review of Anthropology* 18: 401–44.
    1991.   *Stains on My Name, War in My Veins: Guyana and the Politics
                    of Cultural Struggle*. Durham, North Carolina: Duke Univer-
                    sity Press.
    1993.   "The Impact of the Precepts of Nationalism on the Concept of
                    Culture: Making Grasshoppers out of Naked Apes." *Cultural
                    Critique* 24 (2): 143–92.
    1995.   "Classification Systems Revisited: Kinship, Caste, Race, and
                    Nationality as the Flow of Blood and the Spread of Rights." In
                    Naturalizing Power: Essays in Feminist Cultural Analysis. S.
                    Yanagisako and C. Delaney (eds.). New York: Routledge.
Williams, Samuel Cole (ed.).
    1928.   "Alexander Cuming Journal." In *Early Travels in the Tennes-
                    see Country, 1540–1800*. Johnson City, Tennessee: Watauga
                    Press.
    1930.   *Adair's History of the American Indians*. Johnson City, Ten-
                    nessee: Watauga Press.
Wilson, Walt.
    1971.   "Freedmen in Indian Territory during Reconstruction." *The
                    Chronicles of Oklahoma*. Oklahoma Historical Society 49 (2):
                    230–44.
Witthoft, John.
    1983.   "Cherokee Beliefs Concerning Death." *Journal of Cherokee
                    Studies* 8 (2): 68–72.
Woodward, Grace Steele.
    1963.   *The Cherokees*. Norman: University of Oklahoma Press.
Worcester v. Georgia.
    1832.   Peters 6: 515.
Yanagisako, Sylvia J.
    1985.   *Transforming the Past: Tradition and Kinship among Japanese
                    Americans*. Stanford: Stanford University Press.

Index

Compositor:	Binghamton Valley Composition, LLC
Text:	10/13 Sabon
Display:	Sabon
Printer and Binder:	Maple-Vail Manufacturing Group